UNDERDEVELOPMENT AND INDUSTRIALIZATION IN TANZANIA

To my children
KEMILEMBE AND RUSHUMA

JUSTINIAN RWEYEMAMU

UNDERDEVELOPMENT AND INDUSTRIALIZATION IN TANZANIA

A Study of Perverse Capitalist
Industrial Development

Nairobi
OXFORD UNIVERSITY PRESS 1973
London   New York

Oxford University Press, Ely House, London W. 1

GLASGOW NEW YORK TORONTO MELBOURNE WELLINGTON
CAPE TOWN IBADAN NAIROBI DAR ES SALAAM LUSAKA ADDIS ABABA
DELHI BOMBAY CALCUTTA MADRAS KARACHI LAHORE DACCA
KUALA LUMPUR SINGAPORE HONG KONG TOKYO

Oxford University Press, P.O. Box 72532, Nairobi, Kenya

ISBN 0 19 572268 X

Made in East Africa

ACKNOWLEDGEMENTS

This book is a revised version of the doctoral dissertation, 'An Industrial Strategy for Tanzania', which I submitted to Harvard University in 1970. In the period during which the book has been in preparation, the list of persons to whom I am indebted for assistance, criticism and encouragement has grown to unmanageable proportions. I hope I will be pardoned for singling out a few upon whom I have called most frequently for help, and failing to name many others who have given advice.

I am greatly indebted to Professors Albert Hirschman and Thomas Weisskopf, who were on my dissertation committee, for their help and encouragement. Among colleagues and others who have read and criticized earlier drafts I must mention Professor Arthur MacEwan as well as other members of the 'Africa Group' at Harvard including Ivory Robinson, Mahmood Mamdani and Jim Ault. Dr. Giovanni Arrighi of Milan, Italy, Paul Sweezy of the *Monthly Review* and Professor Shigeto Tsuru of Hitotbashi University, Japan, all gave useful criticism.

To my wife Anna and our children Kemilembe and Rushuma who shared the innumerable discomforts of dissertation and book writing, I wish to express my sincere thanks for their endurance.

I cannot conclude this very incomplete account without a word of gratitude and praise for the intellectual and human environment in which I have been privileged to work during the past four years: the Faculty of Arts and Social Science of the University of Dar es Salaam. Its young but firmly established concern with interdisciplinary problems and with the social aspects of all technical work in social science has, I hope, found some reflection in what is stated in this book.

Finally I would also like to express my gratitude to the University of Dar es Salaam for granting me an extended study leave to complete this work; the Rockefeller Foundation that financed my stay at Harvard; the then Principal Secretary, Ministry of Development Planning, Tanzania, for allowing me access to the industrial survey files; the various industrialists in Tanzania who readily responded to my questionnaires; Mrs. Irene Temu for her efficient work in typing the manuscript and to the Eastern Africa branch of the Oxford University Press who readily agreed to publish the book.

I hasten to pronounce the customary absolution, relieving all the persons mentioned above of responsibility for what I have written; but I cannot absolve them of the inspiration they gave me to finish writing the book.

J.F.R.

Dar es Salaam, 1972

CONTENTS

INTRODUCTION   **xi**

PART ONE: THE POLITICAL ECONOMY
           OF TANZANIA

CHAPTER 1   TANZANIA: ECONOMY AND SOCIETY
            IN THE PRE-INDEPENDENCE PERIOD   1

1.1   General characteristics of the country   1
1.2   The traditional economy and society   3
1.2.1 The effects of slave trade and slavery
       on the traditional society   9
1.3   The colonial period   11
1.3.1 The plantation system and the proletarianization
       of the peasantry   14
1.3.2 Cash crop production and class formation   25
1.3.3 The institutional setting: trade and infrastructure   32
1.4   Some concluding remarks   35

CHAPTER 2   ECONOMY AND POLITY DURING THE
            POST-INDEPENDENCE PERIOD, 1962-71   38

2.1   Background to Arusha–I: the international aspects   38
2.2   Background to Arusha–II: domestic policy and
       social differentiation   46
2.3   The Arusha Declaration and after   57
2.4   Some theoretical considerations   70

PART TWO: THE STRUCTURE OF TANZANIA'S
           MANUFACTURING INDUSTRY

CHAPTER 3   A MODEL OF PERVERSE CAPITALIST
            INDUSTRIAL DEVELOPMENT   78

3.1   The conceptual framework   78
3.2   Historical evolution and present trends   80
3.3   The major consequences of the inherited
       structures on the industrialization of the periphery   91
3.4   Some tentative hypotheses   105

vii

CHAPTER 4 THE INSTITUTIONAL AND HISTORICAL
          SETTING OF TANZANIA'S
          INDUSTRIALIZATION PROCESS   111

4.1   The historical setting   111
4.2   Investment pattern in the post-independence period   122
4.3   Incentive structure and performance   130

CHAPTER 5 THE EMPIRICAL RESULTS OF THE PERVERSE
          CAPITALIST INDUSTRIAL DEVELOPMENT
          MODEL: THE CASE OF TANZANIA   138

PART THREE: TOWARDS A SOCIALIST
            INDUSTRIALIZATION
            STRATEGY

CHAPTER 6 TOWARDS A SOCIALIST
          INDUSTRIALIZATION STRATEGY   175

6.1   Preliminary considerations   175
6.2   Tanzania's socialist goals   175
6.3   Planning relations and resource allocation   178
6.4   Socialist production relations   192

Appendix I*   Sources of data   199
Appendix II*   Number of registered factories by
                31 December 1964   204
Appendix III*   Static characteristics of Tanzania's industry   209
Appendix IV*   The inter-industry relations study for Tanzania,
                1966   228
Appendix V**   Classification of ISIC industries into consumer,
                capital, building materials, producers'
                supplies and other industries, 1966   244
Appendix VI**   Export promotion and import substitution   246

Index   265

*Appendixes I-IV are an extension to chapter 4
**Appendixes V and VI qualify chapter 5

LIST OF TABLES

1.1   Population growth of various ethnic groups in
mainland Tanzania, 1910–67   2
1.2   Response to German control in Tanzania, 1888–1906   13
1.3   Principal total exports and exports sent
to Germany, 1911   15
1.4   Production of principal exports by the Africans   18
1.5   African monthly rates of pay in plantations, 1936   20
1.6   Balance of payments of mainland Tanzania, 1912   21
1.7   Allocation of sisal profits, 1951–6   26
2.1   Book value of British direct investment
in selected African countries, 1960–5   41
2.2   Tanzania's terms of trade, 1960–5   43
2.3   Some elements of the balance of payments, 1961–5   44
2.4   Trade in non-traditional markets   45
2.5   Comparative actual and planned structures of GDP   49
2.6   Sectoral distribution of plan investments   51
2.7   Total and sectoral distribution of
wage employment, 1962–6   53
2.8   Income and its distribution in Tanzania, 1961–6   55
2.9   Net earnings of invisibles, 1966–70   63
4.1   Historical review of manufacturing industries
by industrial activity   112
4.2   Distribution of share-holding in manufacturing
processing industries by citizenship and
industrial activity in 1965   115
4.3   Tanzania: inter-East African trade, 1954, 1960, 1966
by SITC sections   119
4.4   Inter-East African trade, 1962–4   119
4.5   Production of selected industries   121
4.6   Cotton piece goods imports   122
4.7   Wireless sets imported by major source, 1958–66   126
4.8   Tariff protection and import substituting industrialization   131
4.9   Effective protection of Tanzania's industry, 1966   134
4.10   Profitability of some of the protected firms, 1966   136
5.1   Distribution sample of 36 firms by ownership and industry   145
5.2   Ownership and capital effectiveness in five firms   149
5.3   Backward linkage effects as measured by equation 5.6   153
5.4   Forward linkage effects as measured by equation 5.7   156

5.5	Backward linkage effects as measured by equations 5.6, 5.8, 5.9	159
5.6	Locational quotients of Tanzania's manufacturing industry	161
5.7	Coefficients of localization of Tanzania's manufacturing industry, 1966	162
5.8	Relationship between location quotients and the share of raw material cost on gross output	164
5.9	Tanzania: sectoral distribution of value added and employment, 1966	167
5.10	Comparative sectoral distribution of value added in manufacturing industry	167
5.11	Japan's machinery production	169
5.12	Capital-labour ratio and capital-output ratio of 36 firms, Tanzania	170
5.13	Structure of non-exportable consumer goods industry: value added and employment as a per cent of total industry	172
A2.1	Number of factories registered as of 31 December 1964 by industry and employment	204
A3.1	The structure of costs in Tanzanian manufacturing industry	210
A3.2	Tanzania: value added per person engaged, in U.S. dollars, 1966	216
A3.3	Value added as per cent of gross output	218
A3.4	Tanzania: the structure of manufacturing input by industrial origin, 1966	219
A3.5	Average labour productivity by sector, 1966	220
A3.6	Value added per person employed in selected countries (in U.S. dollars), in manufacturing industry	220
A3.7	Comparative average labour productivity by industry	222
A3.8	Tanzania: productivity of capital in 36 firms	225
A3.9	Geographical distribution of manufacturing, 1966	226
A4.1	The structure of the economy of Tanzania, 1966	232
A4.2	Table of technical coefficients	236
A4.3	Table of total requirements	240
A5.1	Classification of ISIC industries into consumer, capital, building material, producers' supplies and other industries, 1966	244
A6.1	Comparative structure of exportables	247

INTRODUCTION

Most theories of economic development imply, explicitly or implicitly, that the present underdeveloped countries are historically similar in the sense that their past and present resemble the earlier stages of history of the now developed countries, except that the former fell behind in the process of historical development while the latter 'took off' and passed them by, and that consequently the underdeveloped countries now are at an earlier, lower, though 'natural' stage of the general process of growth. In other words, the starting point is the assumption that capitalism is still a progressive force in the sense that it can lead to a full 'self-generated' and 'self-sustaining' industrialization of the underdeveloped countries, or at least in the sense that it is able to create progressive socio-political forces in these countries that would ultimately lead to similar results. Attention is thus directed to those features which the developed countries possess and the underdeveloped countries lack, viewing the process of development and underdevelopment as *sui generis* to the country concerned.

The point of view advanced here, however, is that the historical pattern of capitalist growth does not and cannot repeat itself because the classical capitalist process of growth itself, as we know it from the economic history of world development, has fundamentally altered the very conditions that spawned it. In order to evaluate meaningfully the development possibilities of the underdeveloped countries, it is imperative to analyse the implications of both their past history and the consequent contemporary reality. In particular, to the extent that their history has been intimately related to the history of the developed ones, at least for several centuries, the relationships which have been established are shown to lead to *perverse* capitalist development— perverse in the sense that within their institutional setting, the reliance on the private enterprise system as the prime mover of social development will not lead to self-generating and self-sustaining growth.

The major factor in the development process of the periphery is that an economic system was *imposed* on it which became the basis for *spontaneous forces* that tend to reproduce and reinforce the system of underdevelopment and its structure. Such built-in factors arising from this structure tend to restrict accumulation, restrict expansion of the internal market and limit the labour absorbing capacity of the economy.

The implication of this analysis is that the observed and well-documented characteristics of underdevelopment are not deviations with respect to the ideal or 'normal' pattern of capitalist development, or problems of infancy which will be healed by economic growth and modernization. Rather, it is argued that behind these observed symptoms there lies a system organized on the basis of certain structures whose functioning inevitably produces such results and will continue to produce them as long as the *system* itself is not changed. In other words, to the extent that it is the inherited structure which constitutes the heart of the system of underdevelopment, then it is by altering that structure that one can hope to overcome underdevelopment.

Moreover, an analysis of the history and the interests of the underdeveloped countries may reveal that capitalism is not a *desirable* social system. At least this is so in Tanzania—a country that has been taken as a case study with respect to the hypotheses advanced above.

This analysis is reflected in the form, content and structure of this book. Part I deals with the political economy of Tanzania from a historical perspective in an attempt to grasp the major forces and structural relations which have defined the trajectory of Tanzania's development, and, *a fortiori*, a delineation of Tanzania's social goals as rooted in historical reality. No doubt to the traditional economist the author will appear as an irrelevant wanderer from his proper territory, and to the historian as an intruding amateur. I have not been unaware of my own imperfect preparation for the task.

I have nevertheless been encouraged to persevere by the obstinate belief that economic analysis only makes sense and can only bear fruit if it is joined to a study of historical development, and that an economist concerned with present day problems has certain questions of his own to put to historical data. After all, the relevance of the questions that a particular theory tries to answer can only be judged in the light of the knowledge about the form of development and the sequence of events in the past. Needless to mention no pretence is made that the study does more than answer certain specific questions. Only certain aspects of Tanzania's economic development have been selected; although the selection has been made in the belief that these aspects have paramount significance.

Part II, consisting of three chapters, analyses the impact of colonialism on the industrial development of Tanzania. Specifically it is shown that the dependency relationship created by the colonial division of labour, dependency on foreign markets for the sale of their output and the provision of basic inputs, technological dependency on the advanced countries and dependency on foreign entrepreneurs, all these work in such a way as to produce perverse capitalist industrial growth. Such growth is characterized by the establishment of a productive structure that (a) is biased against the capital goods industries, thus limiting industry's contribution to the production of farm equipment and transport facilities, (b) utilizes relatively more capital-intensive techniques of production, thus compounding the problem of urban unemployment and the widening of urban-rural differentials, (c) has limited linkage effects, especially with respect to the traditional sector, (d) fosters lopsided development both in terms of geographical location within the country, and sectoral distribution of consumer goods output favouring luxuries, and (e) sets up uncompetitive oligopolistic structures.

In so far as the above characteristics are not a consequence of random policy mistakes by the decision-makers in the periphery but were predetermined to a great extent by the inherited structure of the Tanzanian economy, and in view of society's goals as pointed out in the earlier chapters, part III explores the nature of the contemplated change in the social structure contained in the Arusha Declaration and subsequent policies. The change in social structure is aimed at both liquidating underdevelopment and creating the foundation for the emergence of socialist man. Part III is presented on the assumption, already justified in part I, that the formation and implementation of an appropriate industrial strategy is essential to the attainment of the goal of socialism and self-reliance.

Certainly the emphasis on industrial growth does not imply that substantial growth cannot be achieved, for instance, through an expansion of agriculture, nor that this may be an indispensable precondition or complement of industrial development. In a closed economy, however, there is a fairly low ceiling to the growth that can be achieved through agricultural expansion, which is limited both on the supply side and on the demand side, and although in the open economy these limitations should, on *a priori* grounds, be less severe, this is generally not the case with respect to many of the ex-colonial countries. Growth therefore turns to industry not only in the longer run, after the potentialities of agricultural expansion have already been exploited, but *immediately*, and industry is the dynamic sector which sets the pace and pattern of development.

It is true, of course, that the nature of the industries established, the nature of production relationships in industry and the patterns of ownership and control established, affect the pattern of the industrialization process in overcoming underdevelopment and establishing the necessary conditions for the emergence of socialist man. These are the issues discussed in the final chapter. Tanzania has already taken important steps in implementing some of the policies recommended here. If the observations made sound more critical and prescriptive than laudatory, it is because there is more to be gained from trying to diagnose shortcomings than from celebrating successes. For Tanzania's success in implementing these policies will depend upon the perspective it takes. If an overall perspective is lacking—that is, of viewing the policies pursued from the beginning as successive approximations and stages toward a socialist society which is their meaning—then the sum of changes that have already been undertaken and those which I have suggested, will at best degenerate into perverse capitalist development in which the power of capital and alienated labour will survive and underdevelopment will persist.

The political economy of Tanzania

'We have been oppressed a great deal, we have been exploited a great deal, and we have been disregarded a great deal.'

The Arusha Declaration

INTRODUCTION

This first part of the book is a brief sketch of the historic processes of Tanzania's economic growth. My main concern is to provide as broad a perspective as possible in order to highlight the policies and institutional changes that have shaped the existing structure of the Tanzanian economy. This is made necessary by my belief that no economic system (including components of it such as the industrial structure which is the object of my inquiry) can be studied meaningfully irrespective of the associated social structure. Consequently, any policy of economic growth must be related to the *historical* experience of a given society, to its socio-economic organization. Such an approach is particularly relevant to the study of former colonial economies such as Tanzania's whose present society is a result of a dual evolution: one spreading from endogenous transformation of the traditional social structure and the other from the imposed western capitalist structure.

The impact of colonization had different results according to the indigenous social structures which it met and according to the degree of economic transformation which it brought about. Part I is therefore divided into two chapters. In order to underscore the processes of economic change (as they have been historically manifested) as well as the characteristics of the existing economic structure, chapter 1 analyses the major features of the traditional economy as well as the impact of colonization (and *a fortiori* of capitalist penetration) on the traditional society.

Chapter 2 describes the attempt by the independent government to modify the inherited structure and place the economy on a self-sustaining basis, concluding with the theoretical implications of Tanzania's historical development experience, especially as it affects a possible industrialization strategy.

CHAPTER ONE

TANZANIA: ECONOMY AND SOCIETY IN THE PRE-INDEPENDENCE PERIOD

I.I GENERAL CHARACTERISTICS OF THE COUNTRY

The United Republic of Tanzania came into being on 24 April 1964 when the People's Republic of Zanzibar merged with the Republic of Tanganyika.[1] The former became independent of Britain in December 1963 while Tanganyika (hereafter referred to as mainland Tanzania) became independent two years earlier. Mainland Tanzania, covering an area of 883,589 square kilometres and lying just south of the Equator and between the African Great Lakes and Indian Ocean, was estimated to have a population of 11,763,150 in 1967, implying a density of population of 13.7 persons per square kilometre.[2] The 1967 census indicates that 44.3 per cent of the total population was under 15 and 44.13 per cent was between 16-45. The racial distribution was as follows:

Africans	11,481,595
Asians	75,058
Europeans	16,907
Arabs	29,779
Other	839
Not stated	143,883
Total	11,763,150

The growth of the various ethnic groups since the German period can be seen in table 1.1, p. 2.

It should be noted, however, that despite the African preponderance, the non–African minorities have, as we shall see below, exerted an

[1] For articles of union, see William Tordoff, *Government and Politics in Tanzania* (Nairobi, East African Publishing House, 1967), pp. 205-35.
[2] Although population growth as indicated by the 1957 and 1967 data amounts to 3 per cent per annum, it has been taken by statisticians at about 2.5-2.7 per cent per annum in order to allow for possible improvements in reporting. See Central Statistical Bureau, *Recorded Population Changes: 1948-1967* (Dar es Salaam, Government Printer, 1968).

influence on the economic life of the country which is disproportionate to their number.

An outstanding feature of the country is the very uneven geographical distribution of the population. Density of population varies from 170.1 persons per square kilometre in Ukerewe to 1.3 persons per square kilometre in Mpanda. Two-thirds of the entire population in fact live in one-tenth of the area. In general, the population is concentrated along the periphery on the coast, in the rainy highlands of the South, around Mount Kilimanjaro and Mount Meru, and along the shores of Lake Victoria. This is due largely to the lack of permanent water supplies—a fact which greatly reduces the natural fertility of the country—and also to the tsetse fly, which has rendered large tracts of land uninhabitable. There is thus a parallel between population distribution and the distribution of natural and agricultural resources (if we equate agricultural fertility with the level of rainfall). As would be expected, the geographical distribution of personal income follows the same pattern and this has had a profound effect on the development of manufacturing industry.

TABLE 1.1

Population growth of various ethnic groups in mainland Tanzania, 1910 to 1967
(in thousands)

Year	African	Asian	European
1910	4700	8.7	3.7
1920	4900	9.7	5.3
1931	5800	32.0	8.2
1940	6500	34.0	9.1
1950	7700	76.8	14.9
1958	8700	95.5	20.6
1967	11482	105.0	16.9

Source: C. J. Martin, 'Some Estimates of the General Fertility and Rate of Natural Increase of the African Population of British East Africa', *Population Studies*, XII, (July 1953); Central Statistical Bureau, *Statistical Abstract, 1962* (Dar es Salaam, Government Printer, 1963), p. 11. Bureau of Statistics, Population *Census, Vol. 3, Demographic Statistics*, table 216 (Dar es Salaam, Government Printer, 1971).

The major features of land use are a small land area taken up by urban development (less than one per cent of the land area), a small proportion of cultivated land area relative to the total land area (5.3 per cent) shared between plantation agriculture (European and Asian owned) and African smallholder farming at 0.7 per cent and 4.6 per cent respectively.[3] Mineral production accounts for a very small

[3] L. and E. Berry, 'Land Utilization and Land Use in Tanzania', *Bralup Research Notes*, no. 6 (University College, Dar es Salaam, 1969).

proportion of total product. Diamonds, gold, mica and salt are the important exploited mineral resources. Iron and coal, though they exist in substantial amounts have not yet been exploited.

Zanzibar on the other hand, with an area of 2,640 square kilometres and an estimated population of 354,000 in 1967, has a relatively homogenous density of population of about 135 persons per square kilometre.

The conclusion to be drawn from this brief survey of Tanzania's natural resources is that the distribution of economic activity—and hence of population and purchasing power—is almost entirely determined by agricultural and climatic conditions. This may change as irrigation is extended, but for the industrial development which has so far taken place, it is the historical situation which is important in determining the present pattern. In general, as will be shown in later chapters, this development has taken the form of either processing available agricultural commodities or import substitution.[4] Since both agricultural supply and the pattern of domestic demand are closely related to ecological and climatic conditions, it will be readily apparent how important these have been in the development of manufacturing industry.

1.2 THE TRADITIONAL ECONOMY AND SOCIETY

Any study of the major features of an economic system must take into account the two fundamental problems of political economy. First, it must explore the social relations determining the size of the economic surplus, its distribution and utilization; and this implies the analysis of the conditions of production (the productive forces) and the relations of production. This is because the development of a people is pivoted around the relations they forge in the process of reproducing, sustaining and improving themselves as constrained by nature. The notion of productive forces designates the set of factors of production, resources, tools, men, characterizing a productive society at a given time which must be combined in a specific way to produce the material goods and services necessary to that society. The notion of relations of production designates the functions fulfilled by individuals and groups in the production process and in the control of the factors of production. Secondly, it must study

4 D. S. Pearson, *Industrial Development in East Africa* (Nairobi, Oxford University Press, 1969).

relations governing the adaptation of the society to changing social conditions, especially in confrontation with external threat.[5] It is within this framework that the traditional economy is analysed.

Before systematic European colonization the vast majority of mainland Tanzania consisted of independent producers still involved in pre-capitalist modes of production, generally clustered in various socio-cultural groupings that are normally referred to as 'tribes'. A general characterization of these units is extremely difficult because of their heterogeneity and the inadequacy of available information about them, but a few features that are pertinent to our analysis can be isolated.[6] Firstly, *the dominant productive system was the village community*. This community was based on the fact that its members consisted of working 'owners' of land, small peasant cultivators. Their independence was regulated by their mutual relationships as members of a community, by the need to safeguard common land for common needs. Membership in the community was the precondition for the appropriation of land, but in their capacity as members of the community, the individuals could consider the allotment to them as their own as long as they continued to occupy it beneficially. Security of tenure was, in this way, guaranteed.[7]

Thus, if we consider systems of land tenure as 'clusters' of rights over land and its products, the traditional systems of land tenure are almost universally characterized by (a) the right of every individual to the *productive use* of some land in virtue of his citizenship in a given

[5] For a political economy framework of analysis see especially Paul Baran, *The Political Economy of Growth* (New York, Monthly Review Press, 1957); Oscar Lange, *Political Economy*, vol. I, translated by A. H. Walker (New York, Pergamon Press of the Macmillan Company, 1963); Jan Halpern, 'Traditional Economy in West Africa', *Africana Bulletin*, no. 7 (1967), pp. 91-112; Maurice Godelier, 'System, Structure and Contradiction in Capital', Saville and Miliband (eds.), *The Socialist Register, 1967* (London, Merlin Press, 1967), and Giovanni Arrighi, *The Political Economy of Rhodesia* (The Hague, Mouton, 1967).

[6] Recent publications and current research in this area are enhancing our understanding of traditional societies. See especially Andrew Roberts (ed.), *Tanzania Before 1900* (Nairobi, East African Publishing House, 1968) and Isario Kimambo and Arnold Temu (eds.), *A History of Tanzania* (Nairobi, East African Publishing House, 1970).

[7] J. K. Nyerere, *Freedom and Unity* (Dar es Salaam, Oxford University Press, 1966), pp. 161-71 and Introduction; Karl Marx, *Pre-Capitalist Economic Formations*, translated by Jack Cohen, edited and with an introduction by E. J. Hobsbawn (New York, International Publishers, 1965), pp. 67-93, *passim*; E. B. Dobson, 'Comparative Land Tenure of Ten Tanganyika Tribes', *Tanganyika Notes and Records*, no. 38 (March 1955), p. 35; M. Yudelman, 'Some Aspects of African Agricultural Development', in E. A. G. Robinson (ed.), *Economic Development for Africa South of the Sahara* (London and New York, Macmillan & Co. at St. Martin's Press, 1964); or see below.

socio-cultural group, (b) the overlapping of rights in land and its products among individuals and groups which manifests itself in (c) rigid prohibition against individual alienations of land over which a person has specific but never absolute rights.[8]

It is obvious that a precondition for the continued existence of the community was the maintenance of a semblance of *equality* among its free, self-sustaining peasants, and their individual labour as the condition for the continued existence of their property. This accounts for the frequently noted *absence of classes* in our traditional societies. That is, fundamentally the village community was a system of production without classes in the sense that it lacked social differentiations. It lacked wage labour, the precondition for capital accumulation, since each individual peasant was not separated from his land. The emergence of classes would have dissolved communal landed property and hence the village community as a productive system.[9]

Techniques of production were highly land-intensive. This was due to two factors: people's attitudes towards land which was that of usufruct only, and the existence at that time of unlimited supply of good land. In many cases these techniques of production led to the well-known system of shifting cultivation that made unnecessary any attempts to take steps to preserve the fertility of the soil. The cultivation of annual crops and the general simplicity of houses probably also fostered this mode of production.

There was no serious competition over land use such as might have called for regulation by superior authority. There was thus little pressure for chiefs to exercise authority over large numbers of people. These factors may explain the lack of large, well-organized political units in these areas. Certainly the low level of surplus

---

[8] The literature on this subject is highly scattered. Some standard works include: B. J. Hartley, 'Land Tenure in Usukuma', *Tanganyika Notes and Records* (April 1938); E. B. Dobson, 'Land Tenure of the Wasambaa', *Tanganyika Notes and Records*, no. 10 (1940); Hans Cory and M. Hartnoll, 'Notes on Haya Land Tenure in Bukaria (Bukara) (Musoma)', ibid. (June 1947); E. B. Dobson, 'Comparative Land Tenure of Ten Tanganyika Tribes', *Tanganyika Notes and Records*, no. 38 (1955); A. A. Oldaker, 'Tribal Customary Land Tenure in Tanganyika', ibid.; Nos. 47 and 48 (1957); P. H. Gulliver, *Land Tenure and Social Change Among the Nyakyusa* (Kampala, East African Institute of Social Research, 1958); and Priscilla Copeland Heining, 'Haya Land Tenure; Landholding and Tenancy', *Anthropological Quarterly*, no. 35 (1962), pp. 58-73.
[9] The above is, of course, not true for areas where the communal structure had yielded to feudalism, see *infra*. In general, however, see J. K. Nyerere, *Freedom and Unity*, op. cit., pp. 8-11, 162-71; Samir Amin, 'The Class Struggle in Africa', *Revolution*, vol. I, no. 1 (1964), p. 25; Symon Chodak, 'Social Classes in Sub-Saharan Africa', *Africana Bulletin*, 1966, no. 4, pp. 8-11.

generation tended to sustain such a weak political system.

As mentioned above *production relations* were such that a peasant worker had an objective existence of his own, *independent* of his labour. Moreover, the relationship of worker to objective conditions of his labour was one of ownership. Thus the individual peasants behaved not as labourers but as owners and as members of the community who also labour. Furthermore, the purpose of work was not the creation of value, but the maintenance of the owner and his family as well as the communal body as a whole.[10] It follows that the traditional economy did not have a market for labour, in which labour was treated as a commodity and allocated on the basis of the highest bidder, nor did individuals lose control of the work process by those who owned and controlled capital (including the concomitant loss of control by the worker over his activities during the hours of work). On the contrary, production was often undertaken by intimate communities of persons sharing a multitude of social ties and functions, one of which happened to be the production of material goods. Work was part of the social obligation to kin, friends or even rulers but not for the production of value. There was no alienation from the means of production and as we shall see below the productive system was independent of the impersonal market forces that are unrelated to the indigenous social system.

Market exchanges were peripheral in the sense that most producers did not rely on exchange for the acquisition of the bulk of the means of subsistence. The absence of market exchange as the dominant economic organization encouraged social control of production by kinship, religion and political organization. Primary *factors of production* were never traded. Land was distributed through kinship, chiefs, etc., while labour was appropriated through marriage, kinship and friendship reciprocity, for example work parties to do specific tasks such as the clearing of fields and harvesting. In other words, labour and natural resources did not have a separate economic organization; factor movements and appropriations that took place were expressions of social obligation, social affiliation and social right. Consequently, and in contradistinction to the capitalist mode of production which was to be imposed on our communities during the colonial period, social relationships and values were the most important determinants

---

[10] K. Marx, *Pre-Capitalist Economic Formations*, op. cit., pp. 67-8, *passim*; George Dalton, 'Tribal and Peasant Economies', *Quarterly Journal of Economics*, LXXVI, pp. 360-78; and J. K. Nyerere, *Freedom and Unity*, op. cit., Introduction.

of work organization.

In this social organization that subordinated economic goals to wider objectives of societal consolidation and security, the *distribution of production surpluses* rested on an institutionalized (but by no means quantitatively determinate) system of socially obligatory duties of making, receiving and returning gifts. Investment effort on the other hand was spent on clearing the bush, building, manufacturing or purchasing appropriate tools. The distributive system thus served the purposes of social cohesion and security of subsistence to the individuals.

Thus the village commune, producing agricultural and artisan goods for its own consumption, had all the necessary conditions for the production of a surplus and also for reproduction, and because of this it was very resistant to internal processes of disintegration. The system had very obvious drawbacks. The material level of life was very low, which was a result of the social organization in failing to inspire innovation and technical changes that would have significantly raised society's production frontier. It is important to recall that this inadequacy of the social system was *not incidental* to the system as has been claimed.[11] Rather it was implicit in the social structure itself. The small-scale operations and the failure of the system to reward innovators were essential ingredients of the village economy which hampered accumulation and growth. We shall return to this theme in chapter 2 but it should be noted here that the village community was vulnerable to confrontations against the more technically-advanced modes of production.

Although the village community was the dominant mode of production, there were other modes coexisting with it. At least three such modes can be identified. First is the *pastoral* mode which is found in the drier areas of the country necessitating constant movements in search of water and grass, thus constraining considerably the possibilities of a settled life.

Secondly is the banana culture of present day West Lake, Kilimanjaro and Usambara regions where a more settled, perennial culture emerged, leading to social differentiations based on land holding. The introduction of the banana, a perennial crop which nourishes itself from its own debris of fallen leaves and can continue to bear fruit almost

---

[11] Julius Kambarage Nyerere, 'Socialism and Rural Development', in his *Freedom and Socialism* (Dar es Salaam, Oxford University Press, 1968), p. 34.

7

indefinitely, created an artificial scarcity of land and hence a struggle for its control, which manifested itself in the gradual emergence of feudal oligarchies in these areas. The *nyarubanja* system of land tenure in West Lake is an example of this development. Although it was by no means pervasive, the Nyarubanja had come to embrace a significant part of the peasantry. The peasants (*bailu*) were deprived of their land by the ruling elite who could extract from the former both produce and services in return for security.

Closely related to the banana culture were areas where intensive and often irrigated settlements were established. These were normally a result of population pressure. Here attempts were made to restore fertility to the soil. Thus on Ukerewe a system was evolved of green manuring the shambas (plots) with two indigenous species of legumes which were specifically grown for the purpose. In the Matengo highlands of Songea district steep hillsides were kept in production by an ingenious system of pit-cultivation—pits being dug on the slopes and all crop residues and woods burned in them.[12]

A third mode of production, though it may probably be inappropriate to call it so, is that of artisans and traders. There is now an extensive literature on African trade in the mainland. Of special importance is the regional trade in grains, pots, fish, livestock, such wood products as barkcloth, bark boxes, axe and spear shafts, wood carving, honey, beeswax, etc. There also developed, especially among the Yao and Nyamwezi, a long distance trade in iron products (hoe blades, knife blades, axe heads, spear blades, anklets, bracelets, necklaces, etc.), salt, and later in the nineteenth century, ivory.[13] The existence of trade in such products necessarily implies the existence of artisans and middlemen. Moreover, it implies the existence of a generated surplus over and above subsistence, which may have been appropriated by the rulers but which may also have cushioned social differentiations. Furthermore, traders became agents of diffusion of new products (e.g. maize, rice, cloth, etc.), new innovations and specialized skills. It is, indeed, the dissipation and disruption of these dynamic sectors under the impact of the slave trade and systematic colonization that created the major discontinuities of our societies and deepened the development of underdevelopment with all its

---

[12] Heinz-Dieter Ludwig, 'Permanent Farming in Ukara' in Hans Ruthenberg (ed.), *Smallholder Farming and Smallholder Development in Tanzania* (Munich, Weltforum Verlag for Ifo-Instit., 1968).
[13] R. Gray and D. Birmingham (eds), *Pre-Colonial African Trade* (London, Oxford University Press, 1970).

consequences of uneven development, poverty and a low level technical progress.

Thus the precolonial society was not an undifferentiated, communal society but a complex system characterized by several modes of production. While there is evidence of gradual differentiations, the precolonial economy was *viable* as a unit and certainly did not exhibit tendencies of dependency relations.

1.2.1 The effects of the slave trade and slavery on traditional society

The productivity of the traditional economy was determined by the available manpower. The slave trade, which drained the country of the most active section of its population, seriously undermined the traditional economy by reducing its productivity. Famines increasingly became a problem. In these circumstances, the traditional patriarchal democracies gave way to warrior monarchies. Conflicts between communities, which were encouraged by Arab slavemongers (who provided the guns), were aggravated, thus diminishing trade relations between the various communities. The psychological effects of the slave trade which deprived the people of self-confidence was another factor that was further aggravated by colonization.[14]

Most of the slaves from the mainland were taken to the Zanzibar clove plantations, although some were sent to Muscat, the Middle East and to Europe and America. The clove plantation economy in Zanzibar had been established by Seyyid Said in the first half of the nineteenth century when he extended his sovereignty over the island. The ruler of the Hadimu[15] (the Mwangi Mkuu) is supposed to have 'agreed' to some kind of indirect rule under which the Sultan could govern the Zanzibaris through their traditional systems. However, Seyyid Said's motivation to come to Zanzibar was not only political; it had economic roots as well. Seyyid Said was concerned with controlling the trade between East Africa and the rest of the world in two ways: (a) by collecting duties through control of the ports and *entrepôts* of the coast, and (b) by trading into the interior in his

---

[14] For a succinct analysis of the impact of the slave trade, see Walter Rodney, *West African Slave Trade* (Nairobi, East African Publishing House, 1967).
[15] The Hadimu were the descendants of Zanzibar migrants from the African mainland.

own right.[16] Accordingly he encouraged the expansion of the volume of exports from the East African mainland, introduced a plantation system of cloves and opened up new markets for the products of the territory by welcoming the European, Indian and American traders who were beginning to enter the area.

The introduction of a clove plantation economy in Zanzibar had far-reaching implications. First of all, the Sultan had to encourage *permanent* Arab immigrants into Zanzibar since he limited clove cultivation to the Arabs. Secondly, because of the high labour requirement of the crop, especially during the picking season, the system encouraged the slave trade.[17] The Arab ruler had negotiated with the Hadimu for the provision of *corvée*—the temporary recruitment of forced labour—in their so-called 'treaty'. At first this requirement involved forest clearance and timber-cutting for construction purposes —activities which did not interfere with most of the Hadimu's important daily tasks. But when the plantations began to produce crops, the Hadimu became compelled to work for Arabs during the harvest seasons. Indigenous labour soon proved insufficient and had to be supplemented by slaves from the mainland.

On this basis the Arab community was able to build an expanding and flourishing plantation economy. This development was crucial to the development of an Arab oligarchy in so far as it led to the emergence of a landed aristocracy. Without it, the Arabs might have remained a dominantly urban élite composed of government officials and merchants and only remotely in touch with the indigenous population. But as a rural plantation-owning class, the Arabs were able to continue to impose heavy demands on the Hadimu society both in the expropriation of their best land and in enslaving them.[18]

It must be noted also that Indians played a very significant role in this process. They had traded with the island since earlier times, but they really never settled there. Seyyid Said, however, encouraged more Indian merchants to settle in Zanzibar because he wanted to make use of their commercial skills and capital in the expansion of his own enterprise. The Asian traders became the economic backbone of the entire Zanzibar system, financing virtually all the caravans which

[16] R. Coupland, *East Africa and Its Invaders* (Oxford, Clarendon Press, 1939), chapter X.
[17] Alpers, *The East African Slave Trade* (Nairobi, E. A. Publishing House, 1967), pp. 10-13.
[18] Michael Lofchie, *Zanzibar, Background to Revolution* (Princeton, Princeton University Press, 1967), p. 62, *passim*.

left the coast for the interior to capture slaves and other booty, on credit which they alone could afford to give, meanwhile controlling the export-import trade.[19] Furthermore, the Sultan employed only Asiatics in his newly organized customs and revenue services. He thus inaugurated a practice which has characterized the subsequent development not only of Zanzibar's administrative apparatus—the reliance on Asians in the clerical, auditing and staff positions of the civil service—but of the mainland as well.[20]

When the British took over Zanzibar as a 'protectorate' in 1890, the basic classes of Zanzibari society had been formed. There was an Arab élite which monopolized political power and progressively intensified its domination over an undifferentiated African majority, and an Asian commercial and middle class whose economic and social status was threatened by the Arab planters. Much of Zanzibar's subsequent political economy can be shown to be an interplay of these forces.

1.3 THE COLONIAL PERIOD

The latter part of the nineteenth century witnessed the 'take-offs' of many European economies, stimulating increasing requirements for raw materials.[21] European exploitation then entered a new phase—that of exploiting more systematically, non-human raw materials. 'Humanitarian conscience' was now aroused at the 'inhuman' nature of the slavery institution. The coincidence between the humanitarian sentiment to stop the slave trade and the imperialist necessity to harness African labour for the production of raw materials has rarely been commented upon.[22] Indeed, as Jim Ault points out

> economic, evangelical and humanitarian interests intertwined to articulate a unified, coherent policy towards the slave trade . . . European capitalists found the slave trade incompatible with their interests in a stable wage-labour force. Humanitarian groups glorified the moral superiority of a

---

[19] J. J. Mangat, *A History of Asians in East Africa circa 1886–1945* (Oxford, Clarendon Press, 1969).
[20] J. D. Karstedy, 'Beitrage zur Inderfrage in Deutsche-Ostafrika', *Koloniale Monastsblatter* (Berlin, Süsserott 1913), pp. 337-55.
[21] W. W. Rostow, *The Stages of Economic Growth* (London, Cambridge University Press, 1960), indicates on p. 38 that Germany had its 'take-off' in 1850-73, whereas France and Belgium had theirs in 1830-60.
[22] See, however, Walter Rodney, 'The Imperialist Partition in Africa', *Monthly Review* (April 1970).

system of labour organization based on long-distance migration, wage labour, and capitalist time-discipline exacting high productive performance during the hours of the work day. The missionaries proselytization of the Christian faith could not be undertaken in safety while the slave-hunting raids and tribal wars persisted.[23]

Then followed the military expeditions of the great powers culminating in the 'partition' of Africa.[24] Of course, the African communities were regarded as prepared for this eventuality as their social order had been ravaged by the horrors of the slave trade. Yet it is significant to note that despite the absence of a national revolutionary movement, the degree of resistance which the African people mounted against the intruders was phenomenal. In the case of Tanzania, no less than eleven recorded revolts took place between 1888-1906 when the Germans began to systematically colonize the country (see Table 1.2). This indicates (at least in part) that even though the traditional economies were almost destroyed by slave trade raids, it cannot be claimed—as was to be rationalized by the colonial powers—that nineteenth century Africa, and Tanzania in particular, was necessarily set on a path to destruction from which only European intervention could save it.[25] On the contrary, these economies showed rapid, and at times successful, adaptations to the growing pressures of the outside world.

Systematic European colonization, both German (1884-1918) and British (1919-61) is characterized by the following elements: (a) the establishment of the plantation system, (b) the introduction of metropolitan-oriented cash crops to the African peasantry, with the consequent class formation resulting therefrom, (c) the financial and other infrastructure which was to serve the production structure thus introduced and (d) the establishment of the basic institutions of foreign trade with the metropolis. I shall discuss the economic impact of colonialism on the traditional economy in the above framework.

A clear understanding of the colonial structure, however, impels

---

[23] Jim Ault, *The Political Economy of Zambia*, mimeo. (Harvard University, 1971), p. 12.
[24] See Roland Oliver and Gervase Mathew (eds.), *History of East Africa*, vol. I (Oxford, Clarendon Press, 1963), especially chapters by G. S. P. Freeman-Grenville and A. Smith.
[25] A. J. Hughes, *East Africa: Search for Unity* (Penguin African Library, 1963), p. 35 says that 'British intervention perhaps prevented the extinction of many groups whose lands might slowly have been taken over by the Arabs and their allies.'

TABLE 1.2

Response to German control in Tanzania: 1888 to 1906

Year	Event
1888	Arab revolt at Pangani against German East African Company. Ignites Bushiri rebellion from Pangani to Kilwa. Revolt put down by Imperial German force led by von Wissman, October, 1889.
1889-94	Siki, Chief of Unyamwezi, expresses hostility to Germans in 1889. Closes caravan routes at Tabora in 1892. His son attacks German forces. Defeated by Germans and Tabora occupied in 1894.
1890	Gogo raid in Tabora area. Punitive expeditions sent out to put an end to raids.
1890	Kalemera, Chief of Usambiro, attacks Stilmann's passage in 1890. German troops destroy two bomas and 163 Africans killed and wounded.
1890-8	Ngoni rebellion at Unyanyembe and Urambo. Not subdued until 1897-8.
1891	Sinna of Kibosho tears down German flag. Subdued by Wissman.
1891-8	Mkwawa rebellion destroyed Zelewski's column in 1891. Seriously defeated in 1894 but harassed by Germans until he committed suicide in 1898.
1892	Meli, successor of Mandara as paramount chief of Chagga collides with Germans and kills Baron von Bulow. Punitive expeditions sent.
1894	Sultan Hassin bin Omari tries to take Kilwa from the west in order to re-establish slave trade. Captured in a punitive expedition.
1895	Machembo, Yao chief southwest of Lindi, refuses to pay hut tax. Persists until 1899 when a punitive expedition imprisons his followers and he flees to Portuguese territory.
1905-6	*Maji Maji* resistance war. Begins on cotton plantation and spreads throughout south-east region. Suppressed at an estimated cost of 120,000 lives.

Source: J. P. Moffet (ed.), *Handbook of Tanganyika* (Dar es Salaam, Government Printer, 1958), pp. 56-9, 63, 65, 66; Richard Reusch, *History of East Africa* (New York, Frederick Ungar, 1961), pp. 310, 315, 316, 322-6; Roland Oliver and Gervase Mathew (eds.), *History of East Africa* op. cit., pp. 442, 443, 446.

us to look at a colony in the context of an 'overseas economy', consisting of a metropole and periphery. The metropolis (i.e. Germany or Britain) was the locus of product elaboration and disposal and the source from which the system was provisioned with capital, managerial skill and other ancillary services needed for production. It was, moreover, the locus of initiative and decision, the critical linkage point between international demand and supply and the nexus through which the pattern of resource combination was determined. The colony (periphery, hinterland) was merely an entity for supplying raw materials, land and labour, propelled by specific demands from its metropole, and in return, receiving the supplies needed to fulfil these demands.[26] In this context, it was necessary to designate certain

[26] See Justinian F. Rweyemamu, 'International Trade and the Developing Countries', *The Journal of Modern African Studies*, vol. 7, no. 2 (1969); Andre Gunder Frank, *Capitalism and Underdevelopment in Latin America* (New York, Monthly Review Press, 1969), pp. 6-11.

institutional mechanisms geared to enhance collaboration between the two. In particular, colonialism imposed *exclusive spheres of influence* of the centre on the colony, thus limiting the external intercourse of the colony with other areas. This was particularly noticeable in the specification of origin, destination and carriage of trade, though this factor pervaded the production relations as well, as I shall indicate below. Secondly, it restricted the colony to terminal activity in production, i.e. crude production, some processing and occasional assembly, leaving the product elaboration to the metropole and with that, of course, the lion's share of value added. In other words, the *division of labour* and hence the colony's *specialization* was imposed upon it by the metropolitan power, rather than by objective resource conditions of the colony (e.g. resource endowment). Thirdly, it specified the *monetary arrangements* to be adopted by the colony in the form, for example, of the *currency board*. This entailed the use in the colony of the metropolitan financial intermediaries, the maintenance of free convertibility with metropolitan currency at a fixed rate of exchange, and with that, the assurance that the liabilities of financial operators in the colony were fully matched by metropolitan assets. The effect was to ensure that the colony's assets were readily realizable in terms of metropolitan supplies of goods and services.[27]

1.3.1 The plantation system and the proletarianization of the peasantry

The Reichskolonialamt and the Kolonialwirtschaftskomitee viewed the German colonies chiefly as sources of raw materials.[28] They could also act as markets (e.g. for textiles) and offer opportunities for capital exports and population migration, but their primary function was viewed as that of expanding tropical products over which the

[27] Lloyd Best, 'Outlines of a Model of Pure Plantation Economy', *Social and Economic Studies*, vol. 17, no. 3 (September 1968), pp. 283-4.
[28] John Iliffe, *Tanzania Under German Rule* (London, Cambridge University Press, 1969), p. 77; Eric Moore Ritchie, *The Unfinished War* (London, Camelot Press, 1940), p. 73. Gustav Stolper supports this view when he says of Germany at the turn of the century that '. . . the industrial affluence and exporting capacity of the country were entirely dependent upon the importation of raw materials and foodstuffs, which by far exceeded the exports of finished goods'. See Gustav Stolper, *German Economy, 1870-1940: Issues and Trends* (New York, Reynal & Hitchcock, 1940), p. 53. For the British motives see Lord Lugard, *The Dual Mandate in British Tropical Africa* (London, Frank Cass & Co., 1965).

Anglo-Saxon powers had hitherto exercised a virtual monopoly. However, the Germans were not necessarily interested in cheap materials, rather, they wanted strategic raw commodities, especially cotton, sisal, rubber and gold. These were strategic in the sense that the industries requiring these raw materials, which were of such importance to the economy for political or military reasons, required an independent source which the Germans could effectively control. For example, they started producing cotton in order to have their own independent source of supply, even though on the average American imports were cheaper, since they wanted to reduce the risk of price fluctuations brought about by the American suppliers.[29] An independent supply of these commodities would also ease Germany's foreign exchange requirements. It was for these reasons that practically none of these items was sold to countries other than Germany, as is shown in table 1.3.

TABLE 1.3

Principal total exports and exports sent to Germany, 1911
(in thousands of marks)

Item	Exports (1911)	Exports sent to Germany (1911)
Non-plantation rubber	4781	3511*
Plantation rubber	3610	2539*
Sisal fibre	4532	4423*
Hides and skins	3035	237
Copra and coconuts	1848	185
Cotton	1332	1267*
Coffee	1266	561
Gold	1023	1013*
Beeswax	817	452
Timber	515	460
Groundnuts	490	128
Ivory	485	14
Sesame	404	141
Mica	348	348*
Rice	120	nil
Gum copal	107	13
Wattle and bark	96	27
Total Exports	22438	13207

*Asterisks indicate 'strategic' raw materials to Germany.

Source: Michael J. Yaffey, 'International Transactions Before and During the German Period' (Dar es Salaam, Economic Research Bureau of the University College, mimeo., 1967), p. 8.

[29] Thus although between 1897-1906 the average price of American raw cotton in Hamburg was 70 Pf per kg; in February 1904 it was 170 Pf, in December

The issue that plagued the German administration was one of means; that is whether they should encourage settler plantations or African smallholder production. The problem was finally resolved after the arrival of German settlers (by 1912 there were 758) who wanted to establish plantations. This event necessitated the alienation of community land and the recruitment of African labour to man the plantations. By 1913, 542,124 hectares had been alienated through the eviction of indigenous citizens from their best lands; reserves being created for those evicted. There is no doubt that the German settlers, and the English settlers after them, expropriated the best lands.

Fuggles-Couchman, for example, notes that the soils of the highest fertility in the Northern Region are 'the great areas of plantation coffee production, the centre of large-scale estate farming producing wheat, maize, seed beans, and the first centre of large-scale sugar production'.[30] Graham, referring to British settlement after the war concurs: 'It is a fact', he says, 'that the land already chosen . . . was the *best* in Ubena, and much of it had been in continuous cultivation for 50 years'.[31]

In many areas, the result of these expropriations was to intersperse native reserves with settled 'European' areas. Any native reserve could subsequently be alienated if the governor so decided. In the Kilimanjaro and Meru areas the settlers pushed the displaced Africans further up the mountain between the alienated belt and the Forest Reserve.[32] This clear separation of land between Africans and Europeans made it possible to direct capital expenditure. Furthermore, by depriving the Africans of their best land and confining them to reserves, the colonial powers and the plantation owners restricted considerably the competitiveness of African exports. The plantation owners expansion prospects depended on the labour supply from

---

the same year it was 70Pf, in September 1907 it was 120 Pf. The textile manufacturers, especially Leipzig cotton spinners and Stuttgart millionaire, Olto, sought independent sources of supply in the new colonies. See J. Iliffe, *Tanzania Under German Rule*, op. cit., pp. 77-8.

[30] N. R. Fuggles-Couchman, *Agricultural Change in Tanganyika: 1945-1960* (Stanford Food Research Institute, 1964).

[31] J. D. Graham, 'Changing Patterns of Wage Labour in Tanzania: A History of the Relations Between African Labour and European Capitalism in Njombe District, 1931-1961' (PhD. dissertation, Northwestern University, 1968), p. 178.

[32] Kirilo Japeth and E. Seaton, *The Meru Land Case* (Nairobi, East African Publishing House, 1967); Tanganyika Territory, *Report of the Arusha-Moshi Land Commission* (Dar es Salaam, Government Printer, 1947).

the African peasantry and the reduction of competition for export markets.[33]

One of the characteristics of the plantation system is that production is based on large-scale units utilizing a sizeable resident labour force performing routine tasks for close to subsistence wages. Juxtaposed to the traditional economy, where a proletarian class did not exist, the institution of the plantation system required the creation of conditions for the emergence of free labour that was alienated from the means of production, facing the capitalist who owned and controlled the means of production. At first this was not fully realized by the planter class, who expected the peasants to flock to their plantations through normal market mechanisms.[34] To their surprise, the market mechanism did not resolve the paradox of 'actual shortage in the presence of the deceptive appearance of plenty'. Indeed, Leubuscher notes that:

> ... ever since white settlement became of importance, the question of labour supply for European employers had been one of the main concerns of the Administration of German East Africa .... In the earlier stages of colonial development, the native's unfamiliarity with the work required and therefore unwillingness to undertake it, is the main cause of labour shortage; added to this is a *lack of responsiveness to inducements to earn a money income.*[35]

In general the planters' views coincided with Leubuscher's quoted above though they stressed the inherent lack of capacity of the Africans to improve their well-being. This racial belief crystallized into the convention of maintaining low wages which as Myint points out contrasts with the experience of the 'areas of recent settlement'.[36] It is important, however, to understand the rationale of the African reaction to plantation interests. In the first place, Africans had the alternative of producing cash crops to supplement their income. Moreover, this option was preferable to working on the plantation in that it did not alter the production relations of the community. In other words, given the existence of surplus productive capacity in the form of land and labour, a peasant could grow some cash crops,

[33] Giovanni Arrighi, *The Political Economy of Rhodesia*, op. cit., p. 24.
[34] Nor would standard conventional wisdom have understood the African reaction. See especially, W. Arthur Lewis, 'Economic Development with unlimited supply of Labour', *The Manchester School* (May 1954).
[35] Charlotte Leubuscher, *Tanganyika Territory: A Study of Economic Policy Under Mandate* (London, Oxford University Press, 1940), p. 29.
[36] Hyla Myint, *The Economics of the Developing Countries* (London, Hutchinson University Library, 1964).

augment his income while retaining his status as a non-wage labourer, i.e. controlling the work process. Africans who had access to modes of transportation therefore either extended their acreage to include cash crops or interplanted cash crops within the food crops (e.g. coffee/banana holdings in Moshi and Bukoba).[37] The result of African involvement in cash crop production will be examined in the next section, though its quantitative significance is indicated in table 1.4.

TABLE 1.4

Production of principal exports by Africans
(selected years)
(a) *Kilimanjaro*

Coffee (*in tons*)

Year	Tonnage
1923-24	32
1926-27	80
1929-30	416
1934-35	1275
1940-41	3250
1944-45	3275
1950-51	5670
1955-56	6577
1960-61	8739

(b) *Mwanza*

Cotton (*in kilos*)

Year	Kilos
1905	9975
1908	21496
1911	164402
1913	676000

(c) *Bukoba*

Coffee (*in tons*)

Year	Tonnage
1904	—
1905	234
1909	280
1911	554
1912	681

Source: Kilimanjaro Native Cooperative Union Limited (annual report); Ralph A. Austen, *Northwest Tanzania Under German and British Rule*, pp. 270-1.

[37] This phenomenon is the familiar Myintian 'vent for surplus'. See Hyla Myint, 'The Classical Theory of International Trade and Underdeveloped Countries', *Economic Journal* (June 1958), pp. 317-37.

Secondly, the plantation interests underestimated the level of subsistence wages that would attract the African peasantry. Imbued with their racial prejudices, they discounted the value of the security of subsistence which was provided by the traditional sector. Such real income consisted of the flow of means of subsistence accruing to the peasant family over its 'life cycle', including the support the members would receive from the wider community during their old age or sickness.[38] Wage income promised by the plantation interests not only fell short of what an African would need to support his family but was unreliable as well. Conditions of work in the plantations were also unsatisfactory. Once employed under contract—either written or more often oral—Africans were subjected to harsh sanctions for breaking the contract. The institution of the contract in a preliterate society where employers had monopoly over the ability to read, write and speak the language of the law, provided manifold opportunities for abuses intended to keep Africans in employment longer than they desired. The medical officer, reporting the typical conditions of an African labourer, three decades after the establishment of the plantation system said:

> On arrival at the plantations, the labourers were turned on to build any sort of shelter, and within a day or two were put to work. The diet issued was deficient in quality and variety, and there was no adequate arrangement for hospital accommodation, medical attention, water supplies, kitchens, latrines, etc. As a consequence, dysentery, bowel troubles and deaths ensued, and the proportion rendered unfit was large.[39]

In spite of these problems, the Africans who refused to work on the plantations or who worked there occasionally were regarded as irrational. Indeed by 1936 (after the depression years) the monthly rates were no higher than they had been at the turn of the century (see table 1.5).

The question might be raised as to whether the 'conventional beliefs' of the settlers in their refusal to raise real wages sufficiently to close the gap between supply and demand was against their rational economic interests. From the available evidence it seems that this is not so. The high returns in peasant agriculture and the security afforded by the traditional society contributed to a low elasticity of

[38] G. Arrighi, 'Labour Supplies in Historical Perspectives: The Proletarianization of the Rhodesian Peasantry' (Dar es Salaam, Economic Research Bureau of the University College, mimeo., 1967), p. 28.
[39] Tanganyika Territory, *Annual Medical Report* (Dar es Salaam, Government Printer, 1924).

19

the supply of labour over a wide range of wage rates. Below some very high wage rate at which it would have paid the African peasants to cut off their links with the traditional system, the quantity of labour supplied to the capitalist sector would have been very small. On the other hand, the expected marginal revenue product of labour, which determines the demand for it, must have been low over a wide range of levels of employment due in great part to the initial low productivity of labour. Given this situation, that is, of a high elasticity of demand for labour and a low elasticity of supply, the effect of raising wages sufficiently high to attract permanent African labour, in other words, of proletarianizing the peasantry, would have resulted in an insignificant increase in employment and a drastic reduction of the settlers' short-term profits.

As the settlers aimed at *short-run* profit-maximization (which is evidenced by the profits they repatriated—see table 1.6—where profits can be approximated to about 30 per cent) they were not prepared to increase wages. They therefore resorted to a *political* solution. This took various forms. First, they sought to create conditions that would lead to the emergence of free labour by depriving the peasants of their land. Governor Gotzen took thousands of men from the interior, mostly Nyamwezi and Sukuma, and settled them on the coast where they were bound to work for at least ninety days a year on the plantations.[40] The scheme, however, failed miserably as the transplanted men ran to Kenya where conditions of work were better.

The administration then sought out other measures of increasing labour supply without increasing wages. *Forced labour* was resorted to, at least during the German period. In Western Usambara, for example, each Shambala was issued with a labour card which required

TABLE 1.5

African monthly rates of pay in plantations, 1936

Area		Category of labour		
		Unskilled	Semi–skilled	Skilled
Tanga		shs. 10-12	shs. 12-15	shs. 30
Morogoro	Sisal	shs. 8-12	shs. 10-15	shs. 30
	Cotton	shs. 10-11	shs. 10-15	shs. 30
Kilosa	Sisal	shs. 10	shs. 15-17	shs. 30
	Cotton	shs. 9-12	shs. 15-17	shs. 30

Source: Report by Mr. F. Longland on Labour Matters in Sisal Areas, Tanga (Dar es Salaam, Tanganyika Archives).

[40] R. A. Austen, *Northwest Tanzania Under German and British Rule* (New Haven, Yale University Press, 1968), p. 74.

20

TABLE 1.6

Balance of payments of mainland Tanzania, 1912
(in thousands of marks)

	Cr.	Dr.
Exports	31,418	
Imports		50,309
International		
Investment Income		3,712
Other Head Office Expenses		1,831
Military Grant from Germany	3,618	
Capital Inflow and Errors	20,866	
	55,902	55,902

Source: Michael J. Yaffey, *Balance of Payments of Tanzania* (Munich, Weltforum Verlag for Ifo-Institut, 1970), table 14, p. 44.

him to spend thirty days on the European plantation. In Morogoro the headmen were

> ... instructed to produce a certain number of workers for a specified plantation in proportion to the number of inhabitants of their villages .... These regulations ... [were] carried out with energy, if necessary by an askari ... [and] ... are based on agreement between planters and district officers.[41]

Forced labour, however, became unpopular when it was found to be one of the major causes of the Maji Maji rebellion in 1905-6.[42]

The administration adopted two other measures to influence the supply of labour. First the German administration issued a taxation ordinance in 1897 which was re-enacted by the British in 1922.[43] Areas under full political control were subjected to a hut tax whose main object was to 'oblige Africans to accept paid labour and accustom themselves to European administrative discipline'.[44] Again this mechanism did not work satisfactorily since taxation, by failing to discriminate between incomes derived from the sale of produce and the sale of labour, did not alter the discrepancy between returns to peasants in agriculture

[41] Iliffe, *Tanzania Under German Rule*, op. cit., pp. 136-7, 64.
[42] ibid., p. 23.
[43] J. R. Modi, 'Income Tax Policy Problems in Less Developed Economies of Tropical Africa: With Special Reference to Tanganyika' (unpublished Ph.D. dissertation, University of Edinburgh, May 1964), chapter IV.
[44] Iliffe, *Tanganyika Under German Rule*, op. cit., p. 160. It is interesting to note that the motives of the Germans and British were almost identical. The purpose of the 1922 'Hut and Poll Tax' was 'to assert the colonial authority and thereby cause some psychological effect on the indigenous population so that it will act as a potential instrument for social and institutional changes'. Quoted by Modi, ibid.

and those in wage employment, which was one of the main determinants of the unwillingness of Africans to enter wage employment.[45] Secondly, the colonial government administered a preferential tariff for the benefit of European planters. The annual report of 1911-12 states, for example, that

> the incidence of the export duties falls almost exclusively upon the indigenous population, as the produce of European planters is exempt from duty. Also among the import commodities, most of the duty is borne by necessities imported for the coloured population, especially textiles .... [46]

These measures had the effect of raising the Africans' cash requirements and thus reducing their income from exports. Finally, an attempt was made to prevent Africans from growing certain cash crops, which were supposed to be the monopoly of Europeans[47] though this was not implemented except in Pangani. Wilson and Wilson visiting the country after the Second World War, report that

> settler pressure against the development of market crops by Africans is strong in [Kenya and Rhodesia], and although their influence is less in Tanganyika, settlers there spoke bitterly to us of the *right* of Africans to produce coffee, which they felt should be a monopoly of Europeans.[48]

The effect of this political mechanism was to induce some increment in labour supply, although at no time was it ever sufficient. Moreover, the system attracted the *migratory* type of labour. That is, the low wages and lack of security in the plantations led Africans to seek temporary jobs while maintaining the security afforded by their membership in the rural-based kinship group. In other words, *the plantation system failed to bring about the proletarianization of the African peasantry*. This failure has had long-lasting consequences. In the first place the inability of the planters to attract more permanent and therefore more productive labour (with relatively low absentee rates) led to excessive substitution of capital for labour in the plantation sector. This is confirmed by Fuggles-Couchman.[49] The consequence of these changes was a fall in the number of men employed per ton of output. For example, while estate coffee output increased by 200

---

[45] Arrighi, 'Labour Supplies', op. cit., p. 13.
[46] Quoted by Michael Yaffey, 'International Transactions', op. cit., p. 6. The tariff structure was retained by the British administration for similar reasons.
[47] Iliffe, ibid., pp. 169-70. Tanganyika Territory, *General Administration Memoranda* (Dar es Salaam, Government Printer, 1931).
[48] G. Wilson and A. Wilson, *Social Change* (London, Cambridge University Press, 1945), p. 137.
[49] Fuggles-Couchman, *Agricultural Change*, op. cit., p. 26.

per cent between 1945 and 1960, labour in terms of men employed rose by 33 per cent. It is worth noting that this capital labour substitution took place not as a response to increased labour-cost but to scarcity of additional workers. When, therefore, the labour union and the independent government negotiated and obtained wage increases that could stabilize the labour force, planters were able to massively lay off workers and still maintain adequate output levels.[50] Secondly, the cheap labour policy pursued led to the perpetuation of the unskilled character of the Tanzanian labour force which is still evident today, illustrated by the sisal industry which was a 'leading' industry. The capitalist nature of the production process did not improve the quality of the local factors of production as would be expected.[51] As we shall show later, this factor has significant implications for the industrialization process. Thirdly, it becomes evident that the major cause of absenteeism, lack of initiative, and low productivity of African labour was the nature of the plantation system itself rather than the nature of traditional society.[52] Fourthly, the system of migrant labour impeded innovations in the traditional sector so that a vicious circle was built up with poverty compelling migration and migration in turn hindering the alleviation of poverty.

This section concludes by examining briefly some of the other long term effects of the plantation system. It produced a very narrow range of primary commodities (sisal, coffee, tea) for the export market in the metropolis where in the case of sisal protective shelter was provided.[53] Capital, entrepreneurship, management (the so called 'missing productive factors' in the underdeveloped countries) were all foreign. Such a productive system had a number of growth implications.

[50] They could afford to lay off workers and maintain adequate levels of output because the laid-off workers worked fewer hours per month due to a high rate of absenteeism (over 50 per cent). By offering higher wages and other benefits which will be discussed in later sections, the labour force was stabilized, drastically reducing the rate of absenteeism. See Justinian F. Rweyemamu, 'Some Aspects of the Turner Report' (Dar es Salaam, Economic Research Bureau Paper 69.20 of University College, 1969) for further details.
[51] Albert O. Hirshman, *How to Divest in Latin America, and Why*, Essays in International Finance, no. 76 (Princeton; Princeton University Press for Department of Economics, 1969), p. 4.
[52] I should mention, however, that the above refers to the *particular* plantation system, as it developed in Tanzania during the colonial period rather than plantation systems in general. See Hyla Myint, 'An Interpretation of Economic Backwardness', *Oxford Economic Papers*, N.S. vol. VI, no. 2 (Oxford, Clarendon Press, June 1954).
[53] Until 1967, for example, when the government announced its intention to nationalize the sisal industry, sisal exports enjoyed a 10 per cent preferential tariff in Britain.

Firstly, resource availability was not simply determined by the factor endowments of Tanzania because the system itself was defined as being dependent on factors of production which except for land and labour were drawn from abroad. This aspect of the plantation system might at first sight be seen as a sign of progress since it led to the provision of the 'missing productive factors'. But it will become evident that the usefulness of such investments is highly limited as, by having all supplies and capital goods imported from Britain and Germany, it caused the secondary effects of such investments to be felt in the metropolis rather than in Tanzania.[54] Indeed as Singer remarks

> I would suggest that if the economic test of investment is the multiplier effect in the form of cumulative addition to income, employment, capital, technical knowledge, and growth of external economies, then a good deal of investment in the underdeveloped countries which we used to consider as 'foreign' should in fact be considered as domestic investment on the part of the industrialized countries.[55]

Secondly as resource use was determined by the economic interests of the owners, investment opportunities perception became biased in favour of complementing the metropolitan economies. Intersectoral links within Tanzania have therefore remained weak. Furthermore, the established industries did not always correspond to comparative advantage, however defined. For example, the Germans built up a high cost sisal industry because they wanted to have cordage for their navy from an independent supply which they could control. When Britain took over after the war, she discouraged further investments in the industry (as she had no use for the product at this time), only to encourage it during the Second World War when the British Admiralty adopted the use of cordage after her supplies of manilla hemp-fibre were blocked by the Japanese. The selective perception of investment opportunities (according to the requirements of the metropolitan power) was further evidenced by the granting of more rights of occupancy to European tea growers in the south of Tanzania after the Second World War when South East Asian tea output was disrupted by the war and post-war colonial liberation movements, and

[54] George Beckford, 'Toward an Appropriate Theoretical Framework for Agricultural Development Planning and Policy', *Social and Economic Studies*, vol. XVII, no. 3 (1968), pp. 233-42.
[55] Hans W. Singer, *International Development: Growth and Change* (New York, McGraw-Hill Book Co., 1964), p. 163. It is interesting to note that J. S. Mill makes a similar comment with regard to the West Indies. See John Stuart Mill, *Principles of Political Economy* (London, Longmans, 1929), p. 415.

the establishment of the ill-fated but well-documented Groundnut Scheme.[56]

Thirdly, foreign ownership of the plantations implied that much of the saving and investment potential was depleted by the outflow of factor payments in the form of interest payments to their financiers in the metropolitan powers (the Mincing Lane complex, Wigglesworth, etc.) and dividends to their shareholders (who were also in the centre), while retained earnings tended to be employed for further expansion of the same export industry. This led to very little agricultural diversification in the plantation sector (practically all the new crops that are now being exported were grown by African smallholders or arose out of the inflow of new capital). The survey by Guillebaud of the sisal industry sheds some light on these observations. Table 1.7 shows average profits (*net* of depreciation) of ten plantations between 1951 and 1956 and their allocation. It should be noted that interest income is not indicated, as it is normally treated as an expense of the business for the year. Accordingly the outflow is grossly understated.

Fourthly, the development of the plantation system hindered the diffusion of technological change in various ways. By importing all the capital goods requirements, it failed to develop the technological base of skills, knowledge, facilities and organization upon which further technical progress so largely depends. Moreover, because of the political power the sector wielded, research was concentrated in the crops which they were growing. Consequently very little technical knowledge concerning production of other crops (especially food crops for the internal market) was acquired.

1.3.2 Cash crop production and class formation

Even before the systematic European colonization of mainland Tanzania, the establishment of Europeans and Arabs on the coast for slave trade and commercial activities had profoundly affected the traditional societies of the coast. Iliffe recounts how these communities had

[56] Hans Ruthenberg, *Agricultural Development in Tanganyika* (Munich, Weltforum Verlag for Ifo-Institut, 1964), p. 46. Sir Herbert Frankel, *The Economic Impact on Underdeveloped Societies* (Cambridge, Harvard University Press, 1963), pp. 141-53; Fred G. Burke, *Tanganyika: Preplanning*, National Planning Series of Syracuse University (Syracuse University Press, 1965), pp. 34-9.

begun commercial agricultural production.[57] A further impact of these contacts showed itself in the creation of *akidas* (administrative or commercial intermediaries) who were sent to exploit the hinterland.[58]

It was, however, German and British colonization that reinforced traditional class differences on the one hand and introduced and developed new class differences linked to capitalist exploitation of the country on the other. This class differentiation went hand in hand with the uneven development that is so characteristic of capitalist penetration.[59] The major agents of these class and regional differentiations were: economic, in the introduction of cash crops and labour market; educational, a factor that was highly influenced by missionary activity; and administrative, in the form of indirect rule.

TABLE 1.7

Allocation of sisal profits: 1951 to 1956
(in shs. million)

	Amount	Per Cent of Total
Total Profits	192.6	100
Capital Expenditure	52.5	27
Net Current Assets	11.5	8
Taxation	48.0	24
Payment to Shareholders	72.4	37
Capital Reorganization	8.2	4

Source: C. W. Guillebaud, *An Economic Survey of the Sisal Industry* of *Tanganyika* (London, James Nisbet & Co. for the Tanganyika Sisal Growers Association, 1966), p. 38.

The introduction of cash crops divided the country into two major areas. On the one hand, we find a fairly prosperous peasantry, located in areas with plentiful rainfall engaged mainly in the cultivation of perennials, favourably located with respect to transport facilities (Northern and Central Railways as well as the Uganda-Kenya railway) and with a relatively dense population. For reasons that will be enumerated below, these areas have undergone the most significant class differentiations (that is, in relation to other areas) since class formation

---

[57] Iliffe, 'The Age of Improvement and Differentiation', in I. N. Kimambo and A. J. Temu (eds.), *History of Tanzania* (Nairobi, E. A. Publishing House, 1969). p. 134.
[58] For an exposition of the role of *akidas* see J. Clagget Taylor, *The Political Development of Tanganyika* (Stanford, California, Stanford University Press, 1963).
[59] The nuances of periphery-satellites that emerge from capitalist penetration are fully discussed in Frank, *Capitalism and Underdevelopment in Latin America*, op. cit., pp. 8-12, *passim*.

in Tanzania remains embryonic because of the low level of productive forces. On the other hand, we find a less prosperous peasantry, located in areas with moderate and unreliable rainfall where sparsely-settled peasants still engage in largely subsistence cultivation of food and a few exchange items, and are unfavourably linked with modes of transport and urban market centres. Here land tenure systems remained communal so that they were not affected by the 'Freehold Law' passed after independence. Consequently, class formation in this sector, except that imposed by indirect rule (see below), is almost absent.

In areas where capitalist penetration expressed itself through cash-crop production for export, we find these societies dependent upon one single cash crop and the emergence of non-communal forms of land tenure. Mainly through an adaptation of traditional practices, land (before the 'Freehold Law') had come to be treated as a commodity to be sold, rented or leased, and traditional collective rights and overlapping rights over the land and its products had been replaced by an expanding sphere of *individual* rights. This is confirmed by studies of the Nyakyusa and the Chagga by Gulliver and Fuggles-Couchman respectively.[60] This trend of individualization of holdings, which was encouraged by the Royal Commission,[61] gradually eroded the fundamental feature of communal land tenure and started to create the landless peasant, the proletariat.

The emergence of the proletariat, however, depended upon the intensification of pressure on land, which in turn depended upon the technique of production adopted. That is, to the extent that peasants did not alter their traditional techniques (see above), the introduction of cash crops led to an expansion of acreage thus speeding up the pressures on land. While it is often suggested that colonial imperialism was beneficial because it introduced new methods of production, this view is not supported by available evidence.[62] The acreage for cotton for example increased from 142,000 acres in 1945 to 582,000 in 1960. During the same period, cotton output rose from 7,512 long tons to 34,241 long tons, thus revealing an insignificant change in labour productivity during the period,[63] if we assume a labour force rising proportionate to acreage. Clearly this type of expansion has

[60] Gulliver, *Land Tenure*, op. cit., p. 27; Fuggles-Couchman, *Agricultural Change*, op. cit, p. 65.
[61] *East African Royal Commission, 1953-1955 Report* (London, HMSO, 1955).
[62] Changes in production techniques result in changes in labour productivity. This is the sense in which the above statement refers.
[63] Fuggles-Couchman, *Agricultural Change*, op. cit., p. 22.

very definite limits in the availability of cultivable land and/or in the availability of surplus labour if the productivity of the latter does not rise fast enough to offset the exhaustion of surplus labour time initially available. Indeed in certain areas of Tanzania some of the former constraints were already noticeable before the end of the colonial era. Gulliver for example observes that 'the young Nyakyusa men find increasing difficulty in obtaining arable land rights in favour of the young generation, as they traditionally did . . . . This means that in the high density areas, the majority of men under the age of thirty years have little or no arable land. Nor can they hope for it until the deaths of their fathers'.[64]

Moreover, as commercial agriculture tended to dominate the village economy and the communal system of land tenure began to disintegrate into individual ownership of land, human relationships in the sphere of production also tended to become commercialized at the expense of the old systems of mutual and reciprocal obligations that lay at the heart of the traditional system. In particular, co-operative forms of labour began to be replaced by hired labour. Karl-Heinz Friedrich referring to Bukoba notes that '. . . on the large farms it is the usual practice to supplement the family labour by hired labourers'.[65] This was the nascent rural African *bourgeoisie*, which, like its white counterpart, was beginning to exploit the migrant workers.

The commercialization of agricultural activities stimulated, reinforced, and in many areas created the position of the African merchant class. Squeezing in between the European and Asian wholesalers, and some Asian retailers and the rural producers, the African middlemen developed considerably during the period. Most of the big business continued to be owned and operated by the European and Asian *bourgeoisie*. The African through a variety of laws and regulations was relegated to a very low-turnover retailer and itinerant trader. Nevertheless an embryonic merchant class was in the offing. The 1961 survey of wholesale and retail trade in the country found 34,381 licensed African retail traders out of 48,535 total traders (including wholesalers but excluding itinerant traders).[66] However, all these African traders did less than a third of the total business! This very low turnover has been attributed to a natural lack of inclination to 'barter

---

[64] Gulliver, *Land Tenure*, op. cit., p. 36.
[65] Karl-Heinz Friedrich, 'Coffee-Banana Holdings in Bukoba' in H. Ruthenberg (ed.), *Smallholder Farming*, op. cit.
[66] H. C. C. Hawkins, *Wholesale and Retail Trade in Tanganyika: A Study of Distribution in East Africa*, (New York, Frederick A. Praeger, 1965), p. 34.

and trade'.[67] Such a view, however, is not only a mistake, since at least there are examples of big successful African businessmen outside of Tanzania, but invidious as well. The Tanganyika law on licences declared that 'under no circumstances' was a valid application for a trading licence to be refused. But a study of 'the distribution and consumption of commodities among Africans' carried out in 1952–3 noted that 'in *practice* . . . some administrative officer will effectively discourage an African applicant from pressing his application' (my emphasis).[68] But more serious was the regulation that forbade wholesalers to advance Africans merchandise in excess of six hundred shillings' worth on credit.[69] Furthermore commercial courses in schools were reserved for Asians. These are some of the more serious causes for the low turnover of African businessmen; rules which curbed the formation of an African *bourgeois* class, while breeding an Asian one.

European colonization, by systematically reinforcing and even creating 'artificial' chiefs through the system of indirect rule, created an auxiliary class of privileged people that exploited the peasants. Depending on the level of material forces, it is these 'leaders', authentic or artificial, who have been the principal beneficiaries, taking the best land which they exploit with local serf or migrant paid labour. Coffee, for instance, had long been grown in Bukoba area, the berries being used by chiefs for ceremonial purposes. When coffee became an export crop and the Uganda Railway reached Lake Victoria, the chiefs began to grow it in large quantities. Partly because they had a traditional monopoly and partly because they were supported by the Germans, the Haya chiefs obtained most of the early profits from coffee-growing. They made use of a quasi-feudal form of land tenure (*nyarubanja*) to obtain much of the best coffee land, turning the peasants into tenants and taking a large proportion of their coffee crop.[70] A similar development was taking place in Moshi and Arusha. When coffee was introduced by the missionaries in the 1890s, it was the chiefs and their courtiers who had the best opportunities. Chief Marealle 1 was said to have grown as many as one thousand coffee trees in 1909. Moreover the Germans permitted the Chagga chiefs to distribute

---

[67] 'The Indian Trader', *Colonial Paper*, no. 148, 1938.
[68] F. C. Wright, *African Consumer in Nyasaland and Tanganyika*. (London, HMSO 1955) p. 36.
[69] Wright, op. cit., p. 36; J. Loxley, 'East African Stock Exchanges' in P. A. Thomas (ed.), *Private Enterprise and the East African Company*, (Dar es Salaam, Tanganyika Publishing House, 1969), p. 132-ff.
[70] The *nyarubanja* system of land tenure was abolished by the Tanzanian Government in 1969.

vihamba (clan lands), which they had not been able to do previously.[71] Other privileges which the colonial chiefs obtained included fairly high official salaries, more frequent agricultural assistance, preferential treatment by traders and even cars. The colonial government set up a school for their sons as well, thereby instituting the only 'public school' in the British sense, which ironically enough also educated most of our 'revolutionary' leaders!

Finally, through the educational system that was closely tied to the regional development of the productive system, a salaried African class emerged. This group consisted of minor functionaries, confined for a long time to inferior positions such as postmen, clerks and teachers. It was this class, however, that articulated the anti-colonial consciousness. It is true, of course, that civil servants were not allowed to join political parties—this may explain the low calibre of politicians who emerged on the dawn of independence—but their indirect role and contribution was significant.

These social differentiations among the African population were one tier of a broader stratification of colonial Tanzanian society, which, in comparison was only embryonic. For there had emerged a compartmentalization of society which did not usually cut across racial boundaries but coincided with them. The rural and urban European *bourgeoisie* (owners of capital in the plantation sector, industry and commerce respectively) and the British professional personnel in the civil service formed the top stratum of society in the mainland. The Arab aristocracy and the British professional civil servants played a similar role in Zanzibar. These classes had power, prestige and wealth—the hallmarks of a ruling élite. The Asians' financial strength in commerce, industry and agriculture put them next, as they lacked political power. The Africans, stripped of power, prestige and status, debarred from acquiring wealth, remained at the bottom of the ladder, constantly serving the interests of the ruling élite and the merchant class.

These class divisions were reinforced by economic, social and political discrimination and segregation. There were separate residential areas for the various racial communities; different schools, hospitals, clubs, etc. This separation was intended to minimize competition between the races. On the economic level, the compartmentalization

[71] Much of the material in this paragraph was obtained from Iliffe, 'The age of Improvement Differentiation (1907-1945)', (Conference on the History of Tanzania, the University College, Dar es Salaam, undated), pp. 7-8.

was reinforced by a racial salary structure in the public, and imitatively in the private, sector as well as wide disparities in both quality and quantity of social and economic services funded by government for different races. Typical of the colonial attitudes toward this racial stratification was that expressed by the Holmes Commission 1947–8, which when called upon to inquire into the 'Civil Service Structure and Salaries in East Africa', recommended different salary structures for different races on the ground that 'the European surpasses the Asian in such matters as sense of public service, judgement and readiness to take responsibility, and subject to individual exception the African is at the present time markedly inferior to the Asian in the same educational qualifications, in such matters as sense of responsibility, judgement, application to duty and output of work'.[72]

It was against this background that the independence struggle was waged. The natural desire to achieve political autonomy and self-improvement had resulted in the formation of various local political associations (Bahaya Union, 1926; Kilimanjaro Native Co-operative Union, 1932, Pare Union, 1950) that finally merged with TANU in 1954. In the fight for self-determination that ensued the emerging African social differentiations we have noted above were temporarily submerged, though they have determined the structure of the ruling party. The uneven development produced by capitalist penetration and the heterogeneity of the local party units necessitated a rather weak central structure of the TANU party, a fact that is still observable today.[73] The Europeans formed their own party, the United Tanganyika Party, but despite the colonial administration's encouragement, it was never popular. The lack of support for UTP was due to its largely racial character (which limited its membership) and to the fact that unlike in Zanzibar the *bourgeoisie* could not intimidate and threaten the African into supporting it.

It should be mentioned, though, that the attainment of independence was not primarily the outcome of a domestic class struggle. Rather it was the result of a constellation of various historical circumstances in which *external* forces played an important role: the general crisis of colonialism after the Second War, the pressure of the United States to open up the colonies to all capitalist nations, and the armed struggle

---

[72] Quoted by B. A. Ogot, *East Africa Journal* (August 1967), p. 40.
[73] This is a correction to Henry Bienen's, *Tanzania: Party Transformation and Economic Development*, (Princeton, University Press, 1967), stress on the low level of available resources as the major cause of TANU's weak structure. See especially p. 413.

engaged by some of the more advanced colonies for independence were all contributory factors.[74] The Mau Mau revolt in Kenya and the threat of violence in the other African colonies including Tanzania (in the form of strikes, boycotts, etc.) were certainly instrumental in the rapid 'transfer of power' to Tanzanians. There was, however, no armed struggle and the peasantry was not reorganized into fighting structures.[75]

1.3.3 The institutional setting: trade and infrastructure

During the colonial period a partially inter-linked institutional structure of private trading interests grew up which has shaped the export enclave of the country. Its main East African base was Nairobi, Kenya, where, in conjunction with settlers it was able to pressure the colonial administration to adopt policies conducive to its continued growth.

In the earlier period, the Deutsche Ostafrika Gesellschaft, the oldest chartered company with land concessions and plantation holdings, had the widest trading networks. It had the monopoly of sisal, cotton and most of the produce. In turn, it imported most of the country's requirements. In all its operations, it used the Indian middleman. When the British gained control of the economy, a new network of oligopolistic firms were established. Many of these merchandising companies were subsidiaries of international corporations and had their main offices more often in Nairobi than in Dar es Salaam. Crops such as sisal, for example, were handled by brokers, the most important being Ralli Brothers of Kenya, a subsidiary of Ralli Brothers of London who handled purchasing, transport, warehousing, insurance and shipping of sisal. Coffee and cotton were sold by auction to large foreign buyers, agents such as Tancot Ltd. (Tanganyika Cotton), now part of Lonrho group (London and Rhodesia), and Brooke Bond. Other products (e.g. meat products, pyrethrum) were handled by a foreign-

---

[74] Kwame Nkrumah, *Handbook of Revolutionary Warfare* (New York, International Publishers, 1969), and Claude Meillassouk, 'A Class Analysis of the Bureaucratic Process in Mali', *Journal of Development Studies*, vol. VI, no. 2 (January 1970).

[75] The Tanzanian case is therefore different from that pictured by Romano Ledda in which the nationalist leadership was an urban petty *bourgeoisie*. It is true that some of the leaders were petty *bourgeois* in this sense, but the major support came from the rural peasantry. See Romano Ledda, 'Social Classes and Political Struggle in Africa', *International Socialist Journal* (August 1967), pp. 562-3.

controlled distributive network such as Liebig Extract of Meat Company and Mitchell Cotts. In all these cases, the producer was at the mercy of the monopolistic power of these export firms.[76] The small farmer (or peasant), particularly, lacked any form of countervailing power to defend his interests.

Moreover, the firms which handled exports were invariably involved in the import trade. A significant proportion of private consumer goods (except textiles that were handled mainly by Asian wholesalers) were supplied by a few European-owned firms. Smith Mackenzie, for example, that merged with Dalgety in 1965, is a member of the Inchape Group of London that has been characterized as 'the largest overseas merchandising group in the world', trades in livestock, estates, hides and skins, insurance merchandise, shipping, tea brokerage, coffee, dairy machinery and agricultural engineering.[77] Almost all government imports were purchased through the Crown Agents for Overseas Administration in London. Yet, perhaps a large quantity of goods—probably the majority—were imported under exclusive agency agreements. The overseas manufacturers paid a fixed commission and guaranteed exclusivity. The agent stocked the goods at his own (or his bank's) expense and distributed them. The agent undertook the obligation of not handling similar, that is, competing lines. The result of this system enabled the manufacturers and the merchants to exploit the Tanzanian market with an unusual thoroughness. Yaffey claims, for example, that prior to nationalization 'one expatriate trading company paid its overseas parent company an agency fee of 2½ per cent on the f.o.b. value of *all* its imports and exports (although only 30 per cent of this business was handled in any way by the parent company) and in addition certain suppliers of imports paid *secret* commissions to the parent company which reached 9 per cent in one established case. Allowing, for example, a profit of 10 per cent on capital goods and 2½ per cent on all other imports would provide in 1966 an additional shs. 75 million to the declared shs. 110 million'.[78]

Alongside the powerful firms directly dominating the export-import trade, there grew up in the colonial era a variety of institutions that facilitated and reinforced their role in the economy. Perhaps the most

[76] For an understanding of the rather intricate network of these trading networks see: *Who Controls Industry in Kenya? A Report of the Working Party* (Nairobi, East African Publishing House for the National Christian Council of Kenya, 1969).
[77] *Who Controls Industry in Kenya?* op. cit.
[78] M. Yaffey, *Balance of Payments of Tanzania*, op. cit.

important of these were the banks and other financial intermediaries.

During the period 1919 to 1966, the Tanzania currency supply, together with those of Kenya and Uganda, was under the control of the central monetary authority, the East African Currency Board. Under this system, the shilling issued by the Board was freely convertible at a fixed rate of exchange with sterling. The Board itself was in London and the issue was generally backed by 100 per cent (or over) sterling reserves, contributed largely out of the country's export earnings. This system had a number of implications for trade patterns, monetary equilibrium and economic growth. Firstly, by stabilizing the shilling *vis-à-vis* the pound sterling, it eased both the flow of trade between Tanzania and Britain and the working of the supra-territorial banks (mostly British) with their bases in London without any exchange risk. Secondly, the link between the supply of East African currency and the availability of sterling meant that changes in the former were automatically determined by the state of the country's balance of payments, the public's propensity to hold cash and the commercial banks' lending policy. This meant that the government could not control either its external reserves or the credit policies of its commercial banks and other financial institutions. More serious, however, was the opportunity cost lost in terms of imports as a result of maintaining sterling reserves which had to be held as currency backing.[79] Britain and the more developed Commonwealth members gained in various ways, viz. they were able to change some of their soft currencies by drawing on the gold and dollar earnings of the colonies and to amass windfall gains on the country's sterling reserves as a result of sterling devaluation in 1949.[80]

Under these conditions, the commercial banks played a significant role in fund allocation. Initially, these banks were established for the purpose of providing credit on the basis of funds derived from their London connections for financing the distribution of imports. This accounts for the fact that the most important commercial banks operating in Tanzania were British-owned; Barclays Bank, Standard Bank (formerly Standard Bank of South Africa) and National Grindlays (formerly Bank of India, a British bank despite its name). Their earlier function was, of course, the bridging of the gap between

[79] Arthur Hazlewood, 'Economics of Colonial Monetary Arrangements', *Social and Economic Studies*, vol. III, nos. 3 and 4 (December 1954), pp. 291-315; W. T. Newlyn, *Money in an African Context* (Nairobi, Oxford University Press, 1967), pp. 29-55
[80] M. Barrat-Brown, *After Imperialism* (London, Heinemann, 1962), p. 219.

purchase and sale. But as conditions improved, they began to perform the more general roles of deposit banking. The outstanding characteristic of this phase of their development was that they soon became able to collect deposits locally in excess of what they felt they were able to utilize in Tanzania which they invested in London.[81] The result was that *for a considerable period, they were involved in a process of exporting capital from Tanzania to London.* The quantitative magnitude of these transfers can be obtained by noting that while deposits in Tanzania rose from sh. 36 million at the end of 1938 to sh. 359 million at the end of 1948, local lending by banks rose from sh. 31 million to sh. 36 million.[82] These banks were required moreover to invest at least two-thirds of their savings deposits outside the country.[83] Similar outflows were generated by the insurance companies through their investing insurance income abroad and by carrying an excessive reinsurance programme.

It is thus fair to say that these financial institutions were instrumental in shaping the sectoral pattern of investments and consequently the structure of the Tanzanian economy. For by directing a significant proportion of their loans and advances to the export-import trade and to plantation agriculture, they reinforced the enclave character of the economy.[84]

1.4 SOME CONCLUDING REMARKS

It cannot be denied that some material development took place during the colonial period. This was particularly true of the export sector of the economy on which depended not only the population's purchasing power but also the limited development and welfare projects. Moreover, there was some imposed technological advancement, particularly in the field of transport, in the use of more efficient hand tools and in the adoption of such agricultural machinery as the plough. However, the most important result of the colonial period is the

---

[81] W.T. Newlyn, *Money in an African Context*, op. cit., p. 43.
[82] H. H. Binhammer, 'Commercial Banking in Tanzania' (Dar es Salaam, Economic Research Bureau Paper No. 69.11, University College, mimeo, 1969), p. 3.
[83] Barrat-Brown, *After Imperialism*, op. cit., p. 219.
[84] A thorough re-examination of the major characteristics of such economies has been made by Reginald Herbert Green, *Stages in Economic Development: Changes in the Structure of Production Demand and International Trade* (Yale Growth Center, No. 125, 1969).

nature and direction of that development.

From what has been said it can be asserted that the development of the Tanzanian economy and society was the development of under-development. In particular, the development of the colonial economy was *dependent* on the external (or more explicitly the metropolitan) world. This was quite clear during the depression, and during the Second World War and after. This means that the further development of Tanzania would largely depend not so much on what Tanzanians did but on forces external to it.

Moreover, the development of the colonial economy was such as to generate within the country itself a pattern of regional inequality. There were the periphery centres where the pressures of the world economy were most direct: the major towns, the sisal estates and the main cash-crop areas. These were surrounded by peripheries which supplied them with food and other services, and sub-peripheries which either supplied labour to the periphery centres or stagnated.[85] Each of these subdivisions had problems of its own—problems which could not be tackled effectively by a colonial government.

It is important to realize that the development of underdevelopment of Tanzanian society during the colonial period was institutionalized, and that its essence was *not* the formal political relationship with Britain, but the economic ties that had been forged in the course of its historical development as a colony. Consequently, as we shall see in the next chapter, the attainment of formal political independence *in itself* would not be sufficient to substantially alter these two aspects of the development of underdevelopment.[86]

There were, moreover, deleterious psychological effects as well, including a lack of self-confidence, motivation and innovative conscious-ness as well as the destruction of the people's culture and history.[87] This was achieved through the set-up of segregated facilities already referred to as well as by the treatment of the indigenous citizens by the ruling élite. As Mwalimu Nyerere has expressed it, '. . . years of European domination had caused our people to have grave doubts about their own abilities. This was no accident; any dominating

---

[85] J. Iliffe, 'Agricultural Change in Modern Tanganyika: An outline History' (Dar es Salaam Social Science Conference, 1970), pp. 18-23.
[86] Said Hassan Mwingine, 'Class Conflict and Collaboration in Uganda: An Historical Perspective' (Harvard, 1971, mimeo.), p. 20.
[87] For a concise restatement of the disintegrative forces of colonization and their effects, see Frantz Fanon, *The Wretched of the Earth*, translated by Constance Farrington with a preface by Jean-Paul Sartre (New York, Grove Press Inc., 1966).

group seeks to destroy the confidence of those they dominate because this helps them to maintain their position and the oppressors in Tanganyika were no exception. Indeed it can be argued that the biggest crime of oppression and foreign domination in Tanganyika and elsewhere, is the psychological effect it has on the people who experience it'.[88]

[88] J. K. Nyerere, *Freedom and Unity*, op. cit. p. 3.

CHAPTER TWO

ECONOMY AND POLITY DURING THE POST-INDEPENDENCE PERIOD: 1962 to 1971

In this chapter the process of Tanzania's growth during this period is examined from two fundamental perspectives: Tanzania's relations with the outside world and its internal dialectic. In turn these perspectives are related to the events that preceded and followed the Arusha Declaration. The chapter is subdivided into four sections: Section 2.1 deals with the background to the Arusha Declaration from the point of view of Tanzania's relationships with the external world; Section 2.2 discusses the social differentiations that had begun to emerge during the same period; and Section 2.3 analyses the significance of the Arusha Declaration for Tanzania's future growth and development, and particularly its success in resolving the contradictions (internal and external) that had manifested themselves in the earlier period. Section 2.4 concludes with the theoretical implications of Tanzania's development experience, especially in so far as it suggests a possible industrialization strategy.

2.1 BACKGROUND TO ARUSHA—
I: THE INTERNATIONAL ASPECTS

When mainland Tanzania became independent on 9 December 1961, it inherited its basic position within the international community from the colonial relationship. In economic terms, this meant that a client 'independent' state on the periphery of western capitalism was created. Political independence did not necessarily mean economic independence, namely, control over economic decision-making and the national economy, the establishment of a firm industrial structure leading to a self-generating and self-sustaining growth, and a diversification of external economic contacts consistent with the nation's economic interests. On the contrary, the institutional framework diligently erected by Britain during the colonial period ensured

Tanzania's economic dependence on international capitalism in general and on Britain's in particular. Habit, acquaintances, specifications, lists of firms asked for quotations and similar semi-institutional heritages continually made Tanzanian importers biased towards the United Kingdom. The Commonwealth preference on sisal and other products also tended to attract Tanzania's major exports to Britain. This trading arrangement was made easier by the simplicity of the sterling exchange mechanism that automatically converted East African shillings into pounds sterling, and the nature of the commercial banking system already discussed. Investments, both public and private, were assumed to flow easily from Britain. Nor did the leadership at this time become unduly concerned about these relationships and institutions.

There was in fact a belief that the major impulse to the economy was to come from the foreign sector, *regardless of the form of that sector*. That is to say, there was no expressed intention to alter the ratio of foreign trade to national product, nor was a change in the composition of that trade or the importance of the trading partners contemplated. Secondly it was assumed that foreign private capital would easily flow into Tanzania if favourable conditions, such as were suggested by the World Bank Report and the Arthur D. Little Report, were created.[1] There was no discussion of the nature of such enterprises, nor of their effects on the growth potential of the economy. Both the Three Year Development Plan and the First Five Year Development Plan left the industrial sector to private entrepreneurs (largely foreign) without specifying ownership patterns, techniques of production and product mix.[2] All foreign aid was accepted whatever the terms. The underlying assumption of these early policies was the belief that a temporary sacrifice of economic independence (i.e. by maintaining colonial ties) would, by attracting significant western capital, produce a quicker rate of economic development which would lead ultimately to independence. The strategy also assumed, to a considerable extent, good will in international relations, i.e. the absence of antagonistic contradictions between Tanzania's interests and international capitalism. As will be shown below, these two assumptions were to be rendered questionable

[1] IBRD, *Economic Development of Tanganyika* (Baltimore Johns Hopkins Press, 1961), and Arthur D. Little, Inc., *Tanganyika Industrial Development* (Dar es Salaam).
[2] Government of Tanganyika, *Development Plan for Tanganyika, 1961-1962, 1963-1964* (Dar es Salaam, Government Printer, 1962), pp. 7-8, and the United Republic of Tanzania, *Tanganyika Five-Year Plan for Economic and Social Development, 1st July 1964—30th June 1969* (Dar es Salaam, Government Printer, 1964).

by the events of 1964 and after, thus forcing the leadership to adopt a new strategy that found full expression in the Arusha Declaration.[3]

Yet, perhaps the early strategy seemed to casual observers quite meaningful. The dependence on foreign trade as an 'engine of growth' guaranteed the new government easily collectable revenue, which forestalled the political risk of further taxing the population's income. The inflexibility of the production structure also limited alternative policy options. Moreover, there did not appear to be any reason why foreign enterprise might not be interested in Tanzania, if the latter created an attractive investment climate. After all, factors which were assumed to attract foreign private capital (low relative labour cost, adequate tax incentives, etc.) were amply available. Besides, foreign assets in the economy of Tanzania were relatively minimal. There were thus fewer assets which foreign interests might manoeuvre to protect. Moreover, the colonial power had not left a military base or communications centre—thus rendering the country strategically unimportant.

But such a strategy ignored the dangers implicit in a production structure that is characterized by short-run inelasticity of output. This was to express itself in the form of output fluctuations due to weather (which is both uncertain and uncontrollable), export price and import price fluctuations, thus affecting government revenue and the economy's capacity to import. More serious, however, was the failure to recognize the fact that there are serious (at least in the long run) constraints on the ability of any economy to depend on foreign investment for financing its growth.[4] This failure postponed the mobilization of domestic savings, even though the savings ratio had been declining in the fifties and marginal savings was actually negative between 1961–2.[5]

The leadership's overestimate of international capitalism's interest in the economy and its beneficent role as a growth-promoter was due to a fundamental misunderstanding of contemporary capitalism. It is true of course that there has been a broadening of western capitalism's interests in the underdeveloped countries of the world *in general*, due to the more direct involvement of the multinational corporation

[3] Catherine Hoskyins, 'Africa's Foreign Relations: The Case of Tanzania', *International Affairs*, 1968, pp. 446–62.
[4] O. Aboyade, *Foundations of An African Economy: A Study of Investment and Growth in Nigeria*, (New York, Frederick Praeger, 1966).
[5] Kighoma Malima, 'Trends in the Economy of Tanzania', Dar es Salaam, University College, mimeo. 1968).

in such industrialization as takes place in the periphery. However, its attraction to any particular economy is no longer dominated by such considerations as cheap labour, favourable tax incentives, etc. Rather, the factor of overwhelming contemporary importance is the 'existence of relatively developed and rapidly expanding industrial structure, as the latter ensures the smooth operation of capitalist manufacturing enterprises from the standpoint of outlets for their products and sources of production'.[6] Thus to the extent that the Tanzanian economy lacked an industrial structure, more developed capitalist relations of production, a wide consumer market and important

TABLE 2.1

Book value of British direct investment in selected African countries, 1960 to 1965
(in millions of £)

	1960	1961	1962	1963	1964	1965
Kenya	43.8	46.3	47.0	46.2	46.3	43.2
Ghana	47.8	50.2	53.2	49.9	47.9	53.4
Nigeria	88.0	98.6	94.8	99.8	92.4	96.7
Rhodesia	n.a	n.a	n.a	n.a.	66.1	62.0
Uganda	5.1	5.4	5.8	5.9	6.0	8.0
Tanzania	8.0	8.2	7.7	7.3	6.8	9.3
South Africa	258.3	270.6	290.0	319.4	352.9	391.7

Source: *Board of Trade Journal*, 26 January 1968, p. vii.

minerals, it was unlikely to attract significant capital inflow from international capitalism. Indeed in Africa, international capitalism has become interested in the Southern Africa complex (because of its industrial structure and minerals), and a few countries endowed with known mineral resources of great importance to the world economy (Zaïre, Nigeria, Zambia, Gabon), as well as peripheral centres (owing to their relatively more structured economies) such as Ghana, Kenya and Ivory Coast.[7] It is, however, the Southern African complex (including South Africa, South West Africa, Angola, Mozambique and Rhodesia) that occupies the dominant position in the structure of international capitalists' interests in Africa. Consequently their main interest *vis-à-vis* independent Africa and *a fortiori vis-à-vis* Tanzania is *to prevent the growth of strong politico/economic systems independent*

[6] Giovanni Arrighi and John Saul, 'Nationalism and Revolution in Tropical Africa', *Socialist Register* (1969). See also Hamza Alavi, 'Imperialism, Old and New', *Socialist Register* (1964), pp. 116-17.
[7] The term 'periphery centres' has been borrowed from Ander Gundar Frank, *Capitalism and Underdevelopment in Latin America*, op. cit., pp. 6, 7, *passim*. This pattern of capitalist interests is shown by the *level* of British foreign investments in these areas as shown in table 2.1.

of western capitalist hegemony in the countries bordering the Southern African complex (Zaïre, Zambia, Malawi and Tanzania) which could, among other things, seriously threaten (through their support for the increasingly radical liberation movements) white rule in Southern Africa.[8] Unfortunately some of these nuances of contemporary capitalist penetration were not fully appreciated and more often than not they were misunderstood.

Nothing that has been said should be interpreted to mean that the possibilities of controlling the economy of a former colony, such as Tanzania's, were enormous. Rather, what is being asserted here is that there did not appear to be an overall strategy that examined critically the impact of foreign relations policies to domestic development. In particular, the government did not distinguish foreign investors in terms of their internal need or in terms of their likely prospective impact on growth and income distribution in designing its investment code.[9] Nor did it question the existing pattern of African specialization in low-skilled crop production, leaving foreigners and the Asian minority with a presumed comparative advantage in entrepreneurship, management skills and capital to specialize in commercial and industrial enterprises.

In view of the under-utilization of resources (labour and in some areas land) in the rural sector and the invocations to 'build the nation' characteristic of the early years of independence, there was some increase in crop production as shown in table 2.2. Yet because of the worsening terms of trade (see table 2.2) the value of output in terms of purchasing power (income terms of trade) remained virtually the same between 1960 and 1965 (except for 1963–4). The static income terms of trade implied that the gains from trade were negligible; the country's growth would have to rely on either external financing (inflow of foreign investment and aid) or domestic accumulation. Moreover the price fluctuations of the major crops adversely affected government revenue, forcing the government to institute the unpopular Development Levy in 1965.[10] The remaining shortfall in government revenue was made up by increased import duties on various items.[11] Foreign

[8] Arrighi and Saul, 'Nationalism and Revolution', *Socialist Register*, op. cit.
[9] Ministry of Commerce and Industries, 'A Short Guide to Investors' (Dar es Salaam, 1967, mimeo).
[10] The Development Levy was a tax levied on several export crops (e.g. cotton, coffee, sisal) and on personal incomes. It was particularly unpopular with the cotton growers.
[11] Import duties were placed on shoes (22 per cent), yarn (22 per cent) in 1961; screws, wood (12½ per cent) galvanized gutterings (25 per cent),

capital inflow, though insignificant (13 per cent of total gross capital formation in 1960–2), was expected to rise when the new plan came into effect.

TABLE 2.2
Tanzania's terms of trade, 1960 to 1965
(1954=100)

Year	Net Imports			Domestic Exports			Net Barter Terms of Trade	Income Terms of Trade
	Q	P	V	Q	P	V		
1960	119	99	118	169	89	150	90	152
1961	131	95	124	157	86	135	91	142
1962	139	90	125	162	87	141	97	157
1963	128	99	127	174	100	174	101	176
1964	128	108	138	191	101	192	94	178
1965	127	113	144	187	92	172	81	152

The year 1964, however, witnessed a series of events which were to affect the future of Tanzania's relations with the international community—the revolution in Zanzibar, the army mutiny on mainland Tanzania which also swept through Kenya and Uganda (necessitating an appeal for British troops), the union of Tanganyika and Zanzibar to form the United Republic of Tanzania, the declaration of war on Portugal by Frelimo (a freedom movement which was based in Tanzania), the government support of the so-called rebels in Zaïre, its acceptance of refugees from Ruanda-Urundi, China's firm offer of military and financial aid and the allegation of the United States' attempt to overthrow the United Republic of Tanzania.[12] It is obvious that some of these events brought the cold war struggle to mainland Tanzania as the great powers sought to influence the revolution and to gain a foothold on this portion of eastern Africa. There was no doubt in the leadership's mind that it had responded to these events in accordance with Tanzania's interests. And yet the western press apparently felt otherwise. This evoked an awareness on the part of the leadership that there was a contradiction between Tanzania's interests and those of the West.

In the aftermath of these events, there was a significant capital flight of about sh. 290 million as compared to approximate equilibrium

---

cigarettes and sugar in 1962; and on cloth, blankets, shirts, stockings, builders' requisites, tanks, paints and cement in 1963. See Michael Yaffey, 'External Aspects of the Tanganyika Economy Since 1949' (Dar es Salaam, University College, 1969, mimeo), pp. 18-19.
[12] Catherine Hoskyins, 'Africa's Foreign Relations', op. cit.

in 1963. Since gross capital formation in 1964 was valued at sh. 603 million, this capital flight was of a serious magnitude: one may indeed argue that Tanzania lost about half of her potential capital formation. The economy was further constrained by the fall in the price of sisal in 1965 from sh. 2,094/- per ton in 1964 to sh. 1,507/- per ton in 1965 and the substantial rise of the import price index (a rise of 14 per cent between 1963 and 1965). The increase in the national debt during the period certainly did not lead to greater flexibility in financial allocation. The government found itself helpless in mitigating these new problems: import price rises, lowering of reserves, low capital inflow (both public and private). The failure to generate adequate resources to augment the national income, despite the cautious policy that the government had taken in its relationship with the West, was indicative of the weakness of the strategy hitherto adopted. The intimate relationship between policy and internal development was now seen in a more realistic perspective.

When, therefore, the government rejected West German aid for the latter's invocation of the 'Hallstein doctrine', broke off diplomatic relations with Britain over the Rhodesian issue thus foregoing substantial aid, and made more substantial contacts with socialist countries and the less-committed capitalist countries such as Canada, Sweden, Norway and Denmark, it was acting on the perceived constraints imposed upon Tanzania's potential for development on the chariot-wheel of international capitalism as a satellite. It was in this spirit that the President issued a memorandum entitled *Principles and Development* in which the paramountcy of Tanzania's interests in its relationship with the world is clearly spelt out.

TABLE 2.3

Some elements of the Balance of payments, 1961 to 1965
(million shs)

	1961	1962	1963	1964	1965
Export surplus	+24	+66	+306	+238	+60
Private capital inflow	+15.4	+14	−46.6	−336.4	−89
Net investment income	−62.7	−74.2	−124.7	−93.1	−101.1
Interest payment by government	−27.6	−39.2	−39.8	−46.5	−32.3

Source: IMF, *Surveys of African Economies*, Vol. II (Washington, D.C., 1969), p. 284 and Yaffey, 'External Transactions', op. cit.

As foreign resources became increasingly inadequate to finance the plan which was launched in July 1964, it became necessary to augment the available external finances with a larger proportion of domestic resources. Yet in its endeavour to borrow domestically, the government realized the inadequacies of the inherited institutional framework for domestic borrowing (especially the banking system). In this way the leadership's need to control the economy became translated into its control of important economic institutions in the country.

Mention should also be made of Tanzania's relations with her neighbours: Uganda and Kenya. The three countries, under the tutelage of Britain, had attained their independence with common economic ties including a common market, a common currency and joint management of certain transport, communications and research facilities. It has been claimed that these links served to develop Kenya industrially at the expense of Uganda and Tanzania.[13] It is obvious that these common bonds would remain unimpaired as long as the three countries adopted similar development strategies or entered a political federation. By 1964, however, the pressure for federation seemed to have dissipated. If Tanzania wanted to pursue her new policies towards economic independence it was necessary to alter the existing joint arrangements in order to give her the necessary flexibility to act. Accordingly she initiated discussions which led to the Kampala

TABLE 2.4

Trade in non-traditional markets
(tons)

		1965	1966
Cotton:	Japan	2,414	15,392
	Hong Kong	23,065	33,365
	China	16,182	12,388
Coffee:	Japan	506	1,243
	German Democratic Republic	—	1,777
	China	299	716
Sisal:	China	3,453	6,984
	USSR	2,528	7,414
	Japan	7,261	6,555

Source: M. Yaffey, 'External Aspects', op. cit., p. 36.

Agreement on industrial allocation among the three partner states and the establishment of separate currency and central banks by each

[13] For a discussion of the history and major developments of the East African Common Market and services see Arthur Hazlewood, *African Integration and Disintegration* (London, Oxford University Press, 1967), pp. 69-114.

state.[14] These moves led to a feeling of expected 'dissolution' of the East African Common Services Organization. To counteract this, another round of discussions was initiated that led to a strengthening of the links with the formation of the East African Community.[15]

Yet perhaps the most significant effect of the foreign policies pursued, which we have discussed in this section, was their impact on domestic issues. The expansion of the export sector, the encouragement of foreign capital and dependency on foreign aid had important repercussions on both potential economic growth and social class formation. It is to these issues that we now turn.

2.2 BACKGROUND TO ARUSHA—II: DOMESTIC POLICY AND SOCIAL DIFFERENTIATION

If one examines the economic indices of growth of the national economy of Tanzania between 1962 and 1966, there seems to be no obvious malaise which could have necessitated the proposals embodied in the Arusha Declaration. Indeed many western observers of the Tanzanian economic scene were 'shocked' by the Declaration.[16] Yet the view expressed here is that the Arusha Declaration was born of the historical events preceding it. While the international aspects provided a motor for these changes, the domestic factors largely induced by foreign policy were significant as well. Many of the domestic events are not easily classifiable into simple categories; we shall discuss them here in terms of allocation of resources and social differentiation.

During the early years of independence, resource allocation tended to be both *ad hoc* and *laissez-faire*; the major preoccupation of the leadership at this juncture was the consolidation of the political affairs of the state. *First*, the new government had to tackle the problem of restoring African dignity. This was done by outlawing discrim-

---

[14]The Kampala Agreement set out to (a) arrange a shift in the territorial distribution of production by a number of firms which operated in two or more of the countries, (b) allocate certain major industries between the countries, (c) institute quotas on interterritorial trade, (d) increase sales from a country in deficit in interterritorial trade to a country in surplus, (e) devise a system of inducements and allocations of industry to secure an equitable distribution of industrial development between the three countries.

[15] The Treaty for the East African Community aims at equalizing investment allocation over the area in the form of transfer taxes and through the East African Development Bank.

[16] *The Times* (London), 13 February, *Newsweek*, 20 February, *Der Spiegel*, 20 February, *Frankfurter Algemeine*, 10 February 1967.

inatory practices in social life, in the health and educational services and in wage rates. Closely related to this was the problem of Africanization. This policy could be rationalized as a necessity to build up the self-confidence of the people. However, the major pressure came from the trade unions which had allied themselves with the ruling party in the fight for independence. As Tordoff succinctly puts it, 'At a time when TANU leaders were becoming government Ministers and African civil servants were assuming senior posts, it was natural that union leaders should look with jealous eyes at the lucrative jobs held by European managers, for example, in The East African Railways and Harbours administration and on the sisal estates . . . . Strong dissatisfaction with what was regarded as the TANU government's too leisurely approach to the vital question of Africanization was expressed by several unions.'[17] Eventually, early in 1962, the government took the sting out of subsequent criticism by appointing an Africanization Commission, which issued its report the following year.[18]

However, the strains between the trade unions movement and the new government continued. Wage increases was the next item of disagreement. By the end of 1962, government had accepted statutory monthly minimum wages for employees over 18 as sh. 150/- in Dar es Salaam and Tanga, sh. 125/- in the eighteen other main towns, and sh. 100/- in the other areas.[19] Wage increases in practice were much higher than these figures show.

I should point out that an initial rise of wages in many sectors was necessary as African wages had been kept unusually low by the colonial administration. There was little comparability between labour productivity and wages paid during the colonial era; wages were largely determined by ethnic origin rather than by productivity. This led to the famous vicious circle—low wages-low productivity-high turnover-low wages. But unfortunately the minimum wage policy was not followed up by a more systematic training of the labour force.

The latent strains inherent in the British type of trade union and the new government continued. There were several strike threats, the number of man days lost through stoppages rose from 113,000 in 1961 to 417,000 in 1962. Government therefore took several measures

---

[17] W. Tordoff, *Government and Politics in Tanzania*, op. cit. p. 142.
[18] *Report of the Africanization Commission*, 1962 (Dar es Salaam, 1963).
[19] Wages Regulation Order, 1962, made under S.10 (3) of the Regulation of Wages and Terms of Employment Ordinance (cap. 300).

both to control and contain the trade union movement. These included: the Trade Unions Ordinance (Amendment) Bill to bring trade unions and their finances under a substantial measure of government control; the Trade Disputes (Settlement) Bill which introduced conciliation and arbitration procedures which would have to be followed before strike action could be taken; the Civil Service Negotiating Machinery Bill to settle union civil servant disputes, and finally the National Union of Tanganyika Workers (Establishment) Bill, which dissolved the Tanganyika Federation of Labour (TFL) and its eleven member unions, establishing in its place one central union (NUTA) whose General Secretary and Deputy were to be appointed by the President.[20] This was the end of union autonomy, an inevitable consequence since it is unlikely that government as it was then constituted could tolerate indefinitely the existence of a competing centre of power, strongly entrenched in the urban areas and the sisal estates—the major sources of monetary wealth.

Secondly, the leadership became preoccupied with constitutional matters, this included the establishment of the Republic and a truly representative parliament (one man, one vote) in 1962, the amendment of the TANU constitution, committing the party to a socialist philosophy though, as President Nyerere points out, 'what this meant was not defined';[21] and the establishment of a one party state in 1965.

Land nationalization was also effected in the early days. Freehold land was abolished and development clauses imposed on all leasehold ownership rights. This was not, however, taken as a socialist measure, but rather as a way of eliminating non-indigenous Africans' claims to landed property. There was, moreover, no other policy on land, its distribution or land tenure. People were merely urged to expand their acreage of crops (largely for export) without consideration being given to the eventual effect of these expansions on land tenure and class formation; only seven years after independence was the leadership able to note that this policy had led not only to more individual ownership of land but also to the emergence of an embryo kulak class and a landless peasantry.

The most important governmental policies during this period were embodied in its two plans. The Three Year Development Plan (1961–4) was really a colonial hangover. It was drawn up by the out-

20 Tordoff, *Government and Politics in Tanzania*, op. cit. pp. 144-8.
21 J. K. Nyerere, *Tanzania: Ten Years After Independence* (Dar es Salaam, TANU, September, 1971), p. 8.

going administration on the recommendation of the World Bank. Despite its formal adoption by the government, it should not be considered as an embodiment of their policies—there was never any review of it nor was there any mention of its completion. Instead, the government hired a team of French economists to draft a new plan, which was submitted in May 1964. This is the First Five Year Plan (1964-9), hereafter FFYP, which was a comprehensive plan for all sectors of the economy. It followed the French *indicative* planning method whereby national and sectoral growth and investment targets are established through co-operation of public and private sectors, although in Tanzania, the private sector did not co-operate as assumed. One of the major targets of the FFYP was an increase in *per capita* income from sh. 392/- in 1960-2 to sh. 586/- in 1970 and over sh. 900/- by 1980 (thus implying growth of real product of 6.7 per cent). Its other aims were to make Tanzania self-sufficient in manpower in all economic fields and at professional levels, to increase the number of wage earners from 340,000 in 1960-2 to 800,000 in 1980, i.e. from about 3.5 per cent of the population to 5.7 per cent (half of the 1980 employment was to be in agriculture), and to raise the life expectancy from 35 to 40 years largely through the reduction of infant mortality. These goals were to be met by a 'radical' transformation of the economy which would involve a reduction in the relative contribution of primary production from 60 per cent in 1960-2 to 39 per cent in 1980, and by doubling the share of industrial activities as shown in table 2.5.

TABLE 2.5

Comparative actual and planned structures of GDP

	1960–2 (average)	1970 (target)	1980 (target)
Primary production (incl. mining)	60.0%	50.0%	39.0%
Industrial activities (of which)	13.0%	19.4%	26.7%
Manufacturing and processing	4.0%	7.5%	13.3%
Basic facilities	5.6%	6.3%	7.1%
Construction	3.4%	5.6%	6.3%
Tertiary services	27.0%	30.6%	34.3%

Sources: FFYP, table III, p. 5.

Total plan investment was sh. 4,920 million in the monetary sector (i.e. excluding the subsistence sector); of which 53 per cent would be contributed by the public sector (sh. 2,040 million by central government, sh. 360 million by the East African Common Services Organization and sh. 200 million by the local governments). The remainder was

49

to be contributed by the private sector. These investment figures exclude 'self-help schemes' which characterized the early independence days. While the energies in some of these schemes was dissipated because of lack of adequate leadership and technical assistance they were a considerable contribution to development. The sectoral allocation of the plan investments are 28.4 per cent in social infrastructure (housing and township development constituting 17 per cent of the total), 24 per cent in industry, 13.5 per cent in commerce, 15 per cent in agriculture and 16 per cent in economic infrastructure. These allocations, however, do not reveal the resource contributions by the public and private sectors respectively. This information is contained in table 2.6. As indicated in the table the prime mover for the transformation of the economy was private enterprise as it makes the bulk of industrial and commercial investments, the agents of structural change during the period. Since the private sector was likely to be largely non-African, the government devised means of attracting African entrepreneurs into the commercial sector. The instrument was the co-operative movement. As the Report of the Presidential Commission on the Establishment of a Democratic One Party State stated, the contribution of the co-operatives was to 'enable Africans to participate in and obtain control of certain sectors of the economy which would otherwise have remained in the hands of immigrants or foreign Companies'.[22] Unfortunately, as a result of corruption and inefficiency, as recorded in the report of the *Presidential Special Committee of Enquiry into Co-operative Movement and Marketing Boards*, the co-operative movement has not fulfilled these expectations. Government investments on the other hand were more concentrated in the less directly productive sectors.

The sources of finance for the plan support the view expressed earlier with regard to Tanzania's foreign policy. Seventy-eight per cent of government investment was to be externally financed, 14 per cent was to come from domestic borrowing and only 8 per cent was to originate from taxation. There was, beginning from 1962, a fair introduction of progressive taxation. The poll tax was abolished and replaced by a personal tax system, under which people with an income of less than sh. 2,000/- per annum were exempt from tax. With respect to the private sector at least 60 per cent was assumed to originate from the reinvestment of profits, which would come from existing firms,

22 W. Tordoff, *Government and Politics in Tanzania*, op. cit., p. 133.

mostly foreign. There was little role for monetary and fiscal instruments in the financing of the plan.

It should be noted that although the formulation of the plan was initiated by government, TANU was not involved in its formulation, and indeed its role is not expressed in the plan.[23] This implies that the FFYP did not address itself to any *political* changes that might be required in order to fulfil its objectives. The plan's goals are therefore just quantitative targets involving no choice about the strategy for development or the nature of the future society. One may wonder why the government and especially the party did not articulate their political goals. The answer can only be conjectural. It would seem that on the one hand, the leadership had not at this stage (when the plan was being formulated) fully grasped the nature of structural transformation of society, just as it had misunderstood the realities of international capitalism. On the other hand, however, it may be argued that the leadership was concerning itself with the articulation of what Franz Schurmann terms 'pure ideology', that is, a set of ideas designed to give an individual a unified and conscious *weltanschauung*.[24] This is evidenced by the President's concern with the 'national ethic', and by the tone and character of his earlier papers: 'Ujamaa—the Basis of African Socialism'; 'The Courage of Reconciliation', etc. It was necessary, in other words, for the leadership to outline the basic

TABLE 2.6

Sectoral distribution of plan investments
(in million shs.)

Economic sector	Central government	Private sector	Total
Agriculture	552	168	738
Industry	292	888	1,080
Commerce	72	590	662
Economic infrastructure	392*	NIL	786
Social infrastructure of which housing	580*	674	1,398
and township dev.	210*	600	836
Administrative	156	NIL	156
Total	2,040	2,320	4,920

*The difference is made up by East African Common Services investments.

Source: *FFYP*, p. 98.

[23] Henry Bienen, *Tanzania: Party Transformation*, op. cit., pp. 294-5.
[24] Franz Schurmann, *Ideology and Organization in Communist China* (Berkeley and Los Angeles, University of California Press, 1968).

principles on which to base future action, as it did not adhere to already existing ideological leanings such as Marxism-Leninism. Although a world view may give an individual a certain outlook, *it does not indicate to him how he should act*. For the latter there is a need to articulate a 'practical ideology', that is, a set of ideas that enables an individual to transform the *weltanschauung* into consistent action. This is not merely applying universal truths to real problems, but rather unifying universal theory and concrete practice. The failure to articulate practical ideology may thus account for the inability of the party to play a more prominent role in national affairs.

We are now in a position to evaluate the significance and achievement of the plan. By 1966 real output was growing at 4.8 per cent per annum on a 1960–2 price base (though GDP in current prices increased at 6.7 per cent per annum as planned). Real income growth on the other hand lagged behind real output as a result of the deterioration of terms of trade, maintaining a 3.5 per cent rate of growth. Assuming a 2.5 per cent rate of population growth, real income *per capita* can be taken to have increased at an average rate of 1 per cent per annum. This compares to 4.5 per cent assumed by the FFYP in order to double *per capita* incomes by 1980. Private *per capita* consumption as a result of the acceleration of private investment, rose even more sluggishly at 0.8 per cent per year.

More interesting from the point of view of income distribution was the fact that this meagre increase in real *per capita* income was not evenly spread over the entire population. On the contrary, by 1966 important sectoral differentiations had begun to emerge. In the first place wage earners acquired a significant share of this increase. Between 1961 and 1966 wage rates rose by 80 per cent, while prices went up by 11 per cent, resulting in a significant real income gain for the workers. This was in addition to other welfare benefits which they had come to enjoy since independence. These include severance pay, employment security provisions, fringe benefits, annual benefits and provident fund contribution.[25]

The benefits of wage increments were not shared equally by all wage earners. To begin with, due to the stabilization of labour which was brought about by the above measures, total employment in terms of number of workers fell, as shown in table 2.7. The fall is largely due to the massive lay-offs in the sisal industry due to falling

[25] See, for example, the Security of Employment Act (No. 62), 1964, National Provident Fund Act, July, 1964; and Severance Allowance Act, 1962.

product prices and the structure of the industry, as previously discussed. Secondly, workers in large enterprises, mainly subsidiaries of multi-national corporations—B.A.T. (T), Portland Cement Co., East African Breweries etc.—on which NUTA (the national workers' union) has concentrated its demands, have been able to obtain minimum wages of upwards of sh. 330/- per month while workers in smaller establishments could only obtain half as much or less. Thirdly there was also a continued discrepancy of pay scales among the various regions as well as different economic sectors. Thus the rise in wages in agriculture was only half that for employment as a whole and if the increase is considered on a regional basis, it seems to have been concentrated very largely on people employed in Dar es Salaam and Tanga—wages in other regions having risen comparatively little.[26] One of the results of these wage differentials is the anomaly created whereby equal work now yields very different rewards to the workers. Fourthly, there was the class of senior civil servants as well as senior managers in industry who had inherited a 'European' salary structure. These same people, however, were able to get access to credit facilities and technical advice which enabled them to enter into property-earning activities. These factors fostered great income inequalities, especially in relation to the workers who could not obtain similar credit facilities.

TABLE 2.7

Total and sectoral distribution of wage employment, 1962 to 1966
(in thousands of employees)

Sector	1962	1963	1964	1965	1966
Agriculture	203.8	165.5	163.6	139.2	126.2
Mining	8.8	7.4	7.8	7.2	6.2
Manufacturing	23.4	22.2	23.6	25.7	29.9
Construction	41.2	28.3	33.7	31.5	37.4
Transport	24.3	24.4	25.7	26.4	27.6
Public utilities	4.9	3.9	4.6	4.8	5.3
Commerce	16.9	16.5	17.3	17.8	20.9
Other services	73.7	72.1	74.9	81.3	83.0
Total	397.0	340.3	351.2	333.8	338.5

Source: Background to the Budget, 1967 to 1968.

It should be noted that employment policy was directed towards the creation of a small, comparatively 'high wage' employed population

[26] ILO, *Report to the Government of the United Republic of Tanzania on Wages, Incomes and Prices Policy*, Government Paper no. 3, 1967 (Dar es Salaam, Government Printer, 1967).

instead of a large one at lower wages. Under this policy, recommended by Chesworth, it was hoped that manpower made redundant by increase of wages would be absorbed into settlement schemes which had been recommended by the World Bank (see below).[27] Unfortunately the displaced workers did not go into the rural areas as expected but remained in the towns. This urban unemployed sector was soon joined by school leavers who could not find any jobs. It was this influx of school leavers that pinpointed to the leadership the failure of the Chesworth recommendations. The school leavers are not only numerous, and their numbers are rising each year, but their average educational level is higher than that of workers already in employment.[28] Furthermore, the school leaver problem is complicated by its regional incidence. Owing to the government's decision to hand over primary schools to district councils, the number of school leavers have varied directly with the district's *per capita* expenditure on education which varied in 1966 from sh. 13/40 in Kilimanjaro to sh. 1/08 in Pangani. To the extent that the school leaver problem is potentially explosive in the more advanced areas (and *ipso facto* areas that are highly represented in the civil service), there is a likelihood of manipulating the selection procedure by those in power to maintain the *status quo*. As Art van der Laar puts it, '. . . therefore, those who largely at public expense have received their education which brought them to the position of power in the Government, subsequently have the opportunity to perpetuate the oligarchy. This *a fortiori* is the case *if the economy fails to expand fast enough and does not provide sufficient new opportunities for a growing populace.*' (My italics.)[29]

We have just seen that there were differentiations *among* the workers depending upon size, sector and region. During the same period, there were also significant indices of social differentiation *between* the workers and rural peasants. As shown in table 2.8, while compensation of employees rose from 29.1 per cent of national income (in current prices) in 1961 to 30 per cent in 1966, rural household monetary and subsistence incomes share *fell* from 53 per cent in 1961 to 49 per cent in 1966. The fall in the smallholders' share becomes disturbing

[27] Government of Tanganyika, Chesworth, *Tanganyika; Territorial Minimum Wages Board Report* (Dar es Salaam, Government Printer, 1962).
[28] R. Ray, *Labour Force Survey of Tanzania* (Dar es Salaam, Government Printer, 1966).
[29] Art van der Laar, 'Growth and Income Distribution in Tanzania Since Independence' (Dar es Salaam, University College, 1967, mimeo.) p. 5. See also G. Hunter *The New Societies of Tropical Africa* (London, Oxford University Press, 1962).

when it is noted that the smallholders comprise at least 90 per cent of the working population. It is unrealistic to attribute the fall in the living standards to the workers as Professor Turner unfortunately

TABLE 2.8
Income and its distribution in Tanzania, 1961 to 1966
(shs million)

	1961	1962	1963	1964	1965	1966
GDP at factor cost	3,870	4,189	4,547	4,387	4,894	5,444
Indirect taxes less subsidies	232	281	329	376	410	462
GDP at market prices	4,102	4,470	4,876	5,213	5,204	5,906
Imports of goods and services	1,182	1,232	1,272	1,398	1,548	1,612
TOTAL RESOURCES	5,284	4,702	6,148	6,611	6,852	7,518
Public consumption	480	534	634	706	—	—
Private consumption	3,080	3,484	3,638	3,697	3,708	—
TOTAL CONSUMPTION	3,560	4,081	4,194	4,331	4,414	—
Public investment (gross)	241	249	208	258	313	362
Private investment (gross)	289	239	278	345	525	581
TOTAL GROSS INVESTMENT	530	488	486	603	838	943
Exports of goods and services	1,194	1,196	1,468	1,678	1,600	—
GDP at factor cost	3,870	4,189	4,547	4,837	4,894	5,444
Less net factor payments abroad	54	62	110	76	74	137
GNP at factor cost	3,816	4,126	4,437	4,671	4,820	5,307
Less provision for depreciation	194	202	216	244	255	304
TOTAL NATIONAL INCOME	3,622	3,924	4,221	4,517	4,565	5,003
Total national income	3,622	3,924	4,221	4,517	4,565	5,003
Rural household monetary income	1,346	1,492	1,536	1,413	1,376	1,515
Subsistence incomes	572	600	636	728	807	919
Compensation of employees	1,080	1,126	1,202	1,315	1,418	1,545
Income from property	52	54	58	97	107	115
Government income	72	74	80	155	171	190
Other surpluses of enterprises	450	522	612	701	—	—
Direct taxes on corporations	50	56	94	108	695	719

Source: Background to the Budget (annual).

claims.[30] The smallholders as a group were greatly affected by the worsening terms of trade in the international market. They were also adversely affected by the pattern of surplus utilization in the urban sector which contracted rather than widened the market for their produce.

Nor was the rural sector undifferentiated. There was of course the smallholder peasant producing for subsistence and some limited cash crops. There was also the beginnings of a kulak class, especially in wheat and tobacco growing areas. Garry Thomas, for example, describes the renting of land as commonplace in Mbulu. He says that

> ... this practice is so prevalent today that a large number of farmers with only average-size holdings of from ten to fourteen acres regularly rent out from $\frac{1}{2}$ to $\frac{3}{4}$ of their land to wheat farmers, and are content to cultivate food crops and collect rent in bags of wheat. While a few large landowners are able to earn up to sh. 4,000/- per annum through this practice, those who have been able to rent from five to ten times as much land as they 'own' and with the profits, have been able to buy machinery, and compound their profits by doing contract work .... A private farmer in Mbulu put more land into wheat production in 1966 and earned more money than did the government's higher capitalized pilot village settlement scheme at Upper Kitete.[31]

It should, however, be pointed out that such practices were rare and were confined to a few specific areas.

From the above analysis it is clear that the policies adopted were not likely to gear the economy to self-sustaining and self-generating growth. This was because there had already emerged a contradiction between the rural and urban sector and contradictions among the various sectors. In particular, since the growth of the economy was constrained by the low productivity of the rural sector—a sector that comprised about 95 per cent of the population, and about 90 per cent of the labour force—it was necessary to develop the urban sector in such a way as to induce stimuli that would both exploit the surplus productive capacity of the rural sector as well as raise its productivity. Such a strategy would imply that the pattern of surplus absorption in the urban sector would be geared to maximize both employment creation and internal market expansion.

However, as we have seen, total wage employment fell during the

30 ILO, *Report to the United Republic of Tanzania on Wages, Incomes and Prices Policy*, op. cit., p. 5.
31 Garry Thomas, 'Agricultural Capitalism and Rural Development in Tanzania', *East Africa Journal* (November 1967), p. 30.

period. The fall in the price of sisal obviously precipitated the massive lay-offs as also the introduction and subsequent increases of the minimum wages. However, the pattern of industrial investments also did not favour maximization of employment. On the contrary, the new firms, the most important ones being subsidiaries of the international corporations, tended to employ not only more capital per worker (relative to the nation's average) but also more specialized labour. Furthermore, a large segment of the urban employed tended to have a larger share of their consumption in imports. This fact together with the transfer of investment income referred to in the previous section constrained the widening of the internal market. Consequently the stimulus to increase production came to depend upon international demand. The rural sector's foreign dependency was augmented by the sectoral distribution of the industrial investments. For the bias against capital goods production increased the dependence of the economy on foreign sources for the supply of the requisite capital goods to transform the rural sector. Thus the development of the rural sector would increasingly be constrained by the balance of payments.[32]

It became necessary to find measures which would not only ease the balance of payments constraint but also resolve the non-antagonistic contradictions of society which were beginning to emerge. Meantime, given the spectre of perverse growth, that is, growth which undermines, rather than enhances, the potentialities of the economy for long-term growth, the leadership's ideological articulation was becoming both sharper and more 'practical' in orientation.[33] It is within this framework that we must view the events of the Arusha Declaration and after.

2.3 THE ARUSHA DECLARATION AND AFTER

As shown in the previous subsections, by 1967 there was a realization by the leadership that Tanzania was moving along a familar postcolonial path where the benefits of Africanization and whatever

[32] G. Arrighi, 'International Corporations Labour Aristocracies and Economic Development in Tropical Africa' (University of Dar es Salaam 1967, mimeo). pp. 19-22.
[33] Ignacy Sachs, 'Potential, Proportional and Perverse Growth', *Czechoslav Economic Papers*, No. 6 (Prague, Academia Publishing House and New York, International Arts and Sciences Press, 1966).

development had occurred were enjoyed by only a small, privileged group consisting of the political leaders themselves, senior civil servants, businessmen, traders, and some of the skilled and semi-skilled workers employed by the larger companies. The result of these developments, together with the realization of neo-colonial designs, set the tone and tempo of the events following the Arusha Declaration.

It can be stated that 5 February 1967, when the Arusha Declaration was published, marked a significant watershed in the development of Tanzania. The declaration, by examining the implicit assumptions of past policies, pointed out the inadequacies of (a) relying on *financial resources* (money) as a major instrument of development, (b) emphasizing *industries* at the initial stage of development, and (c) as a consequence of the above, concentration of resources on *urban* development.

The Arusha Declaration argued that

> it is stupid to rely on money as the major instrument of development when we know only too well that our country is poor. It is equally stupid, indeed, it is even more stupid, for us to imagine that we shall rid ourselves of our poverty through foreign financial assistance rather than our own financial resources.

That the country could not in any case get the requisite funds from abroad has already been discussed. More significant was the realization that even if foreign finance were available, this might not be a desirable development as it might jeopardize the country's economic independence. Mistaking the existing pattern of industry (a consequence of the policies pursued!) for any other possible pattern of industrialization, the declaration critized the industrial strategy in these terms:

> The mistake we are making is to think that development begins with industries. It is a mistake because we do not have the means to establish many modern industries in our country. We do not have either the necessary finances or the technical know-how . . . .

Urban development had prospered at the expense of the countryside, a disturbing factor in view of the absolute and relative size of the latter sector.

The declaration charted out a new course of development emphasizing *internal* development. The two fundamental principles were: *socialism* and *self-reliance*. Socialism in this context was defined to mean (a) the absence of exploitation, (b) the people's (workers and peasants) ownership of the means of production and exchange, and (c) the establishment of a genuine political democracy. The major means of production and exchange under (b) above were enumerated. Self-reliance depended upon (a) the people (b) land (c) good policies and (d) good leadership. Because of the centrality of 'good' leadership in the recipe for self-reliance, a rather stringent leadership code was laid down. In particular, every TANU and government leader was required (a) to be either a peasant or worker, 'and should in no way be associated with the practices of capitalism or feudalism', (b) not to own any shares in a capitalist enterprise, (c) not to hold any directorships in any privately-owned enterprise, (d) not to receive two or more salaries, and (e) not to own houses which he rents to others.

Several policies followed the inauguration of the declaration. On 7 February, the Government nationalized all commercial banks (except the Cooperative Bank and People's Bank of Zanzibar), eight export-import firms, including Smith Mackenzie and Co. Ltd.; Dalgety (E.A.) Ltd.; International Trading and Credit Company of Tanganyika; Co-operative Supply Association of Tanganyika Ltd.; A. Baumann & Co. (Tanganyika) Ltd.; Twentsche Overseas Trading Co. Ltd.; African Mercantile Co. (Overseas) Ltd.; and Wigglesworth & Co. (Africa) Ltd. Eight milling firms with associated food manufacturing interests including Tanzania Millers, Chande Industries, Pure Food Products were also nationalized. The National Insurance Corporation was brought wholly under public ownership and was to acquire a monopoly of insurance business in the Republic. Furthermore, the government was to acquire compulsorily up to 60 per cent of the shares in seven industrial firms. These were Kilimanjaro Breweries, Tanzania Breweries, British-American Tobacco (T), Bata Shoe Company, Tanzania Metal Box Company, Tanganyika Extract Company and Tanzania Portland Cement Company. Later in the year (October 1967) the government announced the nationalization of 60 per cent of the sisal industry. This list was to complete the nationalizations implied in the Arusha Declaration. In each case full and fair compensation was guaranteed.

All the commercial banking activities were now vested with the National Bank of Commerce (NBC), the Cooperative Bank and the People's Bank of Zanzibar; wholesale trading of the nationalized export-import firms under the State Trading Corporation (STC); milling and fruit canning of the nationalized firms under the National Milling Corporation (NMC); the nationalized sisal estates under the Tanzania Sisal Corporation and the partially nationalized industrial firms under the control of the National Development Corporation

(NDC).[34] It is interesting to note that in the case of the industrial firms, the parent companies agreed to lend NDC compensation up to twelve years at about $7\frac{1}{2}$ per cent while the parent company would continue to supply the management of the firms under management agreements drawn up for the same period.[35] By mid-1969, with the settlement of the Inchcape Group (Smith Mackenzie, Dalgety, African Mercantile), Barclays Bank DCO and Standard Bank compensation claims, the agreed settlement had been reached on 98 per cent of the value of assets and business acquired in February 1967. The total agreed compensation is in the order of sh. 200 million including NDC share purchase in companies listed above and the government's exercise of option to purchase 50 per cent of the equity of Tiper Refinery Company.

In March 1967 the leadership issued the second policy directive, which was on education. After analysing the system and attitudes of education as they had evolved in Tanzania, the paper demanded an 'educational revolution', meaning a recasting of the educational system in the light of Tanzania's needs and social objectives. The document analysed the inadequacies of the colonial system which had been remedied: the racial distinctions within education which had been abolished; the expansion of educational facilities available (for example primary schools enrolment rose from 490,000 in 1961 to 825,000 in 1967; secondary school enrolment had also doubled to 25,000 and senior secondary enrolment had quadrupled) and the modification of some of the syllabus content. However, these modifications did not significantly alter the colonial nature of the educational system. The skills acquired were not generally related to society as a whole (this reflected itself partly in the school-leaver problem). It was an élitist education designed to meet the interests and needs of a very small proportion of those who enter the school system. This had been corroborated by the university students' boycott of national service.[36] Moreover, it emphasized formal education at the

[34] In Zanzibar, imports were progressively placed under control of official bodies there (Bizanje and Zanzibar State Trading Corporation).
[35] Alan Roe, 'The Company in Tanzanian Development—A Post-Arusha Declaration Appraisal' in P. A. Thomas, *Private Enterprise and the East African Company*, op. cit., p. 247. *Background to the Budget, 1968*, p. 2.
[36] The sending down of the university students in 1966 reflected the contradictions of the Tanzanian society at that time. On the one hand, it was fair for the leadership to expect the intelligentsia to understand the need for 'national service', but it was myopic to expect these students to disregard their interests *vis-à-vis* the fully established civil service and to get over their seventeen-year hangover of colonial education in so short a time.

expense of experience. In consequence the educational system tended to aggravate the crucial problems of economic transformation.

'Education for Self-Reliance' recommended three broad areas that would alter the above trends, (a) content of the curriculum itself, (b) organization of the schools and (c) entry age into primary schools. In view of the financial constraints, it would not be possible to offer universal education for some time. Consequently the new measures were designed to work within these financial constraints. Specifically primary school education would henceforward become both *complete in itself* and *communal* in organization. This would also be true of secondary and teacher training schools. In other words, primary schools (or secondary schools) would no longer be a preparation for secondary schools (or post-secondary education), but rather would be geared to the preparation of the students for life and service in the villages and rural areas of the country. Moreover, they were to contribute to their own upkeep; they were to be economic as well as social and educational communities. This implied a change in age entry (in order to enable school-leavers to become responsible young workers and citizens) and curriculum content. Students would now be taught values and skills that would encourage the 'development of a proud, independent and free citizenry which relies upon itself for its own development, and which knows the advantages and the problems of co-operation'.[37]

In September 1967 the third major policy document, 'Socialism and Rural Development', was issued.[38] This paper after surveying the various social formations that had been taking place in the rural sector recommended the establishment of *ujamaa villages*, i.e. co-operative production units that would foster both socialist principles and rural transformation. They would be promoted through discriminatory extension assistance to those peasants who would opt out of the individualistic system. The major features of the ujamaa village were its emphasis on co-operation, equality and participatory democracy. Village land would become communally owned and would be worked for the common good. Unlike the earlier settlement schemes recommended by the World Bank, the new villages would be less capital-intensive and more spontaneous.

There have been two other important moves by the party since 1967. One was the socialization of the wholesale trade sector and the taking

[37] J. K. Nyerere, *Freedom and Socialism*, op. cit., p. 290.
[38] ibid., pp. 337-66.

over of rent-earning buildings of sh. 100,000/- or over in 1970 and 1971 respectively.

The second policy measure since 1967 whose significance parallels the Arusha Declaration in many ways was the TANU Guidelines of February 1971, variously known as the Mwongozo or the Dar Declaration. These guidelines were issued in the wake of the Uganda Coup and reflect a heightened awareness of the dangers of imperialism, of the need for a tighter control over the economy, the supremacy of the party (TANU) and the introduction of the people's militia in safeguarding the country's independence. The major message of the guidelines was the establishment of socialist production relations to correspond to the mode of production called for by the Arusha Declaration. They call for new attitudes and practices in order to facilitate public participation in all decision-making; for an understanding, both by management and the workers of the real meaning of socialist and democratic activities.

What has been the significance of the Arusha and post Arusha measures? Certainly it is too early to judge the long-term effects of the enunciated policies of socialism and self-reliance. But at least on the theoretical level, certain observations can be made. First, the nationalization measures and the leadership code can be interpreted as being aimed at reallocating the surplus from the export of investment income, invisible payments and conspicuous consumption to serve the requirements of primary accumulation as well as to alter the structure of investments (choice of techniques, sectoral distribution, employment effects, etc.) in order to meet national priorities.[39]

To what extent can these goals be attained? It is important to examine the balance of payments effects of the nationalization measures, as it has often been claimed that nationalization not only discourages foreign capital but also wastes the country's scarce development capital in paying for compensation. It may of course be argued that the possibility of modifying existing investment policies may counter balance of payments losses, but this view as we shall argue is not particularly satisfactory. On the contrary Tanzania's nationalization is likely to have a positive effect on the balance of payments account. This

[39] Politically this might be interpreted to mean that nationalization derived from a belief that if the people were to be called on to make sacrifices in the national interests they would hardly do so if they thought that the cream of Tanzania's wealth was being skimmed off by 'wicked' foreigners. See for example the interview with President Nyerere in *Business and Economy of Central and East Africa*, July 1967.

TABLE 2.9
Net earnings of invisibles, 1966 to 1970
(in shs. million)

	1966	1967	1968	1969	1970
Freight, insurance, etc. on shipping	35.4	82.4	107.4	119.9	133.2
Other invisibles	16.2	−60.7	−58.8	−34.6	−28.5
International investment income	−137.4	−82.6	−27.5	−20.6	−24.9
Total invisible earnings	−61.5	−60.9	+21.1	64.7	79.8
*Compensation payments (including interest) ..		−7.7	−21.2	−61.7	−44.6

 * This is, of course largely a capital item, brought here for purposes of comparison.

Source: Background to Budget 1968-1969 and 1969-1970. Bank of Tanzania, Economic and Operations Report, June 1971.

is largely because most of the nationalized firms produce *services*. To the extent that compensation will be related to capital invested, gains by retention of profits after payment of compensation are likely to be high in services where capital invested is relatively small. For example, in banking, capital invested in Tanzania by the nationalized banks was very small. This was because the banks were mostly branches only. Their creditworthiness was assured by the capital of their head offices. Moreover they had been able to maintain a very high rate of profit on the capital invested through cartel arrangements. In insurance, owing to the practice of reinsuring the bulk of the risks outside East Africa, the insurance companies had been able to operate *de facto* as mere agents, requiring little reserve assets of their own. There were no compensation payments made to insurance companies as no assets were nationalized. In trade also the companies appeared to rely heavily on bank overdrafts rather than on shareholders' capital. Shipping agents required virtually no capital at all, other than expertise and certain personal relationships.

The nationalization measures will reverse some of the past trends with respect to income outflow. Freight and insurance earnings have risen, no doubt boosted by the Zambian traffic, but without nationalization of insurance, part of the earnings would have been exported. As shown in table 2.9 the international investment income has dropped considerably, while compensation payments so far have not been unduly burdensome. The banking system itself has been able to earn a surplus of sh. 139 million, just a little less than the total compensation payments as of 1970. The National Insurance Corporation has also managed to accumulate a surplus of sh. 82 million during its first three years of operation. In the manufacturing sector, almost all the partly nationalized firms have been making profits; a significant part of which is now retained at home. In sum, there is little doubt that the nationalization measures, even with the generous compensations, will succeed in reversing the traditional income drains of the economy.

The nationalization measures are therefore unlikely to have the expected adverse effect on the balance of payments. However, it is questionable whether the nationalization of foreign enterprise will lead to a change in the pattern of investments in the short run. This is for a number of reasons. In the first place because of the lack of sufficiently trained manpower to run the parastatal sector, Tanzania has had to rely more and more on the foreign contractors and suppliers themselves to provide feasibility studies, advice and skilled personnel, as well as machinery and equipment for carrying out investments. Investment decisions have come to be made more on the basis of the existence of a foreign supplier willing to suggest and carry out a project than on the basis of co-ordinated planning. Since high profits were readily available for building the plant and supplying machinery, contractors have had little interest in the economic viability and efficient operation of the enterprises. Needless to say, there has been no significant attempt yet to alter the status of wage and salary earners in the state sector. Minority participation and management agreements will not only ensure the foreign corporations a regular flow of payments in the form of royalties, patent fees, interest and miscellaneous fees, which to some considerable extent will have similar results to the export of capital but will also enable them to pursue autonomous investment policies. And even if the government, through various training programmes, is able to replace some of the managers and reduce substantially the above flows, the bias of investment in favour of capital intensive techniques is likely to remain unaffected not only because of the persistence of managerial constraints but also because the managing corporations profit from the supply of equipment, components, materials and technical services which embody capital-intensive techniques. Finally it should also be noted that unlike the service industries, the undesirable features of the earlier investment decision are ossified in the fixed capital itself. Only in the long run does the opportunity to take different decisions occur.

Nevertheless, one should not overstate these dangers at the expense of the gains of nationalization of industry. First, such a measure secures ownership of capital, *the* instrument of production to the people of Tanzania. This capital and the surplus it generates should therefore be at the service of the nation, with the possibility of utilizing it in accordance with society's needs. These possibilities are not as restricted as pointed out above. The new forms of income drains, for example, are not as effective and long lasting as those built on foreign property. Moreover, with the establishment of a capital goods industry, the *sine qua non* of development, the other problems of factor bias of technological transfer will be gradually solved.

Indeed, *institutionally*, Tanzania is now fairly well equipped for national economic control. For example, with commercial banking, insurance, agriculture and other rural credit and housing finance in the public sector and a strong central bank, Tanzania has the institutional machinery necessary for national credit allocation and its control. The limits here are now basically of personnel, data and detailed thinking out of how to expand the uses made of the existing institutions. The financial institutional field is one which has changed most dramatically since February 1967 but parallel changes of a less sweeping nature have occurred in industry, foreign trade, plantation agriculture and agricultural processing.

However, nationalization and state ownership do not imply a movement towards socialism since the character of the state itself does not necessarily undergo any qualitative change. In particular, state ownership may lead to the creation of a wealthy bureaucratic class which would exploit the masses under the pretext of being guardians of public property. This is the point made by Shivji and is worth considering.[40]

Closely related to state ownership is the nature of the *socialist relations of production*. The ownership of the means of production by the state does not necessarily guarantee workers' control, which is the real meaning of socialism on the economic level. As President Nyerere has pointed out, 'the people who are not in management positions in the public corporations, still do not feel that these corporations are theirs. Even the workers in the organizations frequently feel that they are working for "them" and not for "themselves".'

[40] Issa G. Shivji, 'The Silent Class Struggle' (Dar es Salaam, University of East Africa Social Science Conference, 27-31 December 1970).

The whole problem of workers' control, despite the establishment of workers' councils and the 'TANU Guidelines', still has to be carefully thought out. We shall return to this theme in the concluding chapter.

Secondly, nationalization measures and the leadership code may be interpreted as a means of limiting further expansion of the indigenous capitalist and *rentier* classes and excluding all such groups from access to political power. The implication of such a strategy is that Tanzania will progress from a pre-capitalist to a socialist structure with a bureaucracy in the state sector playing the role of capitalist. The Asian businessman will be absorbed (or replaced?) by the expanding State Trading Corporation while a significant potential African *bourgeoisie* from the party and public sector will be checked by the leadership code. It remains to be seen how these policies will work out in practice.

Thirdly, 'Education for Self-Reliance and Socialism and Rural Development' can be interpreted as outlining measures intended to lead towards the mobilization of the saving potential implicit in the under-utilized productive resources of the rural sector as well as its economic transformation. Yet even here, the policies pursued do not seem to be compatible with this particular goal. It is certainly true that scattered individual peasants can neither practise socialism nor readily improve their techniques of production on a systematic basis. Their degree of self-reliance at anything above subsistence is quite limited, and under such circumstances of geographical dispersion, are unlikely to be serviced by the requisite infrastructure. The policy, therefore, represents for *some* parts of Tanzania a relevant and important insight into one of the major barriers to rural development in those areas, that is, the crippling lack of an intimate community as a consequence of widely scattered settlement.

The policy prescription can be said to suffer from excessive specification. For from the 1967 census 35 per cent of Tanzania's rural population was concentrated in only 5.5 per cent of the land area in densities of 50 persons per square kilometre or higher. Assuming an average cultivable percentage of 46 per cent (with *average* population densities of 81 persons per square kilometre) gives an overall average for available cultivable land of 1.2 acres per person. Obviously in these places, there is little or no surplus land upon which new settlements can be built. To base a programme of socialist development in such areas on *villagization* from the beginning is clearly out of the question if development is to be voluntary and democratic. And in any case people in these areas are already living in villages, or at least they live close enough together. What they require is technical and social services to improve productivity.[41]

If, on the other hand, the policy of rural development is not to be necessarily geared to villagization, then, one can see that it is possible for effectively-organized co-operative endeavour to bring increases in *production*, particularly if it mobilizes under-employed labour, and if it can lead to a solution of certain problems which cannot at present be handled by the individual, such as conservation, reclamation, marketing services and the maintenance of repair workshops. However, such programmes require the imaginative support of local experience from the centre, and the autonomy of making decisions at the district level.

Yet if recent initiatives of the 'frontal approach' in the Dodoma operation are an indication, it appears that it is the 'villagization' strategy, based on the provision of social facilities (which has cost the nation over shs. 40 million at least), rather than the organization of co-operative production involving new settlements, which will be the official policy. These are programmes which are likely to dampen spontaneity and reinforce dependency attitudes; the very problems that affected the earlier, more capital-intensive settlement schemes.

Another danger of the ujamaa policy is its tendency towards autarky, that is, the tendency towards eliminating exchange relations even within Tanzania! The principal task of orientating production toward the internal market through the production of surpluses is in a way blurred.

The path to socialism in the rural areas has been complex for all countries that have adopted a socialist strategy and Tanzania is no exception. The task is perhaps more difficult in Tanzania because of the low level of human and material resources, that is, of the political cadres and the investable surplus. For this reason it is important to dispel illusions about the scale of the problem, to point out the major bottlenecks in the policies. Thus the fact that rural development is not linked to any conscious programme for industrialization limits its adequacy and possibility of success. For rural transformation will mean not only exploiting the existing surplus capacity in the form of land and labour (which are of course limited) but increasing labour productivity as well. As already mentioned, in the absence of a con-

41 W. L. Luttrell, 'Villagization, Co-operative Production, and Rural Cadres: Strategies and Tactics in Tanzania Socialist Rural Development', Economic Research Bureau, Dar es Salaam, Paper 71.11.

sistent industrialization strategy rural transformation will increasingly be constrained by lack of demands for its products as well as acute balance of payments problems.

There has also been a confusion in implementing the policy of education for self-reliance in order to attain the above goals. Virtually all schools now have farms and workshops, but pupils are rarely involved in the learning processes which are the *raison d'être* for their establishment, namely, planning, keeping records and deciding on alternative uses of products. Nor have these farms and workshops been fully integrated into the school routine. The learning by doing process in the workshop or farm still has to be worked out. Similar problems arise in connection with workers' education. As Mwalimu Nyerere points out

'. . . we have not, as a nation, grasped that just as working is a part of education, so learning is a necessary part of working. A factory or a shamba is a place of work; we neither want to change this, nor could we do so. But learning must become an integral part of working; and people must learn as and where they work . . . . We do not think of working and education as being necessarily connected together. But they are connected unless a worker is to become an appendage to a machine.[42]

The policies on education and rural transformation should be geared towards creating a more meaningful economic base (for the leadership) at the level of the peasantry. For though the leadership depends on the peasantry for its existence, it is not sufficiently mobilized to provide an effective counterforce in the event of conflict with the urban classes. Ujamaa villages should provide a more reliable ground for rural mobilization and politicization but the leadership has still the more difficult task of producing cadres who are not merely disciplined to follow the dictates of the party centre but who remain part of the village, being responsive to its needs and values.[43]

We are now in a position to ask whether the Arusha measures (including the policies of rural transformation and education) correctly resolve the fundamental contradictions that were beginning to emerge. There is no doubt that the kind of socialist thinking and praxis evolved in Tanzania, with their emphasis on rural development and elimination of marked income and other differences, are significant and find

[42] J. K. Nyerere, *Tanzania, Ten Years of Independence*, pp. 31-32.
[43] For suggestions along these lines, see the useful paper by W. L. Luttrell, 'Villagization, Co-operative Production, and Rural Cadres: Strategies and Tactics in Tanzanian Socialist Rural Development', op. cit.

few parallels in the whole of Africa. Yet there are a few important areas which have either been incorrectly diagnosed or have been ignored. These include the belief expressed by the leadership that socialist development in a small, underdeveloped economy surrounded by some strong and hostile neighbours can succeed without accelerating industrial development; the failure to specify the crucial role of industry in a development strategy, especially its historic role of raising labour productivity; and the failure to resolve the contradiction between the bureaucracy and leadership on one hand and the bureaucracy and the people on the other. It is indeed strange that despite the Mwongozo, which recognizes the fundamental contradiction between imperialism and Tanzanian development, there is no consideration of how this contradiction is to be resolved! One can only hope that the illusion of a socialism to be built on a 'tortoise tempo', on a pauper basis, in an environment of powerful enemies and demonstration effects will be short-lived. And to the extent that the leadership cannot withstand the effect of economic stagnation in the face of prevailing expectations by the population, it may find itself resorting to non-socialist solutions to maintain its power if it does not immediately attempt to resolve these contradictions. This is the more urgent as the country seems to be in an extreme mood of apathy and insecurity.

Finally, we may ask whether the Arusha measures, however incomplete, are likely to be correctly implemented. This is not an idle question, for these measures cut deeply into the interests and privileges of those who are called upon to implement them. There has been very little overt dissatisfaction, but this may be due to the apathy and insecurity noted above. What is significant in the long run is that the latent internal dissatisfaction coupled with the possibility of the failure of the adopted strategy may be used as a pressure point by outside forces. This aspect needs greater attention than it has so far received. On the other hand, the success of Tanzania's policies will be regarded as a threat, not because outside interests are directly affected, but because of the precedent these policies would set for other countries. As the London *Sunday Times* remarked in a different context, 'if Tanzania gets away with this there are going to be tremendous repercussions all over Africa'.[44]

---

[44] Quoted by Peter Temu, 'Nationalization in Tanzania', *East Africa Journal*, vol. IV, no. 3 (June 1967), p. 41.

2.4 SOME THEORETICAL CONSIDERATIONS

It is now appropriate to take stock of our historical narrative in order to delineate the major forces and structural relationships that define the trajectory of Tanzania's development. This requires, on the one hand, a restatement of society's goals of development as rooted in historical reality and on the other hand an inquiry into the manner of their attainment in view of both the country's colonial background and its place in the contemporary world.

To begin with, as already noted, the Tanzanian leadership has proclaimed the building of ujamaa socialism as the country's ultimate objective. This is the type of socialism that includes the restitution of the egalitarian and humanistic principles of traditional African life within the context of a modern technical society, serving the welfare needs of all its people. Thus, ujamaa socialism affirms both the 'uniqueness' or 'distinctiveness' of traditional African life which recognizes society as an extension of the basic family unit, and the 'independence' or 'invariance' of productive relations and the mode of production at each historical juncture. Before we turn to the development implications of this goal, a few observations on the 'historical' origins of ujamaa socialism are in order.

First, it would appear from our earlier discussion that the production relations observed in the traditional African societies (equality, classlessness, lack of alienation, etc.) are *necessary* consequences of a specific mode of production. In particular, a 'closed' society characterized by a plentiful supply of good land, relatively low population (i.e. relative to land supply), an annual crop culture and the absence of commodity production, would have little pressure for social differentiation. Such may have been the case with a significant proportion of Tanzania's population as we already pointed out, though the introduction of cash-crop production in these areas has profoundly altered some of these features. In these communities it must be admitted that originally there was a unity between the producer, his product and its consumption, since he generally produced for his own use or for those close to him, so that his work possessed a directly functional aspect. However, in the past, a society based on subsistence production has always been an impoverished one. Not only was it subject to the hazards of nature, but it also had to set very narrow limits to man's wants, since these had to conform exactly to its degree of poverty and limited variety of products.

Moreover, this type of social order contrasts with societies such as those of West Lake, Moshi, Usambara, etc., where a more settled, perennial crop culture emerged, leading to social differentiations based on landholding. In this society, the introduction of perennials (bananas, coffee, *et al.*) created an artificial scarcity of land and hence a struggle for its control. The feudal elements in these societies should not therefore be regarded as aberrations of traditional African society but rather as necessary manifestations of the changes in the mode of production on production relations.

This denial of the 'uniqueness' of traditional African societies does *not* imply either that 'Africa has nothing to contribute to the march of mankind',[45] or that the pervasive manifestations of some of the elements of traditional present-day society have no policy implications for the building of socialism at this historical period. Rather, what is being asserted here is that our heritage must be seen in its proper historical perspective if it is to contribute meaningfully to the building of a developed socialism. It must be realized, for example, that the change in the mode of production from subsistence production to commodity production is likely to profoundly affect production relations, unless appropriate policy measures are taken to counteract such effects. This implies that a socialistic 'attitude of mind' cannot be taken for granted as modes of production alter over time, as they are bound to. Of course, the recourse to the traditional origins of the socialist objective by the leadership may have been designed to serve other, more political purposes, for instance seeking to assimilate some of its traditional symbolism in order to broaden or reinforce the basis of its legitimacy; to appear as mitigating the traumatic effects of abrupt or rapid social and economic change, or seeming to present an ideologically-free socialist policy, etc.

Secondly, it is not particularly clear why the goals of society today should rest on such flimsy foundations as the embellishment of our traditional system rather than on the objective conditions of the contemporary world. It is true, of course, that any social order, once established, produces within itself forces that will perpetuate it, so that only internal stresses and contradictions or powerful external shocks are capable of transforming it to a greater or lesser extent. Even then, much of the old may linger on beside the new for many generations. And although our earlier discussion has established that

[45] J. K. Nyerere, *Freedom and Socialism*, op. cit., p. 16.

Tanzania is characterized, historically, by a low degree of direct involvement in the field of international capitalism, so that the crystallization of the interests and the consciousness of the various social classes is still embryonic, nevertheless, it cannot be denied that colonial exploitation and the attendant capitalist penetration has produced economic underdevelopment, the liquidation of which is a prerequisite to the building of any genuine socialism. The ujamaa socialism that is to be the foundation of Tanzania's future (while in many ways an extension of the basic principles of our past social order), must be seen as being primarily justified by the objective conditions of contemporary reality which we now examine.

From the historical survey we have made and as will be shown more rigorously in the next chapter, Tanzania's present state of underdevelopment, which manifests itself in other ex-colonial countries, derives basically from the colonial division of labour, the major features of which we have already described. The most important ones will be summarized here. First, the colonial division of labour, which is of course a feature of the capitalist integument at a certain historical stage, frustrated the natural development of the traditional African economies. Secondly, under colonialism, the political power of the colonized was usurped by the colonizer, who was thus enabled to control effectively the economic development and the social and institutional systems, including the specification of the political boundaries of the colonized. This situation enabled the colonizing power (in the case of Tanzania, Germany and Britain) to develop or suppress in their own interest certain economic sectors by predetermining the economic structure that largely characterizes such economies today. In addition, foreign private capital, flowing into the secured territories and supported by a purposeful economic policy (but also independently of it, by merely relying on the play of spontaneous market forces), developed the export sectors that had no home base but which complemented the metropolitan economy. Thus foreign capital not only distorted the economic structure of the ex-colonial countries with its investment pattern, but within the boundaries of its operation it also built into it, at the same time, the elements of a capitalist mode of production. It suppressed or at least limited to certain fields the rise and development of the local national *bourgeoisie* and occupied the leading sectors of the economy.[46]

[46] Tamas Szentes, 'The System of Underdevelopment: the Roots and Qualitative Features of the System' (University of Dar es Salaam, 1970, mimeo).

In this way, the colonial system created the following features that characterize underdeveloped countries everywhere: economic *dependence* on foreign capitalist powers for sources of capital, entrepreneurship, capital and consumer goods manufactures etc., with the concomitant systematic income drain by foreign capital and various other forms of regular income losses in external relations, the socio-economic disintegration as manifested in the emergence of the 'dual economy' and the persistence of the deformed structure of sectoral distribution of investments.

Given these *ab initio* conditions at the time of independence, it will be shown in part II that the historical capitalist pattern of development was not a viable alternative for these countries. The mechanisms and institutions to liquidate the glaring features of underdevelopment necessarily implied the advisability of a policy of self-reliance *vis-à-vis* international capitalism, and a change in the power base of these countries. It is to the credit of Tanzanian leadership that it was able to perceive these implications in advancing the policies of ujamaa socialism and self-reliance. There is no doubt that these important steps have been taken because of the presence of President Nyerere—a leader of great tactical skill and genuine commitment who might make great use of the opportunities before him to transform the Tanzanian society. It now becomes clear that the goal of socialism is not necessarily a sentimental return to our past but that it arises from the need to liquidate our present underdevelopment. The goals of society must thus be seen in this totality, that is, aimed at eliminating backwardness and building socialism.

Within this totality of goals and objectives, rural development no doubt occupies an important position in that 90 per cent of the population belong to the rural sector where productivity, income and living conditions are particularly low. Its transformation might not only serve to mobilize the implicit potential surplus but might guarantee a more egalitarian distribution of income and of improved living standards. Yet, despite these possibilities, the rural development so far formulated by the leadership (without the strategy of industrial development being outlined) can stand its ground only as a short-term objective; as a future goal it may even jeopardize the chances of liquidating underdevelopment and building socialism. This is because no growth rate (even the highest conceivable) in agriculture can secure the independence of the national economy in the absence of industrialization (since such a situation implies increased dependence on imports and a high sensitivity to changes in the world market), or attain higher productivity necessary to implement the socialist objectives; in other words, it is unable to create the economic preconditions of self-reliance and socialism.[47]

Moreover, rural transformation will be greatly restrained by the pattern of surplus absorption in the modern sector, as already pointed out. For, unless productive investment in the modern sector is directed towards the creation of development stimuli in the traditional sector (such as employment-creating industries, industries using the raw materials of the rural sector), this might lead (as the history of socialist development in non-industrial areas has amply demonstrated) to a restraining of the exploitation of the rural sector's surplus productive capacity.[48] For all the above reasons, the specification of the role and institutional form including the *primum mobile* which industrialization must take under these circumstances attains crucial significance in the over-all strategy that is aimed at liquidating backwardness and building socialism. This 'missing link' in the panorama envisioned by the Arusha Declaration will be explored in the remaining part of the book.

[47] Tamas Szentes, 'Economic Policy and Implementation Problems in Tanzania' (A Case Study) (Budapest, Center for Afro-Asian Research of the Hungarian Academy of Sciences, 1970).
[48] Giovanni Arrighi and John S. Saul, 'Socialism and Economic Development in Tropical Africa', *The Journal of Modern African Studies*, vol. 6, no. 2 (1968), pp. 151-2.

PART TWO

The structure of Tanzania's manufacturing industry

The economists explain to us the process of production under given conditions; what they do not explain to us, however, is how these conditions themselves are being produced, i.e. the historical movement that brings them into being.

Karl Marx, *The Poverty of Philosophy*

INTRODUCTION

The study of Tanzania's manufacturing industry is divided into three chapters. Chapter 3 lays down the theoretical foundations in the form of a model derived from the Tanzanian historical experience, but designed to be applicable to most ex-colonial African countries. This is what I have called the 'perverse capitalist industrial development model'. The industrial development of these countries is called perverse because in their institutional setting, it is unlikely to lead them to the self-generating and self-sustaining stage of development as was the case with classical industrial capitalism. It is capitalist development because the prime mover of industrialization has been the private enterprise system responding to market opportunities. After reviewing the historical origins and differences between the advanced and the now underdeveloped countries, the major part of the chapter analyses the implications of the *ab initio* conditions in which these ex-colonial economies find themselves for their industrial growth. Some of these implications are offered as testable hypotheses in support of the model.

Chapter 4 discusses the industrial development of Tanzania both historically and in its cross-sectional aspects. It provides the basic data about Tanzania's industrial structure and growth, for the purposes of testing hypotheses advanced in chapter 3 and evaluating policy options in part III.

Chapter 5 takes up the testing of the hypotheses put forward in chapter 3 in the Tanzanian context. The major hypotheses are supported by available evidence subject to the constraints of data.

CHAPTER THREE

A MODEL OF PERVERSE CAPITALIST INDUSTRIAL DEVELOPMENT

3.1 THE CONCEPTUAL FRAMEWORK

The formulation of a sound industrialization strategy for any economy involves at least two distinct, though not unrelated, fundamental problems of development policy: (a) the specification of a desirable pattern of industry to be established, and (b) the delineation of the institutional structure and *primum mobile* required to reshape the requisite pattern of industry.

The literature on the industrialization of the periphery, however, has often neglected the latter problem by focusing its major attention on the features and mechanisms that characterize the now advanced countries' industrialization process.[1] In other words, the starting point is the assumption that capitalism is still a historically progressive force either in the sense that it can lead to a full 'self-generated' and 'self-sustaining' industrialization of the underdeveloped countries (as in the case of Japan), or, at least in the sense that it is able to create progressive socio-political forces in these countries that would ultimately lead to similar results. The acceptance of this premise is, in my view, a fundamental misunderstanding of the nature of underdevelopment. For it implies a belief that the present underdeveloped countries are historically similar (in the sense that their past and indeed their present resemble the earlier stages of history of the now developed countries), except that the former fell behind in the process of historical development, lost time and tempo (while the latter 'took off' and passed them by), and that consequently the underdeveloped countries are now at an earlier, but lower, though 'natural' stage of the general process of growth.[2]

[1] See for example, W. Arthur Lewis, 'Economic Development with Unlimited Supplies of Labour', *The Manchester School* (May 1954); Hollis B. Chenery, 'The Role of Industrialization in Development Programmes', *American Economic Review* (May 1955), both reprinted in A. N. Agarwala and S. P. Singh (eds.), *The Economics of Underdevelopment* (New York, Oxford University Press, 1963), pp. 400-49 and 450-71 respectively.

[2] For a contrary view, see Andre Gunder Frank, *Latin America: Underdevelop-*

Yet, the initial position from which the underdeveloped countries start is *not* a given pattern of socio-economic forces handed down by centuries of natural evolution through feudalism and mercantile capitalism, which through their complex interplay laid the basis for the emergence of industrial capitalism; this latter in turn producing, with the unfolding of international capitalism, the system of colonialism. Their starting-point is, on the one hand, premised on the fact that their present condition is a consequence of the international division of labour that was embodied in the colonial system—an inevitable expression of capitalist development at a given historical conjuncture. This international division of labour relegated to the 'balkanized' colonies the supply of primary commodities (extracted largely with foreign capital and by foreign entrepreneurs), while they also served as markets for the centres' manufactures. The colonies were thus transformed as complements to the metropolitan economies because the industrial development of Britain, the leading capitalist country of the period (and to a lesser extent, France and Germany) depended heavily on external sources of food and raw materials as well as on foreign markets for her manufactures.[3]

On the other hand, these countries find themselves confronted with a new form of international division of labour, dating from the end of the Second World War, which has momentous implications for their development. Its major features are: the emergence of the large-scale corporation as the typical unit of production in advanced countries; the consequent shift in the power relations from Britain as the most advanced capitalist country to the United States (a country with the most developed agriculture, rich raw material bases, a much wider internal market and consequently an economy that is less sensitive to foreign trade); the accelerated pace in the conscious, planned application of scientific techniques to industry and its socio-economic consequences; and the advance and unfolding of state monopoly capitalism that has facilitated West European integration, eased her agricultural development through heavy protection and thus minimized Europe's

---

ment or *Revolution* (New York and London, Monthly Review Press, 1969); Paul Baran, *The Political Economy of Growth*, (New York, Monthly Review Press, 1957), and Tamas Szentes, *The Political Economy of Underdevelopment* (Budapest, Center for Afro-Asian Research of the Hungarian Academy of Sciences, 1970).
[3] Karl Marx, *Capital*, vol. I (Moscow, Foreign Languages Publishing House, 1964); Maurice Dobb, *Studies in the Development of Capitalism* (New York, International Publishers, 1963), revised edition.

foreign trade sensitivity (especially with respect to the periphery).[4] Incidentally, this new international division of labour and its consequences was predicted by Marx in the following words:

> Hand in hand with this centralization (of capital), or this expropriation of many capitalists by few, develop, on an ever-extending scale, the co-operative form of the labour process, the conscious technical application of science, the methodical cultivation of the soil, the transformation of the instruments of labour into instruments of labour only usable in common, the economizing of all means of production by their use as the means of production of combined, socialized labour, the entanglement of all peoples in the net of the world market and with this, the international character of the capitalistic regime.[5]

Given these fundamentally different origins of industrialization in the advanced and the underdeveloped countries, two questions emerge: (1) what can the latter learn from the industrialization process of the former in choosing both the pattern of industry and the appropriate *primum mobile* to achieve that pattern, and (2) what industrial structure should we expect to emerge in the periphery, under the above-described *ab initio* conditions of these countries? My contention is that it is the consideration of these two issues that will reveal the *underlying* causes of disenchantment of the little industrialization that has taken place in the periphery—my main concern in this chapter.

3.2 HISTORICAL EVOLUTION AND PRESENT TRENDS

The essential role of industrialization in the development process has been, historically, to raise the physical output per head and to develop economies that become nationally integrated, flexible and capable of self-generated and self-sustaining growth.[6] This has been

---

[4] J. F. Rweyemamu, 'International Trade and the Developing Countries', *The Journal of Modern African Studies*, vol. 7, no. 2 (July 1969), pp. 3-19, reprinted in *International Business—1970. A Selection of Current Readings* (Michigan State University International Business and Economic Studies, East Lansin, Michigan, 1970). Giovanni Arrighi, 'International Corporations, Labour Aristocracies and Economic Development in Tropical Africa' (University of Dar es Salaam, 1967, mimeo); Tamas Szentes, 'The System of Underdevelopment: The Roots and Qualitative Features of the System' (University of Dar es Salaam, 1969, mimeo.).

[5] Karl Marx, *Capital*, vol. I, op. cit., p. 763.

[6] See for example, Alfred Maizels, *Industrial Growth and World Trade* (London, Cambridge University Press, 1963), especially pp. 8–9; Hollis B. Chenery, 'Patterns of Industrial Growth', *American Economic Review*, vol. 50, no. 4 (September 1960), pp. 624–54.

achieved through several mechanisms. In the first place, industrialization leads to the raising of the share of manufacturing in total product. This secular rise of industry's share in gross national product has been noted by several authors.[7] To the extent that the relative product per worker in industry is higher than in primary production, as the work of Professor Kuznets has shown, the sectoral shift noted above tends to raise the average product per worker for the whole economy.[8] In this way, labour made redundant by, among other factors, population growth in the primary sector (which also has a low labour productivity) gets absorbed in the more labour-productive sector. Secondly, the productivity of the manufacturing sector itself increases over time due to technical progress which might be embodied in the factor inputs thus increasing their efficiency, or due to increasing returns to scale, increasing elasticity of factor substitution (where the stock of capital is growing more rapidly through time than the labour force), or increased reproducible capital per worker. Thirdly, industrialization raises the productivity of other sectors through the provision of such external economies as new skills and attitudes to work, increasing the supplies of agricultural inputs such as insecticides, fertilizers, etc. and cheap and appropriate agricultural and transport equipment. Finally, industrialization makes it possible to alter the pattern of output (since alternative usability of resources is great enough) in response to changes in the structure of demand, without either significant relative price shifts or substantial loss of total productive capacity. This aspect—the flexibility of the industrial structure—is of considerable significance in long term growth for, according to Engel's law, variations in levels of income express themselves only partially as differences in the quantities consumed of similar goods; their main effect being to alter the composition of the consumption basket.[9]

This historical role of industrialization in the development process

[7] A. G. B. Fisher, 'Production: Primary, Secondary and Tertiary', *Economic Record* (March 1939); E. A. Ojala, *Agriculture and Economic Progress* (London, Oxford University Press, 1952), and Colin Clark, *The Conditions of Economic Progress* (London, Macmillan, 1957), third ed.; Chenery, 'Patterns of Industrial Growth', op. cit.

[8] Simon Kuznets, 'Quantitative Aspects of the Economic Growth of Nations, II. Industrial Distribution of National Product and Labour Force', *Economic Development and Cultural Change*, July 1957. Analysis of intersectoral differences in product per worker is based on a ratio of the per cent of the national product in a given sector divided by the per cent of the workers in that sector.

[9] Hendrik Houthakker, 'An International Comparison of Household Expenditure Patterns: Commemorating the Centenary of Engel's Law', *Econometrica*, XXV (1957). The role of foreign trade in augmenting capital formation will be discussed subsequently.

implies a specific configuration of the industrial structure made possible by specific, propitious circumstances at that historical conjuncture. In particular, the type of industrialization that has played a progressive role in the development process of capitalism (as indicated above) was such that it augmented capital formation through the production of appropriate capital goods. The growth of this sector in these economies—which in those days was the prerequisite to the production of final consumption goods—contributed to the flexibility and even viability of those industrial economies. Rosenberg even suggests that the degree of development of this sector, is *the* critical factor accounting for differences in the growth performance of industrial economies and primary producing countries in which little structural transformation has taken place:

> It is probable that one of the most important factors contributing to the viability and flexibility of industrial economies is the existence of a well-developed capital goods sector possessing the technical knowledge, skills and facilities for producing machinery to accommodate the changing requirements of productive activity plus the ability and the incentive for raising productivity of machinery production itself—thereby reducing its cost and encouraging its further adoption. Herein may be the most important feedback of all which is central to explaining the differences in behaviour between industrial and primary producing economies. Industrial societies through the role of their highly developed capital goods producing industries, have, in effect, internalized in their industrial structure a technological capacity which undertakes technological change and adaptation almost as a matter of course and routine. Underdeveloped economies, of course, import much of their capital goods from abroad, but this expedient deprives them of a learning experience in the production, improvement and adaption of machinery which may be vital to economic growth.[10]

There are a number of significant features of the capital goods sector mentioned by Rosenberg, which deserve our attention especially if we are to understand the dilemma which the underdeveloped countries face in their industrialization process. First, the capital goods sector is intimately connected with capital formation. On a flow input-output table we observe very little direct impact of the capital goods sector on final demand. But when we examine a capital input-output table, then we recognize the characteristic dependence of all sectors of the economy on the capital goods sector.[11] This primary and essential role

[10] Nathan Rosenberg, 'Neglected Dimensions in the Analysis of Economic Change', *Bulletin of the Oxford University Institute of Economics and Statistics* (February 1964).
[11] Capital input-output tables have been prepared for a number of countries,

of the capital goods sector has also been noted by Abramovitz who argues that if a backward country wishes to attain a high rate of growth fairly quickly, 'what is necessary is not simply capital formation but capital formation directed to the capital goods industries'.[12] This view has been examined more rigorously by Mahalanobis, Findlay, Feldman, Dobb and Domar among others who have concluded that diverting investment into the capital goods sector will ultimately generate a higher level of consumption at some future date than would be the case otherwise.[13]

The second characteristic of the capital goods sector is its ability to transmit technological diffusion. Nathan Rosenberg, whom I quoted earlier, notes that in the early stages of American industrialization, the skill acquired in the production of one type of machine was transmitted to the production of other types of machines.

> Industrialization [was characterized by] the introduction of a relatively small number of broadly similar productive processes to a large number of industries. Throughout these sectors there are common processes, initially in the refining and smelting of metal ores, subsequently in foundry work whereby the refined metals are cast into preliminary shapes, and then in various machinery processes through which the component metal parts are converted into final form preparations to their assembly as a finished product.[14]

Because of this similarity of technical processes (power transmission, feed mechanism, control devices, etc.) the capital goods industry creates an industrial structure that is 'technologically convergent', i.e. it sets up a complex of industries which though apparently unrelated from

---

notably U.S., Japan, India. See Anne P. Carter and W. W. Leontief, *The Position of Metalworking Industries in the Structure of an Industrializing Economy* (MS., Harvard Economic Research Project, 1967), and P. N. Mathur and R. Bharadwaj, *Economic Analysis in an Input-Output Framework* (Poona, Input-Output Research Association, 1967).

[12] Moses Abramovitz, 'Economics of Growth' in Bernard F. Haley (ed.), *A Survey of Contemporary Economics*, vol. II (Homewood, Illinois, Richard D. Irwin, 1952), p. 156.

[13] P. C. Mahalanobis, 'The Approach of Operational Research to Planning in India', *Sankhya*, vol. 16, Parts I and II (1955), pp. 3–130; R. Findlay, 'Optimal Allocation Between Consumer Goods and Capital Goods', *Economic Journal*, vol. LXXVI, No. 3101 (March 1966), pp. 70–83. Feldman's essays in N. Spulber (ed.), *Foundations of Soviet Strategy for Economic Growth* (Bloomington, Indiana University Press, 1964); Evsey Domar, *Essays in the Theory of Economic Growth* (New York, Oxford University Press, 1957); Maurice Dobb, *An Essay on Economic Growth and Planning* (New York, Monthly Review Press, 1960).

[14] Nathan Rosenberg, 'Technological Change in the Machine Tool Industry, 1840–1910', *The Journal of Economic History*, vol. XXIII (December 1963), no. 4, p. 422.

the point of view of the nature and use of final products, are very closely linked technologically.[15] This degree of technological convergence has important consequences both in generating new techniques and diffusing them once developed. This is because the capital goods industry has an internal dynamic to improve its own techniques of production in the production of durable goods themselves.

It is for this reason that Strassman, examining the inter-industrial relations of the capital goods sector notes that each innovation in that sector is 'likely to have more repercussions in this sector than would be the case in textiles, leather, paper, etc. . . As a result of greater interrelatedness, therefore, the rate of technological change will tend to be greater in the production of the most basic types of capital goods'.[16]

In addition, there is an important third characteristic, that of the learning process involved in machinery production and a high degree of specialization which is conducive not only to an effective learning process but to an effective application of that which is learned.[17] Cheng Chu-Yuan found that in the case of China (1952–66) the correlation between labour productivity in industry and the rise in machine-building output was very high (R=0.99) which suggests that the advancement of labour productivity in the industrial sector was closely associated with the increase in machine-building output.[18] This highly developed facility in the design and production of specialized machinery is perhaps the most important single characteristic of a well-developed capital goods industry and constitutes an external economy of enormous significance to the rest of the economy.

Fourthly, there is another feature of the capital goods industry which I shall comment upon in another context. The literature on underdevelopment is obsessed by the observation that although it would be optimal (from a neo-classical viewpoint) to establish labour-intensive industries in the underdeveloped countries because of their resource-endowments, this has not happened either because of market

[15] For measurement of 'technological convergence', see E. Ames and Yan Chiou-Shuang, 'Economic Interrelatedness', *Review of Economic Studies* (October 1965).
[16] W. P. Strassman, 'Interrelated Industries and the Rate of Technological Change', *Review of Economic Studies* (October 1959), p. 16.
[17] Nathan Rosenberg, 'Capital Goods, Technology and Economic Growth', *Oxford Economic Papers* (NS), vol. 15 no. 15 (November 1963), pp. 217–27.
[18] Cheng Chu-Yuan, 'Growth and Structural Change in the Chinese Machine-Building Industry, 1952–1966', *The China Quarterly*, no. 41 (January–March 1970), p. 51.

imperfections or because of the limited range of techniques available to many industries.[19] This conclusion would seem to be unwarranted because the substitutability often pointed out is by no means inherent in the nature of the goods produced. Rather, the actual range of available techniques is largely dictated by the source of existing capital equipment. As long as capital goods continue to be imported from the industrially advanced countries, machinery embodying techniques that correspond to the factor proportions of the periphery will be difficult to realize. In other words, given the existing structure of world trade, as long as capital goods production is concentrated almost exclusively in the industrial centres, the relatively insignificant demand of the periphery for these goods will have only a negligible impact on both current production decisions about the types of machines to be produced and more importantly on the direction that factor-saving bias will take in the future. This trend is likely to continually hurt— indeed, threaten the viability of—the periphery's economies.

The setting up of capital goods industries, or rather the production of capital goods in the advanced countries, was made easier by two considerations, (a) the objective necessity to produce these goods in the absence of any alternatives (such as imports, as in the case of the underdeveloped countries today). Stigler has described this objective necessity in these terms:

> Young industries are often strangers to the established economic system. They require new kinds or qualities of materials and hence make their own; they must overcome technical problems in the use of their products and cannot wait for potential users to overcome them . . . . These young industries *must* design their specialized equipment and often manufacture it . . . .[20]

(b) The disparity between the traditional and modern technologies was not very large; certainly not as large as it is today. David Landes points out, for example, that 'the early machines, complicated though they were to contemporaries, were nevertheless modest, rudimentary, wooden contrivances, which could be built for surprisingly small

---

[19] The classic article by Eckaus and subsequent discussion have generally assumed away the possibilities of an endogenous capital goods industry in the periphery. R. S. Eckaus, 'The Factor-Proportions Problem in Underdeveloped Areas', *The American Economic Review* (September 1955). The above argument holds true also for the size aspect of production techniques (see below). For the neo-classical argument in favour of capital intensity in order to increase the saving potential, see below.

[20] George Stigler, 'The Division of Labour is Limited by the Extent of the Market', *Journal of Political Economy*, LIX (June 1951), p. 190.

sums'.[21] This has two consequences. First, the capital requirements of the early innovations were small, 'usually within the reach of a single person or family, and the successful enterprise could build the framework of each period on the profits of the one before'.[22] Bairoch found, for example, that the investment per worker in nineteenth century Britain was equivalent to four months' wages. This compares with that of United States in 1953 which had risen to 29 months' wages, and of the typical underdeveloped country of today of about 350 months' wages.[23] Secondly, the production of capital goods for the advanced countries did not require such heavy investments in human capital as is the case today in the underdeveloped countries. Thus it seems to me that these differences in *ab initio* conditions of the industrialization processes may explain better the difficulties encountered by the underdeveloped countries in setting up capital goods industries, than the tariff distortions arguments that one frequently hears from the import-substitution critics.[24] It is, incidentally, these considerations that account for the 'highly sequential or tightly staged' phenomenon of import-substituting industrialization in the periphery that Professor Hirschman has pointed out which forecloses, for a considerable period, any fundamental adaptation (involving sustained technological experimentation and concomitant training in innovation) to the characteristics of the periphery's economies.[25]

The second feature of the industrialization process of the advanced countries was such that it contributed to the augmentation of agriculture's labour productivity and assisted the breakdown of such bottlenecks as would have thwarted the growth of the exchange economy, such as transport. Japan is probably the most well-known capitalist country that doubled its agricultural labour productivity in one decade

---

[21] David S. Landes, *The Unbound Prometheus: Technological Change and Industrial Development in Western Europe from 1750 to the Present* (London, Cambridge University Press, 1969), pp. 64–5.

[22] Landes, ibid., p. 78.

[23] Paul Bairoch, *Révolution Industrielle et Sous-Développement* (Paris, Société d'édition d'enseignment supérieur, 1963).

[24] See for example, Gordon C. Winston, 'A Preliminary Survey of Import Substitution', *Pakistan Development Review* (Spring 1967); John H. Power, 'Import Substitution as an Industrialization Strategy', *Philippine Economic Journal* (1966); John B. Sheahan, 'Imports, Investment and Growth: the Colombian Experience Since 1950' in Gustav F. Papanek (ed.), *Development Policy—Theory and Practice* (Cambridge, Harvard University Press, 1968); and Henry J. Bruton, 'The Import Substitution Strategy of Economic Development: A Survey of Findings' (Williams College, mimeo. 1970).

[25] Albert Otto Hirschman, 'The Political Economy of Import Substituting Industrialization in Latin America', *The Quarterly Journal of Economics*, vol. LXXXII, no. 1 (February 1968), pp. 8–10.

from the time of its 'take-off'.[26] In Britain, output per head in agriculture doubled between 1815 and 1880—a growth which was relatively slow.[27] It was for this reason, coupled with the rather low mineral materials base, that Britain sought for these materials abroad. This situation contrasts with that of the United States today; the most advanced capitalist country with little foreign trade sensitivity with respect to the underdeveloped countries. This is the aspect that has triggered a wave of comment both in the literature on international trade and in the international forums such as the United Nations Conference on Trade and Development.[28] In the field of transport, 'the growing supply of ever-cheaper metal did facilitate enormously the mechanization of other industries, the shift from water to steam power, and eventually the transformation of the means of transportation'.[29] Evidently, industry's contribution to these sectors depended upon the growth of the capital goods sector. This again contrasts with the experience of the underdeveloped countries that are always advised to 'modernize' their agriculture on the basis of expensive, and factor and climate inappropriate, imported technology.[30] Moreover, the underdeveloped countries suffer from reduced natural protection due to the lowering of the costs of transportation from the middle of the nineteenth century onwards.

A third feature of the advanced countries' industrialization process was that their exports were combined with a highly important factor — autonomous investment and technological change—thus making it possible to take advantage of the opportunities offered by the external markets and to diversify and integrate domestic production capacity. There was thus no rigidity created in the production structure such that there was one sector to meet domestic demand and the other to meet external demand. In Britain, even cotton and woollen textile exports at no time constituted more than 70 per cent of total production capacity.

[26] Kuzashi Okhawa and Henry Rosovsky, 'The Role of Agriculture in Modern Japanese Economic Development', *Economic Development and Cultural Change*, IX, no. 1, Part II (October 1960), pp. 43–67; and Gustav Ranis, 'The Financing of Japanese Economic Development', *Economic History Review* (2nd Series), IX (1959), pp. 440–54.
[27] E. L. Jones and S. L. Woolf, *Agrarian Change and Economic Development: The Historical Problem* (London, Methuen & Co.), p. 11.
[28] Ragnar Nurske, *Patterns of Trade and Development* (New York, Oxford University Press, 1961); R. Prebisch, 'The Role of Commercial Policies in Underdeveloped Countries' *American Economic Review*, Papers and Proceedings (May 1959); J. F. Rweyemamu, 'International Trade', *The Journal of Modern African Studies*, op. cit.
[29] Landes, *The Unbound Prometheus*, op. cit., p. 89.
[30] René Dumont, *False Start in Africa* (London, Andre Deutsch, 1966).

The base was the home market. Foreign trade augmented the size of the market in the real Smithian sense. In these countries there has not developed an export sector as such; manufactures are consumed in large quantities within the country and any specialization for the external market that has existed has had a home market base.[31] This is not to mention the fact that the bulk of their exports were manufactures. In the underdeveloped countries, on the contrary, one finds exports of primary production, without a home-market base. There is thus created a fragmentation of the production structure in these countries, and as already mentioned, this inflexibility of the productive system of the ex-colonial countries was due to the fact that the perception of investment opportunities was 'selective' in the sense that it was only those opportunities that would complement metropolitan needs that were adopted.[32] It is obvious that such development has significant implications for the pattern of industry developed.[33]

The fourth and last aspect relates to the *primum mobile* of the advanced countries' industrialization. Unlike the presently underdeveloped countries, the industrialization of the advanced countries was carried out by an *indigenous* capitalist class spawned of the feudal and mercantile systems, which was able to expand productive capacity in response to domestic market demand—a factor of major importance in the eventual national integration of these economies. Consequently, the bulk of output and most individual lines of production were and have been home-directed, while the majority of the national demands for most lines of production were met by national production. The external markets, as we have seen, played a significant part in the advanced countries' industrialization. But these markets were sought only as an expansion of domestic markets. With the help of government intervention in such matters as protection (such as the Corn Laws, etc.), provision of cheap land, low taxes on property, and the external markets (through conquest, settlement, etc.), the

---

[31] Phyllis Deane, 'The Output of British Woollen Industry in 18th Century', *Journal of Economic History*, XVII (1957); D. E. C. Eversley, 'The Home Market and Economic Growth in England, 1750–1780' in E. I. Jones (ed.), *Land, Labour and Population in the Industrial Revolution* (London, Barnes and Noble Inc. 1967), pp. 206–59; United Nations, 'The Growth and Decline of Import Substitution in Latin America', *Economic Bulletin for Latin America*, IX (March 1964), pp. 2–3.
[32] Examples of such 'selective' perception of investment opportunities in the case of Tanzania were given in part I.
[33] Such effects include weak incentives for creating local industries, little technological diffusion, minimum impact on inter-sectoral branches of the economy, etc.

capitalist integument, fuelled by profit expectation, has been able to expand enormously these countries' productive forces.

It should be pointed out, however, that this industrialization process generated certain elements of 'uneven development' that characterize capitalist growth everywhere. These include the development of productive facilities at the expense of the welfare of human beings and their environment; in fostering lopsided development, both in terms of geographical location within the country and sectoral distribution of output favouring luxuries; and in the exploitation and subjugation of 'colonial peoples'. While government intervention has attempted to ameliorate some of these ill-effects of industrial capitalism, it would nevertheless seem that they are an inherent component of the industrial structure whose *primum mobile* is the profit-motive of private enterprise. This becomes even more obvious if we recall that private capital in its endeavour to earn maximum profits seeks to build on the best. Thus a businessman locates a new factory in an urban environment where there are other existing ventures, rather than in the hinterland (unless it is a raw-material based industry), in order to gain access to supplies, a skilled labour force, high income consumers and so on. Similarly, a banker extends loans to those who are already successful, etc. The result is 'uneven development'.[34]

In contrast to the advanced countries, the industrialization of the periphery has been undertaken mainly by foreign entrepreneurs from the centres.[35] The result has been a more visible 'uneven development', described in a different context by Fanon as follows:

> The settler's town is a strongly-built town, all made of stone and steel. It is a brightly-lit town; the streets are covered with asphalt, and the garbage-cans swallow all the leavings, unseen, unknown, and hardly thought about . . . The settler's town is a well-fed town, an easy-going town, its belly is always full of good things. The settler's town is a town of white people, of foreigners
>
> The town belonging to the colonized people, or at least the native town, the Negro village, the medina, the reservation, is a place of ill fame, peopled by men of evil repute. They are born there, it matters little where or how; they die there, it matters not where nor how . . . . The native town is a hungry town, starved of bread, of meat, of shoes, of coal, of light. The native town is a crouching village . . . . It is a town of niggers

[34] Stephen Hymer and Stephen Resnick, 'International Trade and Uneven Development' (Yale University Economic Growth Center, Center Discussion No. 83).
[35] There are a few exceptions to this general pattern, such as India, Brazil etc., though even here local enterprise was weak relative to foreign enterprise.

and dirty Arabs. The look that the native turns on the settler's town is a look of lust, a look of envy ... [36]

Thus it can be inferred that the historical pattern of capitalist industrial growth, as it has evolved in the developed countries, is unlikely to, indeed cannot, repeat itself because the unfolding of industrial capitalism in the world economy has fundamentally altered the very conditions that gave rise to it. This is shown by the consequences of the colonial division of labour which it introduced in these countries, and also by the new international division of labour the main features of which were described earlier.[37] It follows, therefore, that in order to evaluate the industrial structures that have been established in the periphery, one must analyse the implications of both their past history and their contemporary reality.

In the remaining part of this chapter, I first discuss some of the important consequences of the inherited economy on the industrial structure that has developed. This discussion lays down the background of the institutional framework within which industrialization in the periphery has taken—and indeed is still taking—place. Secondly, the implications of the inherited economy (in view of the new international division of labour), are examined in terms of testable hypotheses. I believe that such a procedure is necessary in order to unravel the underlying causes of the observed structure and as a basis for more fundamental structural change. Before I proceed in this section, however, one procedural point needs to be made. In order to concretize the discussion, I restrict my discussion to the African countries that have recently attained their independence, bearing in mind that the model that emerges grows out of Tanzanian experience and reflects the Tanzanian past, its recent and prospective economic history. *A fortiori*, any economy that resembles Tanzania in her historical perspective will find the model relevant. The main reason for this restriction stems from my belief that the historical basis of systems are important; any discussion about them must therefore be constrained by their historical similarity. Generalizations about the system among various countries becomes meaningful, then, once the initial historical conditions are ascertained as generally similar.

[36] Frantz Fanon, *The Wretched of the Earth* (London, Penguin Books, 1967), p. 30
[37] See pages 78–80.

3.3 THE MAJOR CONSEQUENCES OF THE INHERITED STRUCTURES ON THE INDUSTRIALIZATION OF THE PERIPHERY

The discussion that follows is therefore directed to those newly independent countries of Africa. These are countries that had suffered the ravages of the slave trade and slavery, a process that destroyed their socio-economic institutions and arrested their growth. There followed the partition of Africa that further deformed these societies. In particular, during the colonial period *political power* was usurped by the metropolitan powers, so that the direction of the economic development of these countries, their social and institutional systems, their cultural development, and even their political boundaries could be controlled and directly influenced by the centres. This situation enabled the metropolitan powers to develop or suppress in their own interest certain economic sectors, that is, to determine the economic structure, and by fixing the boundaries of the country, they could even lay down the framework in which the development of the national economy could be imitated.

These developments created a *dependency* relationship between the colonies and their mother-countries: *dependency* on their *markets* (since the exports that were developed had no home base; they were established to complement the metropolitan's economies), dependency on imports of capital goods (or what Meir Merhav has called '*technological dependency*'),[38] since the above-mentioned disruptions had destroyed the periphery's rural industry and crafts without substituting domestic capital goods in their stead, and *dependency on foreign entrepreneurs* since, as in Tanzania, colonization tended to destroy the confidence of the colonized.[39] These dependency relationships have had very grave consequences on the industrialization processes of these countries, and some of these are outlined below.

Given the fact that these countries are small in terms of population— a result of 'balkanization' that is so eloquently described by Nkrumah[40] — and that they have low *per capita* incomes, a fact that accounts for their being designated as underdeveloped; it follows tautologically that their national market sizes are necessarily small. Moreover, to the

[38] Meir Merhav, *Technological Dependency, Monopoly and Growth* (London, Pergamon Press, 1969).
[39] See part I.
[40] Kwame Nkrumah, *Neo-colonialism: The Last Stage of Imperialism*, (London and New York, International Publishers, 1965). Nigeria is the only exception.

extent that the size of the national markets constrains the size of the commodity markets, which in turn limits the size and/or number of business enterprises, one should expect the objective conditions of these economies to affect the character of competition (market structure) and productivity.[41] This argument is strengthened by the pervasive 'technological dependency' of these countries. Lacking capital goods industries of their own, they are forced to import them from the advanced countries.

Yet, in so far as these capital goods are produced by capitalists (in keeping with any other goods), they are solely adapted to their home market requirements. With the secular expansion of markets and scales of production, plants and equipment are designed to meet the requirements of their main users—the producers in the next stage of manufacture. Although older techniques designed for a smaller scale of output may for a while coexist with the newer, their reproduction ceases as old equipment wears out, and demand for both replacement and net investment shifts to more modern plants. The design of the capital goods currently produced thus becomes increasingly adapted to the demand for the latest technical methods and scales of production. Older techniques gradually fall into disuse and, after a lapse of time (which may not be greater than the normal life span of the equipment) become extinct. Nor is this process simply a passive compliance of equipment producers with the demand from its users. Their own competitive advantage lies in being able to offer goods which, at constant costs to their customers, will yield them a greater value—a larger physical output. In short, the techniques and scales of production appropriate to the early stages of industrial development—sometimes no more remote than a twenty or thirty years' interval—pass out of existence as part of the operative current stock of knowledge and practical arts. Producers no longer make the equipment, engineers forget the techniques and workmen lose the skills which were needed for the older processes.[42] The under-developed countries are thereby forced to purchase plant and equipment that is far from 'size appropriate'.[43]

[41]The above consideration is premised on a closed economy. The question as to what extent market size bottleneck can be eased through production for export must be deferred for the time being.

[42] H. Pack and M. P. Todaro, 'Technological Transfer, Labour Absorption and Economic Development', *Oxford Economic Papers* (November 1969), and Netherlands Economic Institute, 'Second Hand Machines and Economic Development' (May 1958).

[43] See the problem of 'capital intensity' below, pp. 95-6.

This technological dependency leads, on the one hand, to the emergence of a monopolistic, or rather oligopolistic, structure because the scales of output that must be adopted to introduce modern methods of production are large relative to the extent of the initial market; and on the other hand, these markets will be only partially expanded through income generated by investment, since a large proportion of the capital goods must be imported. In addition, the monopolistic structure itself will restrict the volume of investment, so that the two effects reinforce each other: investment is less than it could be with the existing resources, and such investment that does take place expands domestic income only partially, and vice versa.[44]

The above factors are self-reinforcing in the absence of a change in the entire system that produces them. This can be explained as follows. Given that the markets for final products are small (which is ensured by the lack of a widening impact of investment, described above, and the nature of the commodities produced—the latter being a reflection of the class structure, see below), it follows that the markets for the equipment necessary to make the products (assuming a *primum mobile* that expands productive capacity in response to market demand), are even narrower in comparison with the scales of production which prevail in the advanced countries. It is, of course, well-known that the number of units of any one type of machine that will be demanded in the underdeveloped countries is small because the existing stock of capital is small and generates little demand for replacement. Thus these countries' difficulty to produce capital goods becomes a fetter on their growth process in so far as the domestic output and employment generated by a given amount of investment will always be diminished proportionately to the share of capital goods imports in total investment expenditure. This is partly what prompted Baran to say:

> Thus in most underdeveloped countries capitalism had a peculiar twisted career. Having lived through all the pains and frustrations of childhood, it never experienced the vigour and exuberance of youth, and began displaying at an early age all the grievous features of senility and decadence. To the dead weight of stagnation characteristic of pre-industrial society was added the entire restrictive impact of monopoly capitalism . . .[45]

The second consequence of technological dependency and limited market size on the industrial structure relates to efficiency. If an industry requiring a certain technologically acceptable minimum scale

---

[44] Paul Baran, *The Political Economy of Growth*, op. cit., p. 174, and Meir Merhav, *Technological Dependence*, op. cit.
[45] Paul Baran, *Political Economy of Growth*, op. cit., p. 177.

is established in response to existing inadequate domestic demand (either in anticipation of future growth in scales or for other reasons I shall discuss presently), it will necessarily have a high level of costs in comparison with similar industries in the more developed countries; these higher costs are generally offset only to a limited degree by lower wages or by natural advantages which the developing countries have. Such industries are moreover barred from competition in the export markets because of the existence of restrictions such as tariff barriers, quotas, etc. This exclusion from the international markets in turn restricts the development of manufacturing industries in the small domestic markets and perpetuates the high level of costs.

Thirdly, technological dependency of the underdeveloped countries implies that they have little or no influence on either factor bias or speed of technological change—the important dynamic aspects of growth. In the literature on choice of techniques, there have been three schools of thought. The first school bases its argument on neo-classical theoretical assumptions about factor substitutability, contending that the underdeveloped countries should use more labour-intensive techniques because of the very different 'shadow' factor price ratios that prevail in these areas. The economic rationale usually provided for this argument is that static efficiency requires the equilibration of marginal rates of factor substitution with the (implicit) wage-rental ratios. Consequently, since wage-rental ratios are relatively low in less developed countries, more labour-intensive techniques of production would seem desirable. Supporters of this view, in trying to reconcile their attitudes with the reality of the technical form of investment actually in use in the underdeveloped countries, suggest that the divergence observed is due either to market imperfections or to a narrow range of available techniques, or both.[46]

Yet as already pointed out, this recommendation fails to recognize that the underdeveloped countries, to the extent that they have no capital goods industry of their own, are unable to influence the factor bias of these capital goods. This is because labour-intensive techniques are probably not infeasible technically. Rather, they are inefficient from the point of view of the advanced countries where they are produced.

[46] J. J. Polak, 'Balance of Payments Problems of Countries Reconstructing with the Help of Foreign Loans', *Quarterly Journal of Economics* (February 1963); N. S. Buchanan, *International Investment and Domestic Welfare* (New York, 1945); and Eckaus, 'Factor Proportions', *The American Economic Review*, op. cit.

The second school of thought, again based on neo-classical assumptions, arrives at a contrary conclusion, namely that the underdeveloped countries should use more capital-intensive techniques. The argument is based on the choice of technique's influence on income distribution and the size of the investible surplus, and hence its effect on growth of income and employment. More specifically, it is argued that since capital-intensive techniques imply a smaller share of wages in output, they will yield a larger investable surplus and a faster rate of growth of employment.[47]

As Arrighi and Bator have pointed out, this argument is based on a number of very restrictive assumptions, which may not be valid in the conditions of the underdeveloped countries.[48] Specifically, it assumes: (a) that the real wage rate is fixed whatever techniques of production are adopted and is constant through time, (b) that the re-investment of the larger surplus associated with capital-intensive techniques is feasible in the sense that either the productive capacity of the capital goods sector is sufficiently large to supply the capital goods required by such re-investment; or foreign exchange is available to make up the deficiency of capital goods through purchases abroad, (c) that the re-investment of the larger surplus is not only feasible but desired by whoever controls its utilization, and (d) that the rate of saving is a function of the choice of technique. The non-fulfilment of the underlying assumptions in the periphery might turn out to mean that though these countries adopt capital-intensive techniques (not because of the reasons given, but because of technological dependency), these techniques are not necessarily growth-promoting. The consequence of these techniques on urban employment has been extensively documented.[49]

---

[47] W. Galenson and H. Leibenstein, 'Investment Criteria, Productivity, and Economic Development', *Quarterly Journal of Economics* (August 1955); A. K. Sen, *Choice of Techniques: An Aspect of the Theory of Planned Economic Development*, (Oxford, Basil Blackwell, 1960).

[48] Giovanni Arrighi, 'International Corporations', op. cit., pp. 24–5; Francis M. Bator, 'On Capital Productivity, Input Allocation and Growth', *Quarterly Journal of Economics* (February 1957).

[49] The evidence relating to this point is the widely discussed problem of unemployment in these countries. See for example, D. Turnham and J. Jaegar, *The Employment Problem in Less Developed Countries: A Review* (OECD Development Centre, Paris, 1969, mimeo.); Werner Baer and Michael E. A. Herve, 'Employment and Industrialization in Developing Countries', *Quarterly Journal of Economics*, vol. LXX, no. 1 (February 1966), pp. 99–107; Charles R. Frank, 'Urban Unemployment and Economic Growth in Africa', *Oxford Economic Papers* (NS), vol. 20, no. 2 (July 1968) and Arrighi, 'International Corporations', op. cit.

Professor Hirschman also favours the adoption of capital-intensive techniques in the periphery, especially the large-scale ventures; in activities which must be maintained in top-working order; in activities that must observe high quality standards for their output; in machine-paced operations and process-centred industries. This is based on his belief that the modern technology embodied in capital equipment helps management in the countries perform unfamiliar and uncongenial tasks and co-ordinate the internal activities of the firm, while it is precisely these management skills which are most scarce in underdeveloped countries.[50]

These arguments are concerned with the techniques of production which *should* be chosen *in vacuo*, or probably in the institutional contexts of the advanced countries, where one would expect an indigenous entrepreneur class to select techniques of production consistent with the factor endowment of the economy. His decision will be implemented by the machine-producers. This situation, however, contrasts with that of the underdeveloped countries, where there is no capital goods industry and as we shall see below, where the major investment decisions are made by the foreign entrepreneur. It is for this reason that while the debate on capital intensity (or more generally on the choice of techniques) has accumulated a set of theories that pertain to development, there is also no doubt that it has been most difficult to disentangle in the debate valuable insights from needless ingenious elaborations which are strictly applicable to the more structured, fully-integrated economies of the more developed countries. Certainly labour-capital substitution may change the performance of a task, the design of a factory, the structure of an industry, of the output-mix of an economy. The crucial issues, however, are the exploration of the reasons underlying the choice of techniques that are actually taken in these underdeveloped countries. Here, as I will show later, the nature of the entrepreneurs plays a significant role.

An important implication of the above discussion which need to be emphasized strongly is that, regardless of which technology is most efficient from the static context, the fact that the range of choice is being dictated by the technological mandates of factor price configurations and expectations in the developed nations, demonstrates that over time there will be an inherent labour-saving bias in the

---

[50] Albert O. Hirschman, *The Strategy of Economic Development* (New Haven, Yale University Press, 1957).

technology transfer process.[51]

Another important factor that has affected the pattern of industry of the ex-colonial economies is the fact that at the time of independence, they did not have an indigenous capitalist class that would have carried out industrial investments in a *national* context. While this may have been a blessing in disguise, it has in fact meant that a significant portion of the manufacturing industry has been undertaken by foreign private entrepreneurs. What has been the effect of having an extra-national *bourgeoisie* on the industrialization process of these countries? In order to throw light on this question, I will first explore the specific motivations of these foreign investors when investing in the under-developed, ex-colonial countries.

While the literature on industrialization of the periphery has generally assumed that the inducement to invest is largely determined by the extent of the market, that is, industries are supposed to be established in any economy when the market demand corresponds to a size which can support a plant at optimum efficiency, it neglects the specification of the behavioural variables which determine the entrepreneur's perception of investment opportunities and investment decisions.[52] There has, in fact, been a tendency to confuse investment opportunities and investment decisions in received theory. Ideally, this problem does not arise. That is, in a world in which entrepreneurs instantly respond (in the fashion of the Schumpetarian innovator) to any change of condition on the basis of full, costless, instantaneous information, there is no place for any analysis of the stimulants that bring the possibilities of investments to the attention of the decision-maker.[53] However, in the setting of these ex-colonial countries where an

[51] This can be shown very simply by assuming (a) that all capital goods are produced in the developed countries where labour-saving technological progress is embodied in new vintages, and (b) equilibrium prevails in the capital goods market in the developed countries so that prices of equipment of different vintages adjust so as to equalize all profit rates in the developed countries, and (c) the underdeveloped countries import all their capital goods requirements from the developed countries. See Michael P. Tadaro, *Some Thoughts on the Transfer of Technology From Developed to Less Developed Nations* (University College of Nairobi, Institute for Development Studies, 1969, mimeo.).

[52] Examples are Ragnar Nurske, *Problems of Capital Formation in Under-developed Countries and Patterns of Trade and Development* (New York: Oxford University Press, 1967), pp. 4–31, Henry G. Aubrey, 'Investment Decisions in Underdeveloped Countries', *Capital Formation and Economic Growth* (Princeton, Princeton University Press for the National Bureau of Economic Research, 1955), pp. 397–440. See also the voluminous literature on the balanced-unbalanced growth controversy.

[53] Joseph A. Schumpeter, *The Theory of Economic Development* (Cambridge, Harvard University Press, 1934), especially, pp. 61–90.

indigenous capitalist class failed to emerge, one cannot meaningfully assume the Schumpetarian world view. Thus the problem of investment motivation of the foreign investor has to be faced. How have development economists attempted to deal with this problem?

In his search for efficient mechanisms that maximize induced investment decisions, Professor Hirschman has singled out the 'progressive' role of imports in the industrialization process. Observing that imports 'still provide the safest, most incontrovertible proof that the market is there', and that they condition the consumer to the product, breaking down his initial resistance, he concludes that imports thus 'reconnoiter and map out the country's demand. They remove uncertainty and reduce selling costs at the same time thereby bringing perceptibly closer the point at which domestic production can economically be started.'[54] Professor Hirschman's hypothesis can be reformulated as follows: when the market, as mapped out by imports, has reached or is approaching that size which will support a plant at optimum or near optimum efficiency, an investor who is in search of profitable opportunities will come forward, given appropriate publicity and provision of reasonable tariff protection and other fiscal incentives.[55] The hypotheses can be tested empirically by correlating a measure of technological threshold with the time period at which the first import-replacing investment occurs.[56]

While there is little doubt that imports can act as proxies for market size, it is by no means obvious that knowledge of opportunities revealed by import size will lead to investment decisions in the ex-colonial countries. In fact to the extent that such opportunities are likely to be perceived by those engaged in the foreign sector, there is no *a priori* reason, except under certain special circumstances, to expect foreign interests (in the absence of an indigenous capitalist class) to undertake local production of the goods they formerly supplied.[57]

Indeed in the case of Tanzania and Nigeria, where information on this question has been collected, there is sufficient evidence to indicate that

[54] Albert O. Hirschman, *The Strategy*, op. cit., pp. 61–90.
[55] Minimum economic size is defined, *à la* Hirschman, as 'the size at which the domestic firm will be able to secure normal profits and to compete with existing foreign suppliers, taking into consideration location advantages and disadvantages as well as, perhaps, some infant industry protection'. See Hirschman, op. cit., p. 101.
[56] However, Professor Hirschman points out in his book, especially page 125, that imports are not sufficient conditions for inducing investment opportunities.
[57] One of such features is the existence of any lasting disequilibrium that disrupts the balance between demand and production. See next chapter.

in a number of industries there has been a considerable lag between the technological threshold and the establishment of import-replacing industries in specific product lines.[58] This may not imply that Professor Hirschman's view of the mechanism for inducing investment decisions is wrong, since he may not have designed his theory to apply to either ex-colonial countries, or to foreign investors. It does indicate, however, that the attainment of technological threshold, though a necessary condition for investment decisions in a number of cases, is certainly not sufficient in the case of the ex-colonial economies. The next problem is then to examine the sufficient conditions, if any.

In a survey conducted by Hakam on the motivations to invest in Nigeria, he found that by far the most frequently cited reasons were the following:

(a) 'The firm had long held a good export relation with Nigeria. Aiming to preserve the market for the company in face of rising duties, possible rise in duties or local competition' (58 per cent of all firms);

(b) 'Aim to expand sales into a new market otherwise difficult by just exporting' (30 per cent of all firms);

(c) 'As a result of the parent company's strategy of investing in key global areas. Convinced that Nigeria is a very important area and that it may be too late to gain entry profitably into the market if the decisions were postponed too long' (28.3 per cent of all firms); and

(d) 'Aim at forestalling a major competitor's move or possible move into Nigeria' (26 per cent of all firms).[59]

All these motives indicate acting from fear of being pushed out of the export market either by external restrictions or by a monopolistic situation developing within the country. There is thus a considerable element of strategy involved in some of the investment decisions, that of now or never. Obviously, in an area as complex as international investment one ought not anticipate that any hypothesis will have more than a limited explanatory power. The decision-making sequence that is used in connection with international investments, according to various empirical studies, indicates a complex set of motives some of which are not readily quantifiable or even predictable. But there is one theme which emerges again and again from such studies. Any threat to the established position of an enterprise is a powerful galvanizing

[58] For Tanzania see next chapter; information on Nigeria is provided by Peter Kilby, *Industrialization in an Open Economy: Nigeria 1945–1966* (London, Cambridge University Press, 1969).

[59] A. N. Hakam, 'The motivation to Invest and the Locational Pattern of Foreign Private Industrial Investments in Nigeria', *The Nigerian Journal of Economic and Social Studies*, vol. 8, no. 1 (March 1966), pp. 50–1.

force to action. In fact, one might say that threat in general is a more reliable stimulus to action than opportunity is likely to be.[60]

The notion that a threat to the *status quo* is a powerful galvanizing force for international investments also seems to explain what happens after the pioneering investment. Once such an investment is made by a former major exporter, other major producers in that specific product line (who are in some way connected with the particular market) see it as a threat to the *status quo*. They see themselves as losing position relative to the pathfinder with a vague intimation of further losses to come. Their share of the market is imperilled. The uncertainty can be reduced by emulating the pioneering investor and by investing in the same area.[61]

Moreover, such motivation to invest, i.e. protecting one's stake in the market by going into local manufacture, has obvious implications for tariff policy. The investor will demand a certain level of tariff protection in order to eliminate the competition of other sellers. In consequence of the elimination of competition, a firm will be able to expand its total sales and increase its earnings by an even greater proportion as a result of a tariff-enhanced unit profit margin. Not only does the tariff secure the seller who makes an industrial commitment against the competition of similar products, but it also shields him to a substantial degree from technically more advanced varieties or otherwise superior articles which in the absence of fiscal discrimination might pre-empt the market. The overall effects of such investment on market structure will be discussed subsequently.

I note, finally, that this way of looking at investment decision sheds some light on the observed delay in establishing locally certain industries (in Tanzania and Nigeria) whose technological threshold had long been attained. To the extent that the competitive pressures to set up the industrial establishments will express themselves in the changing market shares, volume of sales and distributive margins, it is likely that for any product line, if market shares of overseas supplies

[60] See for example, Yair Aharoni, *The Foreign Investment Decision Process* (Cambridge, Harvard Business School, 1966); Seev Hirsch, *Location of Industry and International Competitiveness* (Oxford, Clarendon Press, 1967); Raymond Vernon, 'International Investment and International Trade in the Product Cycle', *Quarterly Journal of Economics*, vol. LXXX (May 1966), pp. 190–207; Robert B. Stonbaugh, Jr, 'The Product Life Cycle, U.S. Exports and International Investment' (unpublished doctoral dissertation, Harvard Business School, Boston, 1968).
[61] This is what Aharoni terms the 'bandwagon effect'. See Aharoni, *The Foreign Investment Decision Process*, p. 55. For its appearance in Tanzania, see next chapter.

are small and if technical skill barriers are sufficiently high to preclude deploying merchant firms, import substitution may long be delayed because the interests of no single firm are materially jeopardized.[62]

Several other consequences for the pattern of industry that emerges, flow from the above-described investment decision mechanism. I have argued above that foreign investors tend to invest in the periphery in response to, or in anticipation of, protectionist policies on the part of the national governments in order to secure their own export interests or to establish themselves anew in the area. This implies that for the foreign concern, the existence of a local market is not a sufficient though a necessary condition to actually establish a plant. The sectoral distribution of investments will be determined largely by this consideration. Specifically goods that are standardized (and hence subject to competition) and involve minimum risks will normally be established first. This accounts for the generally observed fact that import-substituting industrialization favours consumer goods or rather that it is biased against the production of capital goods.[63]

Secondly, in conjunction with the technological dependency argument discussed earlier, the above process is likely to lead to an oligopolistic structure, which will tend towards inefficiency and become a fetter on market-widening investment either because of the bandwagon effect, which creates excess capacity, or because of the incentive structure, which caters for both efficient and inefficient producers.

Thirdly, the linkages will probably be low because establishments set up as a result of the above motivations are unlikely to be interrelated from the point of view of factor supplies and factor demands.

Fourthly, there is another feature which, though it is not related to the motivation to invest, is nevertheless connected with the 'foreign' character of the industrialization process—the problem of choice of techniques. Studies by Maurice Bye and François Perroux have shown that (a) technology transfer by foreign firms to the periphery, either in the form of private subsidiaries or joint ventures, tends to perpetuate the techniques of production derived from the advanced countries, and (b) any technology transfer to the developing countries, to the extent that that technology is developed and initiated within the factor

[62] Peter Kilby, *Industrialization in an Open Economy*, op. cit.
[63] For a concise analysis of the arguments that indicate the bias against capital goods production with respect to the investment pattern of the multinational corporations, see Arrighi, 'International Corporations', op. cit.

endowments of the industrial countries is *a priori* likely to be biased against the use of labour.[64]

Fifthly, so long as these foreign entrepreneurs have acted as private entrepreneurs, that is, so long as they have been guided by demand considerations in their search for profitable opportunities, it is likely that the type of goods they have produced, the location of their economic activities, etc., have tended to correspond to these requirements. A few examples are given below in order to specify the implications of the private enterprise effect on the pattern of investment in the ex-colonial countries.

As I pointed out in part I with respect to Tanzania, colonization created a small high money-income group which consists of civil servants, workers in commerce and industry, and after independence, politicians. For as long as this upper-income group is likely to have a high import propensity, diversification through the substitution for these imports can be successful only if the new domestic production does not diverge too far from the previous imports in terms of quality, function and appearance. For this to be possible, the new substitutes will generally have to contain a sizeable proportion of imported inputs. A good part of this type of production will often be no more than that which is commonly called 'last-touches import substitution', in which domestic value added does not consist of much more—if that—than the profit margin provided by the tariffs. Moreover to the extent that such commodities are likely to be price inelastic, import substitution on a scale that is at a cost disadvantage by comparison with similar goods produced in the advanced countries will therefore require very high protective tariffs. As a result one would expect luxury consumer goods produced in these countries to be characterized by relatively high tariffs and high import content.

Moreover, as I have already pointed out, the moving force of private enterprise is such that it wants to capitalize on whatever external economies exist. It therefore sets up industries in the 'export enclaves', since these are the only segments of these countries' economies that can provide them with skilled manpower, markets, service needs, etc.

Thus, in conclusion, the discussion above points to the major aspects pertaining to the structural features that characterize the

[64] Maurice Bye, 'Self-financed Multi-territorial Units and Their Time Horizon', *International Economic Papers*, VIII (1957), pp. 147–78; François Perroux and R. Demonts, 'Large Firms—Small Nations' *Présence Africaine* (Paris), X, 38, (1961).

industrialization process of the ex-colonial economies. These features include the establishment of a productive structure that (a) is biased against capital goods industries, thus limiting industry's contribution to the production of farm equipment and transport facilities, (b) utilizes relatively more capital-intensive techniques of production (that is, relative to their resource-endowment), thus compounding the problem of the urban unemployed, (c) has limited linkage effects, especially with the traditional sector, (d) fosters lopsided development both in terms of geographical location within the country (especially the concentration of industry in the export enclave) and sectoral distribution of consumer goods output, favouring luxuries, and (e) sets up uncompetitive, oligopolistic structures.[65]

While conventional economic wisdom has traced the underlying factors responsible for the generation of the above features to 'a consequence of the activities selected for domestic development and of methods employed to provide the incentives to bring about their development'[66] (implying that it is simply the result of random policy mistakes), the above analysis indicates that the policies pursued were predetermined by the inherited structure of those economies. This is what explains the similarity of the import-substituting industrialization processes in the various countries. Moreover, the analysis not only diagnoses the malaise of the ex-colony economies' industrialization, it suggests a more meaningful remedy. This will be taken up in part III.

The above analysis indicates many implications for the industrial structure we would expect to emerge given the *ab initio* conditions of the ex-colony economies, for both short term and long term growth. I have therefore selected those implications that are amenable to testing, given the data I have. The selection of the hypotheses, in other words, has been constrained by the available information. They should not be taken as exhausting the full theoretical implications underlying the model.

[65] For an exposition of these features see Celso Furtado, *Diagnosis of the Brazilian Crisis* (Berkeley and Los Angeles, University of California Press, 1965); Albert O. Hirschman, 'The Political Economy of Import-Substituting Industrialization'; R. Soligo and J. J. Stern, 'Tariff Protection, Import Substitution and Investment Efficiency', *Pakistan Development Review*, V (Summer 1965), pp. 249–70; Henry J. Bruton, 'The Import-Substitution Strategy of Economic Development: A Survey of Findings' (Williams College, 1969, mimeo.); Ann Seidman, 'Comparative Industrial Strategies in East Africa', University College of Dar es Salaam, 1969, mimeo.).
[66] Henry J. Bruton, 'The Import-Substitution Strategy of Economic Development: A Survey of Findings', op. cit., p. 2.

The characteristics of perverse capitalist industrial development as presented above should ideally be observed and tested in any ex-colonial African country that has had a sufficiently long period of time to industrialize. In such a case, the results of the tests of hypotheses advanced below could be interpreted unambiguously. However, in the case of Tanzania, the interpretation of the testing of hypotheses presents several problems of identification. First, Tanzania has only been recently industrialized. The data presented are for 1966, five years after the country became independent. Secondly, the country as a colony had been a periphery-satellite of Kenya, as explained in the next chapter. For these reasons, it might be inferred that some of the characteristics of perverse capitalist industrial development (as set out in terms of hypotheses below) are either natural deviations from the normal pattern (because of Tanzania's union with her neighbours) or due to problems of infancy which will be healed by economic growth and modernization. In other words, it may be argued that behind these symptoms of youth there does *not* lie a system organized on the basis of the model I have presented, whose functioning inevitably produces such results and will continue to produce them as long as the system itself is not changed.

It is thus important to delineate three aspects of the significance of the tests to be presented in the case of Tanzania.[67] First, while it is true that some of the characteristics mentioned below, taken individually may be symptomatic of youth, collectively they would tend to support the theory advanced. Moreover, even problems of infancy are likely to differ between systems. For example, under conditions of central planning it is possible to have relatively higher linkage effects than under conditions of private enterprise. Similarly, there is likely to be a difference in the nature and extent of problems of infancy between classical and perverse capitalist industrial development. Metaphorically, what is being asserted here is that baby behaviour varies partly on the framework in which specific categories of babies are being brought up. Secondly, in so far as some of the ex-colonial countries of Asia, Latin America and Africa (e.g. United Arab Republic) which have had a relatively longer period of industrialization exhibit similar tendencies as formulated in the hypotheses below, it would appear that symptoms of perverse growth which are still embryonic in Tanzania are more deep

---

[67] The term 'significance of tests' is not used in its statistical sense. It merely refers to the meaning to be attached to the interpretation of the results of the tests.

rooted.[68] While a more unambiguous verification of the model must await further tests especially relating to those economies with the *ab initio* conditions here described but with a longer period of industrial development, it is our conviction that the characteristics of industrial development that are displayed by Tanzania's industrialization experience emanate from the model we have specified above. Finally, and most important from our point of view, it should be noted that the model presented aims at identifying the specific characteristics of a system that logically flows from a set of existing initial conditions and a definite prime motive force. The exploration of such a model is deemed to be a necessary prerequisite to the specification of any meaningful industrialization policy for an economy that has resolved to transform into a different economic system. For only then can the key parameters of transition to the desired social system be identified. To this we shall, however, turn in the concluding chapter.

3.4 SOME TENTATIVE HYPOTHESES

The hypotheses presented below are derivable from the above model and deal with such issues as market structure, sectoral distribution of output, capital intensity, location, inter-industry relations, etc. Since the general argument has been sketched above, a summary of it is presented below in each particular case.

Hypothesis 1
A part of the profits of large oligopolistic foreign firms in the ex-colonial countries are not shown as profits in the accounting records of the ex-colonial countries but instead are realized through over-invoicing of equipment, parts, raw materials, etc.

This hypothesis is derived from the postulated behaviour of international firms when such investment is protected by means of tariffs. To the extent that these firms are motivated to invest because of fear of losing the market and are protected to retain these markets (rather than because of their efficiency), they will endeavour to keep themselves by showing minimum profits in the receiving country. This does not mean that they do not benefit from the investment decision. Rather,

[68] For an exposition of these features in Asia and Latin America see footnote 65, p. 103.

they are motivated to keep their balance sheet profits to a minimum, embodying their profits through 'over-invoicing' of raw materials, machines, components, parts, etc., especially if these happen to be subsidiaries.[69]

As a result of this pattern of behaviour, only a small portion of realized profits of the firms operating in these ex-colonial countries is reinvested in the country. This is certainly a fetter to further industrial growth.

Hypothesis 2
Foreign-owned firms tend to be more capital-intensive than locally-owned enterprises.

This hypothesis is a direct consequence of technological dependence and foreign investment dependence in that the local entrepreneur is more likely to shop around for older and less capital-intensive equipment which is less expensive. The foreign entrepreneur, on the other hand, wants to maintain similar techniques to those he uses in the more developed countries (where they were developed) either because he believes they are more factor productive or because of institutional rigidities such as the convenience of having the same maintenance team all over the world, etc. In any case, he is less constrained financially than his local counterpart.

The capital-intensive bias of foreign-owned enterprises has several consequences as a result of its effects on both the nature and volume of employment it induces. With respect to the volume of employment, the capital-intensive bias of foreign investment tends, *ex hypothesi*, to narrow employment opportunities and *a fortiori* a mass-based internal market. Moreover, because capital-intensive techniques tend to employ a semi-skilled and professional type of labour (which receives relatively higher wages in the ex-colonial economies because of its scarcity), it tends to accentuate the disparities in income between town and country and encourages the formation of a 'labour aristocracy' which is not only socially undesirable but also has a demand structure that reinforces the mis-utilization of the country's surplus.[70]

[69] For an empirical study of the various ways of earning monopoly profits by international firms in the periphery, see Constantin V. Vaitsos, 'Transfer of Resources and Preservation of Monopoly Rents' (paper submitted at Dubrovik Conference of the Harvard University Advisory Service, April 1970, mimeo.). For evidence of over-invoicing in Tanzania, though in the trade sector, see M. J. Yaffey, *Balance of Payments Problems*, op. cit.
[70] For a full discussion of the various types of labour required in capital-intensive and labour-intensive industries, see Giovanni Arrighi, 'International

Hypothesis 3
Foreign-owned firms, though capital-intensive (and therefore relatively more labour-productive) are not necessarily more efficient in terms of total factor productivity than locally-owned enterprises.

This hypothesis is derived from the realization that the 'factor bias' of equipment is inappropriate. The technological dependency aspect of the hypothesis has been fully discussed elsewhere.

The inefficiency of capital-intensive investments by the foreign firms, in addition to the employment effects mentioned in the previous hypothesis (b), lead to a mis-allocation of the country's resources.

Hypothesis 4
Linkage effects of the industrial structure of the ex-colonial countries are limited and there is a high dependence on imports.

Limited linkage effects may be due, of course, to the embryonic nature of the industrialization process. However, they may also arise from the nature of the motivations to invest, already described, which allows investment decisions to materialize in those cases where there is a 'threat'. It is unlikely from the logic of such a behaviour that there will be any consideration of inter-industry linkages. There is no reason to expect private entrepreneurs to be interested in inter-industry linkages, though for an economy with a national *bourgeoisie* or where modern international capital is particularly attracted, such linkages may be realized sooner or later.[71] Given the motivation to invest discussed above and the conditions of Tanzania's economy as already explained in part I, it is less likely that linkage effects in the absence of government intervention would be greatly increased. The consequences of limited linkages is, of course, less rapid industrial growth.

Hypothesis 5
Modern industries of ex-colonial economies are located in the export enclaves.

This hypothesis is derived from the *modus operandi* of private enterprise. That is, it is a logical consequence or normal pattern of capitalist

---

Corporations, Labour Aristocracies and Economic Development in Tropical Africa' (University College of Dar es Salaam, 1967, mimeo.).

[71] As explained in part I, the character of modern international capitalist investment does not favour an economy with features such as those of Tanzania.

development, and may be expected to occur during the industrialization process under that system. Lest it should be argued that the new 'development corporations' that have mushroomed in these countries should have corrected this bias, let me add here that I consider their operations as 'private' in character. Briefly my main reason for upholding this view is that it is the rules of the game appropriate to a given property system that I define as characterizing the *modus operandi* of the system. In this sense, an economy may be of a private enterprise character even though its public sector is large, or even growing, *if* the mode of operation of its public sector follows the rules established by the private sector.[72] The crucial distinction, in other words, is what guides the accumulation of capital. If it is the pursuit of private profit (and studies that I have made indicated so, especially in Tanzania)[73]—private here in the sense of the particularistic interest of each enterprise (irrespective of its stockholders)—then the economy is a private enterprise system.

The significance of this hypothesis is the consideration to be taken up in part III that changes in location which might be required by socialist planning of industry will necessitate basic changes in these rules of the game. Concentration of location as such is not the most characteristic aspect of perverse growth, though it is a distinctive feature of capitalist industrial development. Rather the significance of the hypothesis must be seen in the light of possible locational changes in the implementation of socialist objectives.

Hypothesis 6
The system of industrial production of the ex-colonial countries is characterized by (a) a low percentage share of capital goods, and (b) a high percentage share of luxury consumer goods relative to the world average, for given income and population.

This hypothesis is derived from the motivation to invest and the nature of private enterprise. In the first place, it asserts that perverse capitalist industrialization tends to produce a minimum of capital

---

[72] For example, the National Development Corporation (NDC)'s enabling Act provided that 'in carrying on its business the corporation shall *have regard to* the economic and *commercial merits of any undertaking* it promotes, finances, develops, manages or assists and the economic positions and potentialities of Tanzania as a whole, and the corporation shall raise its best endeavours to secure that its business as a whole, is carried out at *net* profit, taking one year with another'. (My italics.)

[73] Ann Seidman, 'Comparative Industrial Strategies in East Africa' (University College of Dar es Salaam, ERB Paper 69.27, 1969, mimeo.); and K. E. Svendsen,

goods. To the extent that these goods involve greater gestation risks and are non-standardized, low tariffs (which historically were adopted to enable planters and miners to lower their production costs), discourages the setting up of such industries. Secondly, the production of relatively more luxury consumer goods is due to the income distribution that has emerged. To the extent that private enterprise is guided by the presence of demand, it is only reasonable that it will tend to produce goods with a relatively high anticipated (monetary) demand. As pointed out in the earlier parts of this chapter, this demand, made evident by the structure of import data, generally favours the production of luxuries.

Several significant consequences follow from this hypothesis. On the one hand, the bias against the domestic production of capital goods enhances the dependence of the rural sector on world demand for its expansion, especially when this factor is complemented by the foreign investment's tendency to set up capital-intensive industries. While trade may be relied upon to play some role in adjusting the rural sector's growth requirements, the realities of the existing international division of labour militate against our expecting the export sector to play the role of the domestic capital goods sector. This is briefly due to the following reasons. To begin with, the metropolitan countries are their own largest customers for their manufactured products (capital goods as well as consumer goods), so that cost and price movements initiating from their internal markets become transmitted to their external markets. These prices and costs are affected by the labour scarcity and pervasiveness of monopoly (or oligopoly) in the metropolitan countries and are biased upwards for obvious reasons. The internal markets of the metropolitan powers are monopolistic so that even if their export markets are competitive, there is a tendency for the price level of their goods to rise over time, either directly or indirectly through the effects of monopolistic prices on the cost levels of competitive industries. Moreover, since these countries have a scarcity of labour, and wages are inflexible downwards (because of labour unions' countervailing power), the wage increases which occur have a ratchet effect.

In contrast to the metropolitan countries, the ex-colonial countries

---

'Decision-Making in the National Development Corporation' (University College of Dar es Salaam, ERB Paper 68.4, 1968, mimeo.); and A. J. M. van der Laar, 'Perspective on the Parastatals: NDC' (University College of Dar es Salaam, ERB Paper 68.5, 1968, mimeo.).

have no significant home markets for their products and they operate under conditions close to atomistic competition in their export markets. In addition, they have an elastic supply of labour which keeps costs down. Furthermore, the income and price elasticities of the products of the ex-colonial countries are low compared to those of the metropolitan countries. As a result of all these factors, not only does the centre fail to pass on to the ex-colonial countries the gains from its own productivity increases, but the ex-colonial economies are unable to retain the benefits of their own rise in productivity.[74]

While, of course, individual ex-colonial countries' gains from trade differ depending upon their specific resource endowment, level of development, trade policies, etc., the general argument that the ex-colonial countries' opportunities for trade expansion are more limited than the free traders care to admit is at least relevant to Tanzania. Almost all of Tanzania's exports face declining market demand either because of Engel's law (e.g. in the case of coffee) or because of the gradual substitution of the agricultural products by synthetics (e.g. sisal and cotton). This is in addition to the rising import price index, turning the terms of trade against Tanzania as discussed in part I.

Thus, the possibility of the bias against the production of capital goods engendering the growth of the rural sector is a real one. This is in addition to the fact that the export sector is not in any case a really good substitute for the domestic capital goods sector because unlike the latter, it does not *automatically* widen the domestic market through the realization of its proceeds. The other major implications of the bias against the production of capital goods have already been discussed at length.

On the other hand, the excessive production of luxuries tends to reduce the growth potential of the economy since these luxuries are not used either as 'instruments of production or as articles of subsistence in the production of others'.[75]

[74] This is a familiar Prebischian argument. See especially, Raul Prebisch, 'Development Problems of the Peripheral Countries and the Terms of Trade' in James D. Theberge, *Economics of Trade and Development* (New York, John Wiley & Sons, 1968), pp. 287–97; G. Meir, 'International Trade and International Inequality', *Oxford Economic Papers* (October 1958), and J. Rweyemamu, 'International Trade', op. cit.
[75] P. Sraffa, *Production of Commodities by Means of Commodities* (London, Cambridge University Press, 1960), p. 7. For an exposition of the concept of 'growth potential', see I. Sachs, 'Potential, Proportional and Perverse Growth', *Czechoslav Economic Papers*, no. 6.

CHAPTER FOUR

THE INSTITUTIONAL AND HISTORICAL SETTING OF TANZANIA'S INDUSTRIALIZATION PROCESS

This chapter is devoted to a descriptive assessment of the pattern and behaviour of industrial growth in Tanzania in a historical perspective. In particular the causes for slow industrial growth in the pre-independence period and the circumstances that have contributed to an industrial 'spurt' thereafter are explored.

4.1 THE HISTORICAL SETTING

Industrial development in Tanzania on any significant scale is of very recent origin. As indicated in chapter 1, there existed during the pre-colonial period such 'cottage' industries as weaving, blacksmithing, pottery and woodworking. Many of these crafts, however, did not survive the competition of imports and colonial regulation. The only manufacturing establishments set up were concentrated in the urban areas, and they were few before 1940. This is for a variety of reasons. The urban population was very small, most needs were met by Kenyan imports, export processing, because of the change in colonial administration described earlier, was still embryonic. This is, however, to anticipate the story. The 1949 *Colonial Report* succinctly summarized the state of manufacturing industry in Tanzania in these words,

> Sisal is decorticated, cotton is ginned, rice flour, maize flour, sugar and timber are milled, oil of groundnut, coconut and sesame is expressed, tea is processed, coffee is hulled but exported in the bean, tobacco is cured but exported in the leaf, papain is extracted from pawpaw and ghee and clarified butter is separated from milk. Soap made from local coconut oil and imported caustic soda has the largest market. There is also a brewery, furniture establishments as well as leather goods, shoes and boots establishments.

As shown in table 4.1, this picture altered significantly between 1950 and 1965.

The table reveals that of the 569 establishments employing 10 or more persons in 1965, only 18 per cent were established before 1946. Almost half of the total establishments (48 per cent) were set up between 1946-1960, and over one-third of the total appeared during the four years after independence. This is indicative of an acceleration of industrial development in the post-war period generally, with an observed higher rate of growth in the post-independence period. Of course, the above assumes that the newer establishments were at least as large (in terms of either value added, output or employment) as the earlier ones—an assumption that is examined below. Part of my inquiry therefore endeavours to unravel the causes and 'sources' of this growth.

TABLE 4.1

Historical review of manufacturing industries by industrial activity
(Establishments employing 10 persons or more)

Code ISIC	Industrial activity	Number of establishments 1965	Year of commencement of production		
			Pre-1946	1946-60	1961-5
20	Food manufacture	125	15	71	39
21	Beverage industries	11	4	3	4
22	Tobacco manufacture	3	1	2	—
23	Textiles*	158	50	66	42
24	Footwear and clothing	10	—	3	7
25	Wood except furniture	73	10	33	30
26	Furniture and fixtures	17	1	13	3
27-28	Paper, printing, publishing	22	—	13	9
29	Leather products	8	4	3	1
30	Rubber products	5	—	2	3
31	Chemicals and products	18	—	11	7
33	Non-metallic mineral products	9	1	5	3
34-35	Metals and products	19	1	5	14
36-37	Repair of machinery	12	1	6	5
38	Repair of transport equipment	73	11	43	19
39	Miscellaneous manufacture	6	2	—	4
	Total	569	101	279	189
	Per cent	100	18	48	34

* Textiles include sisal decortication (110 establishments) and cotton ginning and cleaning (30 establishments). There was no textile establishment other than these two activities prior to 1961.

Source: United Republic of Tanzania, *Survey of Industries* (Dar es Salaam, Central Statistical Bureau, 1967), table 5.

Secondly, one notes from the same table that prior to 1946 about 50 per cent of the establishments were involved in sisal decortication and cotton ginning. This means that at least half of the industrial activities prior to 1946 were export-oriented. Of the remainder, 30 per cent of the establishments were concentrated in food processing, beverages and repairs, both of machinery and transport equipment. In the post-war period, on the other hand, there has been a proliferation of new industrial activities such as paper, printing and publishing, rubber products, chemicals and chemical products, clothing and footwear. The two-digit classification, however, conceals the diversity of new products that have recently been introduced. For example, while the metal and products industry included only metal containers as late as 1958, by 1965 this industry was producing also aluminium sheets, screws, nails, wire, enamelware and razor blades. A noticeable feature of the post-war industrial development is the emergence of import-substitution activities not only for final consumption goods but also of certain intermediate products such as paper, glass, printing and wood products.

Unfortunately, there is no record of the value added data of the above establishments by industrial activity over a given period. There is reason to believe, however, that the relatively large establishments were set up in the post-war period, and especially in the post-independence period. This observation is indirectly supported by the pervasiveness of foreign interests in the newer establishments, since, as I will show later, foreign-owned plants tend to be relatively bigger. Table 4.2 gives some indication of the extent of foreign ownership in Tanzanian manufacturing industry as of 1965, in which most of the new activities noted above are shown to be predominantly foreign-owned. Foreign ownership is particularly concentrated in the following industries (at least from the point of view of number of establishments, though, as I will show later, the ranking may not be significantly altered if one considers total assets, since foreign enterprises tend to be relatively more capital-intensive): non-metallic mineral products; repair of machinery and manufacture of metals and metal products; rubber products; chemical products; tobacco and textiles. This is not surprising, as many of these industries are generally capital-intensive. It is also interesting to note that foreign ownership is dominant in some of those industries with relatively high growth elasticities as compared to average manufacturing.[1]

[1] Growth elasticities are taken from Chenery's study, 'Patterns of Industrial Growth', *American Economic Review* (September 1960), and they are as follows: metal products, 2.143, chemicals and petroleum, 1.65 and 2.22 respectively, rubber 2.0 as compared to the average of all manufacturing, 1.44.

A better picture of manufacturing industry in Tanzania is revealed in table A2.1 in appendix II, as the previous tables conceal the available range of product diversity within the two-digit ISIC classification and restrict observations to those plants employing 10 persons or more. Table A2.1, in contrast, records every known registered establishment as of 31 December 1964, regardless of size. There have been some significant additions since then, the most important ones being cement, petroleum refining, radio assembly, glass products, diamond cutting and larger textile plants.

Despite the observed industrial tempo in the post-war period, industrial output in Tanzania at independence was considerably low, and, in fact, the share of industrial output in total production was significantly below the expected 'normal pattern'. I am using the concept of 'normal pattern' as developed by Professor Chenery, purely in its descriptive sense.[2] According to him, the degree of industrialization among countries is closely associated with income *per capita*. This is indicated by the regression equation he fits to cross-country data of 53 countries at various levels of development;

$$\log Y_i = \log A_{i0} + A_{i1} \log Y + A_{i2} \log N \qquad (4.1)$$

where $\qquad Y_i$ = value added *per capita* in the ith sector,

Y = national income, $\quad N$ = population.

He obtains a good fit which he calls the 'normal pattern', with the following interpretation. Any economy with a given population and national income can determine its 'expected' share of industrial output in total product. In the case of Tanzania in 1966, the actual share of industrial output in total production was 6.6 per cent as compared with an 'expected' share of 10 per cent. It is appropriate therefore to examine the causes of this deviation from the 'norm', though it should be mentioned that Professor Chenery's 'norm' is merely descriptive and implies no normative interpretation.[3]

---

[2] Chenery, ibid.

[3] This can be shown by a careful examination of his basic regression equation. From it one would say that value added *per capita* in the ith sector, such as manufacturing's share *per capita*, is determined by income and population levels. Such an interpretation, however, would have no policy implication since the basic issue is how to raise income *per capita*. In other words, the only normative interpretation which is derivable from Chenery's equation involves the belief that the independent variable can be increased or rather altered, by altering the dependent variable. Without illegitimately using his regression results, Professor Chenery's equation lends no more support to the view that in order to industrialize one must be rich than common sense. For a further critique along these lines, see G. C. Archibald, *Industrialization and Capital Requirements in Greece* (Athens, Centre of Economic Research, 1969).

As is now well-documented, industrialization in underdeveloped economies stems from (a) any lasting external disequilibrium that disrupts the balance between demand and production (wars, depressions, chronic balance of payments deficits etc.), (b) export growth leading to an expansion of the domestic market, (c) deliberate official development policy and (d) gradual processing into higher forms of traditional exports.[4] In the Tanzanian context, wars, depressions and balance of payments deficits have played a minor role in inducing industrial development. It is true, of course, that the First World War brought

TABLE 4.2

Distribution of share-holding in manufacturing processing industries by citizenship and industrial activity in 1965

(Establishments employing 10 persons or more)

Code ISIC	Industrial activity	No. of est.	% 0*	Shares of non-citizens by no. of est.		
				1-50	51-99	100
20	Food manufacturing	125	46	14	19	46
21	Beverage	11	5	1	—	5
22	Tobacco	3	1	—	1	1
23	Textiles	158	37	26	34	61
24	Footwear and clothing	10	4	2	—	4
25	Wood except furniture ..	73	27	7	11	28
26	Furniture and fixtures	17	6	—	—	11
27-28	Paper, printing, publishing	22	10	4	1	7
29	Leather products	8	3	—	—	5
30	Rubber products	5	—	1	3	1
31	Chemicals and products	18	4	1	5	8
33	Non-metallic minerals and products..	9	1	—	2	6
34-35	Metals and products	19	6	3	1	9
36-37	Repair of machinery	12	2	1	1	2
38	Repair and assembly of transport ..	73	27	6	1	2
39	Miscellaneous manufacturing ..	6	2	1	1	2
	Total	569	181	67	95	226

* Although all 181 establishments listed in this category are owned by Tanzanian citizens, it is only fair to state that the majority of these businessmen are of Asian descent who have acquired citizenship during the last few years.

Source: United Republic of Tanzania, *Survey of Industries*, 1965 (Dar es Salaam, Central Statistical Bureau, 1967).

a short burst of activity when the attempt was made to make the country economically self-sufficient. The production of articles which had become scarce owing to the allied blockade was improvised and

---

[4] Hirschman, 'The Political Economy of Industrialization', op.cit.

considerable ingenuity was shown in producing manufactured goods and medical supplies normally imported from Europe. At the Amani Agricultural Research Institute, quinine, sixteen varieties of foodstuffs, twelve of medicines and medicaments, five of rubber products, two of soap, oils and candles, three of materials used in making boats, and ten miscellaneous substances were made. At Mpwapwa, cloth for garments and bandages was woven by hand, the spinning wheels being produced in Dar es Salaam. However, these activities were abandoned after the war, domestic production being replaced by imports.[5]

There was little industrial development during the inter-war period, even during the depression. This was due to several interrelated factors. Firstly, foreign investments tended to flow to Kenya rather than Tanganyika. The British settlers in Kenya were a well-established pressure group in London while Tanzania's settlers were of mixed nationalities, without a cohesive force. Moreover, Tanzania was merely a conquered territory with less value to Britain during this period since her economy had been partly moulded to suit the needs of the German market. Thus, partly because of the uncertainty of the status of the country (especially after Hitler came to power and threatened to reconquer Germany's lost colonies), the administration's pessimism about the viability of investment opportunities and the centripetal pressures converging on Kenya to which the common market arrangements gave full play, industries tended to be established in Kenya. The adoption of a common external tariff with the other East African territories (a tariff structure which was conceived in the interests of Kenyan industrialists) and the elimination of all trade barriers among the partner states, not only deprived Tanzania of a significant amount of customs revenue but by protecting Kenya's industries, forestalled for a considerable period their establishment in Tanzania. These factors also explain the relative industrial stagnation of Tanzania during the depression and the Second World War when considerable industrialization took place in Kenya, Rhodesia, South Africa and in various countries of Latin America.[6] Andre Gunder Frank's hypothesis that 'satellites experience their greatest economic development and especially their most classically capitalist industrial

---

[5] Michael Yaffey, *Balance of Payments Problems of a Developing Country: Tanzania* (Munich, Weltforum Publishing House, 1970), p. 46.
[6] Giovanni Arrighi, *The Political Economy of Rhodesia* (Mouton, The Hague, 1967); Andre Gunder Frank, *Capitalism and Underdevelopment in Latin America* (New York, Monthly Review Press, 1969, 2nd ed. rev.).

development if and when their ties to their metropolis are weakest',[7] certainly has to be qualified when there is a neighbouring 'periphery-center'.

It must be pointed out, though, that the common market arrangements provided some significant external economies to Tanzania through joint common services in such fields as transport and communications. The spread effects (sometimes called the spill-over effects) of an industrializing Kenya to her less developed neighbours, however, tended to strengthen the satellite-periphery-centre relationship. Kenya's industrial growth merely provided access to Tanzania's primary produce—a fact that is revealed in the structure of their inter-country trade. Some of these problems were pointed out at the time the common market arrangements were being set up. In 1924, for example, the Treasurer and Comptroller of Customs in Tanganyika officially 'advised against a customs union on the ground that it would make this country a commercial satellite of Kenya, and subordinate Tanganyika to Kenyan influence'.[8] Because of the strong political power of the Kenyan interests in the United Kingdom, the British Secretary of State for the Colonies directed that the institutions of a complete customs should no longer be delayed. And so in 1927 the articles of the customs union were brought into force. Eleven years later, another Comptroller of the Customs commented on the effects of the common market arrangement in these terms:

> There is evidence . . . that local production is effectively displacing imports of many articles of food which can be manufactured equally well in the territory. It is indeed in these items that increases are shown in 1938 (*viz.* in interterritorial imports). The position is one of the results of the customs arrangements with Kenya and Uganda under which the products in these countries are either of older development or more effectively organized marketing.[9]

Since then there has been a continuing debate on the detrimental effects of the *colonial-based* common market arrangement on Tanzania's industrialization.[10] I do not wish to go over that debate. Rather, I only wish to assert that regardless of whatever other benefits the common market arrangements may have generated in Tanzania, it

[7] Andre Gunder Frank, 'Development of Underdevelopment', *Monthly Review* (September 1966), reprinted in his *Latin America: Underdevelopment or Revolution* (New York and London, Monthly Review Press, 1969).
[8] Michael Yaffey, *Balance of Payments*, op. cit., p. 231.
[9] M. J. Yaffey, *Balance of Payments*, op. cit., p. 230. 'Local production' refers to interterritorial production.
[10] For a review of the debate on this question see Dharam Ghai, 'Territorial

contributed relatively little to the latter's industrial growth in the colonial period. This is partly shown by the data presented in table 4.4 which displays the significant changes in the inter-East African trade in 1954, 1960 and 1966—changes which inevitably reflect variations in industrial structure (and protectionist policies) over the period. 1954 is the base year in this table because it was the first period when the SITC classificatory system was adopted by the East African Customs and Excise. The satellite status of Tanganyika is shown by the fact that in 1954, her exports of food, crude materials and animal vegetable oils (SITC 0, 2 and 4) was 80 per cent of her total inter-East African exports while her imports of beverages, tobacco and manufacture (SITC 1, 6-8) was 60 per cent of her total imports. By 1960, this pattern had not changed substantially, the import declines in beverages were made good by the diversification of the industrial base in Kenya and Uganda as shown by the rise of the SITC 6-8 from 12 per cent in 1954 to almost 36 per cent in 1960. Tanzania's manufacturing exports, on the other hand, grew from 3 per cent to 9 per cent, recording an equivalent growth rate over the period, but on a very slender base.

By 1964, the interterritorial imbalance in trade and industrial structure had reached a point which is indicated by the data in table 4.4. As shown in that table, Tanzania's deficit especially with Kenya was rising to significant proportions, which led to Tanzania's immediately initiating negotiations with her East African neighbours (after Kenya became independent at the end of 1963) with a view to redressing the noted trade imbalances. These difficult negotiations culminated in the Kampala Agreement, which, among other things, (a) urged a shifting of the productive facilities or capacities in certain industries (cigarettes, footwear, beer, cement) in such a way as to increase production capacity in deficit countries and thereby reduce imports from the surplus countries; and (b) inter-regional allocation of major new industries including aluminium, bicycle manufacture, electric light bulbs, radio assembly, nitrogeneous fertilizers and motor vehicle tyres manufacture. It was agreed that these would be distributed

Distribution of the Benefits and Costs of the East African Common Market', *The East African Economics Review*, vol. 11, no. 1 (June 1964); Arthur Hazlewood, 'The East African Common Market: Importance and Effects', *Bulletin of the Oxford University Institute of Economics and Statistics* (February 1966), and Alan R. Roe, 'Terms of Trade and Transfer Tax Effects in an East African Common Market: An Empirical Study' (Economic Research Bureau, Dar es Salaam, 1968, mimeo.).

TABLE 4.3

Tanzania: inter-East African trade, 1954, 1960, 1966 by SITC sections
(percentage of total)

SITC section				Exports			Imports		
				1954	1960	1966	1954	1960	1966
0. Food	..	..	..	34	40	22	32	27	18
1. Beverage and tobacco	..	..		6	17	9	48	24	6
2. Crude, non-fuel, inedible materials		..	..	30	11	10	2	1	1
3. Mineral fuels, lubricants, etc.	..			4	3	0	0	0	13
4. Animal and vegetable fats & oils				16	12	10	4	4	0.6
5. Chemicals	..	..	..	6	4	2	2	6	12
6. Manufactured goods by type of material				1	7	36	6	24	37
7. Machinery and transport		..		1	0	2	0	0.6	1
8. Miscellaneous manufacture		..		1	2	9	6	11	10
9. Miscellaneous transactions		..		1	0	0	0	0.4	0.4
	Total	..	..	100	100	100	100	100	100

Source: East African Customs and Excise, *Annual Trade Report* (1954, 1960, 1966).

TABLE 4.4

Inter-East African trade, 1962 to 1964
(in sh. million)

Year	Exports from Tanzania to		Imports to Tanzania from	
	Kenya	Uganda	Kenya	Uganda
1962	56	9	207	35
1963	62	10	216	42
1964	87	20	271	49

Source: Annual Trade Report (1962-1964).

under the Territorial Industrial Licensing Ordinance on the basis of an exclusive licence to a firm basing operations throughout the region. Tanzania was allocated the manufacture of aluminium sheets and foil, tyres and tubes, and radio assembly and parts production. Although the Kampala Agreement was not ratified by Kenya; it was effective in inducing the industries mentioned in the agreement to be set up in Tanzania.

Partly because of the Kampala Agreement, partly because of other government measures taken to accelerate the industrial tempo of Tanzania, and partly because of the foreign investors' motivations to invest, which received a new impetus after independence, Tanzania's industrial growth soared between 1961 and 1966. This can be seen in table 4.3 which indicates differences in trade patterns between 1960 and

1966 and *a fortiori* in industrial structure. As shown in that table, by 1966 Tanzania exported 47 per cent of manufactured goods and imported 48 per cent of manufactures—which compares very favourably with the developments in the 1950s which I noted above.

After the Second World War, there was an upsurge of export earnings ignited by post-war shortages in raw materials, the devaluation of the pound sterling and shortages of materials due to the Korean War. The earlier post-war industries to be established in Tanzania were supply-based and were prompted by shortages of certain products in the sterling block. This is at least true of Tanganyika Packers—a meat extract company which was established jointly between the colonial government and Messrs. Liebig's Extract of Meat (with 51 per cent and 49 per cent of the shares respectively) in 1949 in order to relieve Britain's shortage of meat and dollars. With Tanganyika Packers came Metal Box Company (T), a subsidiary of Metal Box Overseas of London to manufacture cans that could be used to pack the farmers' meat output. There followed a number of demand-based industries such as Tanzania Bottlers' Company, Sapa Chemicals Ltd., East African Vegetable Industries, Robbialac Paints, Express Dairy and Tanzania Millers. This industrial upsurge of the early fifties, however, began to subside toward the end of the decade owing to the worsening of the terms of trade.

From what I have said above, one important consideration emerges. The low industrial level of the economy, that is low with respect to her expected 'normal' pattern is largely explained by the satellite status of Tanzania *vis-à-vis* Kenya's peripheral-centre position. Of course, the lack of an indigenous capitalist class to champion industrialization played an important role here. In any case, it is possible to argue that the high rates of industrial growth (as shown in table 4.5) experienced in the post-independence period may be interpreted as an adjustment to the disequilibrium in Tanzania's productive structure engendered by her association with Kenya and Britain, after the country became an independent entity. If this is so, then one would expect Tanzania's industrial growth to slow down considerably after approaching her normal pattern, unless the new opportunities of investment planning acquired after nationalization enables her to sustain the present tempo. These conclusions, however, neglect to take into serious consideration the part played by the foreigner's motivations to invest, especially after independence. To this I will now turn.

TABLE 4.5
Production of selected industries

Industry	Unit	1963	1964	1965	1966	1967	1968
Textiles	'000 sq. yds.	6,225	8,930	12,126	17,121	18,277	34,519
Beer	'000 gallons	1,962	2,249	2,673	4,139	5,120	5,413
Cigarettes	millions	1,144	1,535	1,869	2,049	2,044	2,137
Paints	gallons	95,357	96,981	162,573	221,020	274,623	317,948
Plywood	'000 sq. ft.	2,004	6,573	7,794	10,247	8,808	10,658
Sisal twine	tons	—	658	5,778	10,138	14,887	16,454
Saw milling	'000 cu. ft.	3,676	4,675	5,029	5,026	4,585	5,029
Wheat flour	tons	28,378	29,818	38,433	39,714	41,159	42,238
Pyrethrum extract	tons	99	107	174	200	287	187
Canned meat	tons	n.a.	n.a.	11,109	9,162	9,520	6,716
Cement	tons	—	—	—	49,324	144,612	153,894

Source: Background to the Budget (1968-9, 1969-70).

4.2 INVESTMENT PATTERN IN THE POST-INDEPENDENCE PERIOD

It is often said that investment decisions are largely influenced by the extent of the market. However, in the case of Tanzania, there is some evidence to indicate that in a number of industries, there has been a considerable lag between the technological threshold and the establishment of import-substituting industries in specific product lines. Thus, although textile imports have occupied an important place among imports since the early days of colonial rule (in 1897 textiles and clothing imports accounted for 52 per cent of the country's total imports), the first textile mill was established only after independence. From table 4.6 it is seen that textile import capacity must have attained a technological threshold before the 1940s, since the first textile mill's capacity was 8 million square yards. Yet between 1961 and 1968, no less than five textile plants had been established in the country. Table 4.5 also suggests that investment decisions delayed after a technological threshold has been reached, when finally taken are followed by a sudden cluster of investments in that industry. This is shown in the case of textiles, plywood, sisal twine and cement. Moreover, the import statistics show that the delay in investment decisions also occurred in clothing, blankets, maize flour, and cement.

It appears that the major industrialization that has taken place, though influenced by the size of the market, was also affected by the changes in government that took place when transferring political power from Britain to the people of Tanzania. Certainly the import

TABLE 4.6
Cotton piece goods imports
(in '000 square yards)

	1942	1949	1959	1965
Grey unbleached	12,722	6,983	11,654	9,603
White bleached	1,822	3,236	2,376	3,737
Printed, khangas	1,296	1,449	10,793	8,060
Printed, other	4,248	9,904	5,097	12,952
Dyed in the piece	7,805	19,843	17,982	22,140
Coloured	9,572	11,027	4,678	2,244
Other	323	221	45	65
Total	37,792	52,681	52,625	58,801

Source: East African Customs and Excise, *Annual Trade Reports* (1949, 1959, 1956); HMSO *Colonial Report* (1942).

substitution that has taken place during the post-independence period has been largely carried out by the former suppliers and has been ignited by both deliberate government policy and the suppliers' eagerness either to keep their stake in their former export market or to establish new market links. These two factors were largely complementary. Unlike the colonial government which hoped that industry would seek the country 'naturally when it sees, through the growth of purchasing power of our people, an expanding market which will assure them a reasonable prospect of profitable operation, and we may have to await that time before we see a really big increase in industrial manufacturing',[11] the independent government went out of its way to attract new investments by designing a tax incentive structure, by publicizing existing investment opportunities, by guaranteeing foreign investors against nationalization, by establishing industrial estates, etc. Moreover, the country's trade deficits with Kenya and Uganda were instrumental in the government's efforts to shift industry to Tanzania. On the supply side, the former exporters' fear of losing their market as a result of expected moves to alter the trading partners after independence, and offers to break into the market, explains the upsurge of industrial activity noted in table 4.5.

The available information about the sequence of Tanzanian industrialization, at least in the post-independence period, suggests (though of course it does not prove), the significance of the above-mentioned motives and policies. The textile industry, as I pointed out before, was long delayed because of the absence of threat to the existing suppliers. After independence, however, the traditional suppliers feared the invasion of their markets from new sources (USA, China, etc.). As a result, Tasini Textiles was set up in 1961 and is owned jointly by a Netherlands Textile consortium, Smith Mackenzie and Co., Dalgety (E.A.), Victoria Federation of Co-operative Unions (VFCU), and the Tanganyika Development Finance Company (TDFL). Both Smith Mackenzie and Dalgety were import agents of textiles among other things. VFCU is a cotton marketing co-operative (which would ultimately become the supply base) and TDFL a government financing agency, partly owned by the Netherlands government.

In 1966, the Mwanza Textile Mill was set up, being 40 per cent owned by the National Development Corporation (NDC); 40 per cent by VFCU; and Amenital Holding Registered Trust, 20 per cent; and

[11] Budget speech by the Finance Minister, 1960.

managed by Sodefra, Maurer Textiles S.A. of Geneva and Textil Consult of Vaduz (the representatives of Amenital). (The same managing agents are partners to the Nigerian Textile Mills.) It is likely that the motive for Amenital's participation (which probably explains its meagre share capital participation) was to dispose of Société-Alsacienne des Constructions Mécaniques de Mulhause's (SACM) machinery. The fact that machinery was obtained with a supplier's credit of sh. 60 million, repayable over eight years, with three years of grace and an interest of 5.7 per cent per annum, may suggest that the profits of Sodefra must have accrued through over-invoicing of the machinery. Moreover, this venture has consolidated Sodefra's position in Tanzania. It has been given sh. 3.5 million as fees for carrying out industrial tests and preparing a detailed final engineering report on NDC'S sisal pulp project and has also already won the contract for the Mwanza Hotel.

In the same year (that is, 1966), the Chinese built the Friendship Textile Mill Limited in Dar es Salaam. These two latter mills are fully integrated, will produce 24 million square yards of cotton fabrics annually, each using local cotton and will manufacture printed textile products, such as the *kitenge*, *khanga* and dress print styles. The two firms, however, differ in their organization and financing. Friendship employs 3,000 people as compared to 1,200 by Mwanza Textile, and is financed on an interest free loan; whereas Mwanza Textile is financed by suppliers' credit and equity. In 1967, Kilimanjaro Textiles was set up as a joint venture of Industrial Promotion Services (IPS)—a 51 per cent share; German Development Corporation (26 per cent); the textile trading firm of Jos Hansen and Soehne of West Germany (8 per cent); Ploeger, the German textile manufacturer (7 per cent); and TDFL and the Commonwealth Development Finance Limited ($4\frac{1}{2}$ per cent each). There have also been smaller establishments, including Tanganyika Textile Industries Ltd. based in Dar es Salaam (550 employees, production: 3 million square yards); Tanganyika Dyeing and Weaving Mills, also in Dar es Salaam (510 employees, production: 3 million square yards); Calico Textile Industries Ltd., Dar es Salaam (275 employees, production: 2 million square yards) and Moshi Textile Mills Ltd. in Moshi (100 employees, production: 1 million square yards), which belonged to the former Moshi Trading Co. All of these latter establishments belong to local Indian entrepreneurs, who were former textile importers. Thus in the few years since independence, one notices a sudden cluster of investments in the textile industry.

The case of radio assembly provides some empirical evidence of the 'threat to market' hypothesis that was advanced in the last chapter. As indicated in table 4.8 below, Netherlands (of which Philips Industries' sales account for over 90 per cent) had maintained a fairly stable share of wireless sets imports between 1958 and 1962. In the following year, however, Japan overtook her by a substantial margin, due probably to the relatively low prices of her imports and the aggressive marketing strategies of the Matsushita Electric Co. of Japan. Between 1958 and 1964, Japan's market share in the Tanzanian market rose from 1.4 per cent to 68 per cent! The Netherland's share correspondingly fell from its peak level in 1962 (58 per cent) to only 21 per cent in 1964. It was around this period that the Kampala Agreement was drafted which, among other things, allocated 'wireless receiving sets and components thereof' to Tanzania. In view of the fact that the share of Tanzania in the East African radio market was relatively small, and the short term interval between the Tanzanian government's initiative to establish the plant and its hasty set up, there seems to be a *prima facie* case for believing that Philips Industries had already decided to build the plant in order to avert the loss of the market to the Japanese. Consequently Philips formed Philips Electronics (EA) Ltd. which, with a 50 per cent tariff protection, was able to break down Japanese competition. The Matsushita Electric Company of Japan, having lost its radio market, immediately set up a battery factory in Dar es Salaam.

There have been some cases in which gaining a foothold on the potential new market has been significant to an international firm, especially if it is less established internationally. The oil refinery (TIPER) built by the Italian government firm, ENI (which has built several refineries in various parts of Africa in order to effectively break the monopolistic position of the big British and American companies) can be said to belong to this category. Consolidated Petroleum Company, a consortium of Shell, British Petroleum, Caltex and another American company, had built a two million ton capacity oil refinery at Mombasa in 1964 which might have satisfied—at least for some time—a greater part of East African needs. ENI, however, wanted a foothold in Tanzania which has given it the opportunity to build a sh. 160 million pipeline to Zambia with plans to build a refinery there.

Supply based or 'export propelled' industrialization has taken place in meat and meat preparations; pyrethrum extract, wattle extract;

TABLE 4.7

Wireless sets imported by major source, 1958 to 1966

Year	Item	U.K.	W. Germany	Japan	Netherlands	Total(T.)	Total(E.A.)
1958	a*	2,452	2,265	241	4,404	9,421	36,267
	b*	25,349	33,852	1,402	36,290	97,650	375,531
	c*	10.34	14.94	5.82	8.24		
	d*	26	34.6	1.4	37		
1959	a	3,169	2,668	219	5,059	11,173	41,659
	b	29,630	32,218	1,708	43,750	108,364	551,002
	c	9.35	12.07	7.8	8.65		
	d	27	29.7	1.6	41.4		
1960	a	2,854	2,836	1,414	5,363	12,479	71,477
	b	29,224	34,275	12,836	50,275	126,971	725,341
	c	10.23	12.08	9.67	9.37		
	d	23	27	10	39		
1961	a	1,962	2,001	3,596	6,540	14,488	83,050
	b	20,682	23,619	30,923	61,186	149,333	764,707
	c	10.54	11.8	8.6	9.35		
	d	15	17	22	44		
1962	a	859	724	6,778	13,905	22,520	119,709
	b	11,763	11,285	56,523	116,997	220,127	960,298
	c	13.69	15.58	8.33	8.41		
	d	5.9	5.6	28	58		

Year							
1963	a	430	937	15,527	9,919	27,892	191,319
	b	9,317	13,147	101,129	83,870	216,376	1,381,313
	c	21.67	14.03	6.51	8.45		
	d	4.3	6	47	39		
1964	a	1,100	1,625	65,448	17,175	86,502	291,230
	b	24,716	27,925	424,681	128,322	613,755	1,949,742
	c	22.47	17.18	6.49	7.47		
	d	4	4.5	69	21		
1965	a	373	2,278	35,691	16,902	58,371	254,923
	b	6,335	38,665	263,863	149,592	494,640	1,738,561
	c	16.98	16.97	7.39	8.85		
	d	1.2	7.8	53	30		
1966	a	168	3,936	9,162	5,238	26,009	93,866
	b	3,444	67,909	72,609	75,243	281,622	857,658
	c	20.5	17.25	7.92	14.36		
	d	1.2	24	26	27		

*a=number of wireless sets

*b=value of wireless sets in £

*c=average unit price per wireless set in £

*d=share of the Tanzanian market per source of imports. The share is computed from value figures rather than from quantum.

N.B. In 1965, Phillips Electronic (EA) Ltd. began production of wireless sets at Arusha.

Source: Annual Trade Reports (1958-66).

meerschaum pipes; cashew nut processing; cordage, rope and twine; coffee and tea, and diamonds. I have already noted the external circumstances that led to the establishment of Tanganyika Packers, the only meat canning and packing plant in the country. The establishment of Tanganyika Meerschaum Corporation was rendered possible by the discovery of exploitable pipemaking meerschaum in the fifties.

The case of cordage, rope and twine is particularly interesting. Fearing competition from a local manufacturer and wishing to be closer to the supply source, British Ropes Limited which controls 80 per cent of the British sisal twine market and is a previous buyer of more than 35 per cent of Tanzania's sisal output, established Craven and Speeding in 1964 just before Noorani (an Indian sisal plantation owner) was able to install his plant supplied by James Mackie and Sons of Belfast. Immediately, the Tanganyika Sisal Spinning Company joined the bandwagon. This company is owned by a consortium of P. Baumheuter, a German industrialist with sisal interests in West Germany; United Rope Works which has sisal spinning mills in Holland, Belgium and Germany, and the German Development Corporation. Yet the biggest and youngest rope factory and one of three ventures of the Tanganyika Industrial Corporation, TSSC, began operating in 1966 in Tanga. Capacity is reported to be between 24,000 and 36,000 tons of sisal products per month. Apart from the small shareholders, Karimjee Jivanjee (the firm of the leading Indian businessman in the country, Director of NDC, former chairman of the University Council etc.), Sachak, Bird & Co. and the Industrial Promotion Services (IPS) have been the main participants in the shs. 1 million investment.[12]

It is of interest to note, however, that during the colonial period in the 1930s a firm to manufacture binder twine, the Tanganyika Cordage Company of Tanga, had been formed but when it began exporting its products to the United Kingdom, a strong representation to the British government by the British Rope, Twine and Net Makers Federation was made to the effect that 'their home market [was] being menaced by the sale here by the Tanganyika Cordage Company of binder twine produced by the low-paid African labour in Tanganyika'. The Secretary of State for the Colonies in considering his countrymen's position (in spite of the fact that the factory's capacity was no more than 10,000 tons), concluded that 'in the interests of the sisal producers themselves, there is no alternative but to inform the Tanganyika

[12] Karl Schadler, *Manufacturing and Processing Industries in Tanzania*, (IFO Institute, 1969), p. 15.

Cordage Company that, failing an agreement between them and the Federation, I should not be able to oppose the imposition of a prohibitive duty on binder twine imported to this country from the colonial dependency'.[13] As would be expected, there was no amicable agreement and a 100 per cent *ad valorem* duty was imposed on binder twine imported from Tanganyika. The factory was closed down the following year. When the British Ropes Ltd. came to Tanzania to establish its subsidiary in 1964, it enjoyed an effective protection of about 15 per cent!

Finally, another important motivation that has played some role in investing in export-processing industries is the desire on the part of the investors to dispose of their machinery, both old and new. And as I have already noted, this motivation also plays a role in import-substituting industrialization as for instance the Mwanza Textile Mill. In the exporting field, the same motivation is illustrated by Tanita (a cashew-nut processing plant). Cashew-nut processing had remained, until quite recently, the monopoly of Indian producers who imported raw cashew-nuts from Tanzania and Mozambique (Msumbiji), combined these imports with their own local production, and after processing the nuts, exported them mainly to the United States. In Tanzania, a small hand-processing plant existed before independence but due to increases in wage rates (noted in part I) the plant went into financial difficulties and stopped production in the early 1960s. Actually the basic wage rate in Tanzania is nearly treble that of India and 30–50 per cent higher than in Mozambique. In this situation, it was out of the question that Tanzania could compete with the other two countries in the hand-processing of cashew-nuts. The only possibility for processing its raw materials lay in mechanization.

For technological reasons (largely due to the toxic nut shell liquid which can spoil the kernel in the process of decortication), the mechanization of cashew processing was very difficult and was successfully resolved only at the beginning of the 1960s by an Italian firm 'Oltremare' SPA of Bologna. It was then decided to build in Tanzania, the *first* large-scale mechanized plant for cashew processing in the world. A company—Tanita—was incorporated in 1963 as a joint venture between the government of Tanzania (40 per cent of the shares), Oltremare (31 per cent, over half of which was know-how) and Carlo Martelli (29 per cent, one-third in know-how), the former owner of the

---

[13] Statement by the then Secretary for the Colonies, Sir Philip Curtiffe-Loeler, House of Commons (15 November 1934), *Hansard*, p. 2166 *et seq.*

hand-processing plant who became the Managing Director of the new company. So far the venture has proved a financial failure. By 1968 40 per cent of the total capital invested in Tanita had been lost.[14] Another company, Mtwara Cashew Co. Ltd. has now been formed in partnership with the Cashew Company of Japan.

As is evident from the above discussion of the motivations to investment, tariff protection played an important part in the realization of investment opportunities in Tanzania. Before I conclude this historical review, I would like to discuss the nature, mode and effects of tariff protection in the post-independence period.

4.3 INCENTIVE STRUCTURE AND PERFORMANCE

It has already been noted that the motivations to invest by foreigners indicate acting out of fear of being pushed out of the export market by either external restrictions or by a monopolistic situation developing within the economy. In such a situation, the competition-restricting effect of a tariff is a factor of central importance for the foreign investor. For the price of an industrial investment, including the risk of its possible failure, a seller can transform the competitive market he currently faces into a monopolistic (or at least oligopolistic) one. In consequence of the elimination of competition, a firm will be able to (a) expand its total sales, and (b) increase net earnings by an even greater proportion as a result of a tariff-enhanced unit profit margin. Not only does the tariff secure the industrialist who makes an industrial commitment against the competition of similar products, but it also shields him to a substantial degree from technically more advanced varieties or otherwise superior articles, which in the absence of fiscal discrimination might pre-empt the market.

There is little doubt that the import-substitution industrialization which has taken place in Tanzania has been conditional on granting the industrialists adequate tariff protection. Table 4.8 below shows some of the most obvious cases. The data on this table show the simultaneous establishment of industrial projects and the granting of tariff protection. This suggests that protective tariffs are *not* set by government on its own initiative but rather by a process of negotiation between the potential investors and public officials. Indeed, from accounts given by the

[14] Zofia Dorbska, *Criteria for Public Investment in Manufacturing; Five Tanzanian Case Studies* (University of Dar es Salaam, 1968, mimeo.), pp. 71-2.

TABLE 4.8

Tariff protection and import-substituting industrialization

Budget Date	Amount of Tariff	Product	Firm Established &	Date
1961	22 per cent	textiles (yarn)	Tasini Textiles	1961
1962	44/- per lb.	cigarettes	British-American	1961
1963	-/70 per sq. yd.	blankets	Blanket Manufacturers	1962
1963	33 per cent	paints	Leyland Paints	1963
1964	40 per cent	clothing	Kamyn Industries	1965
1965	33⅓ per cent	aluminium products	Aluminium African Ltd.	1964
1965	30 per cent	polyethylene	Tiper	1966
1965	37½ per cent	radios	Philips Electronics	1965
1966	30 per cent	coffee extracts	Instant Coffee	1966
1966	40 per cent	cotton piece goods	Mwanza Textiles	1966

Source: *Directory of Industries* (1967), Finance Ministers' Speeches, annual.

officials of the Ministry of Commerce and Industry who deal with these issues, the initiative orginates with the potential investors who submit a request for a tariff increase (and perhaps also for duty relief on imported raw materials, component parts or machinery), supported by an accompanying investment proposal and set of cost estimates. Invariably, due to the officials' ignorance of the cost estimates, the investor normally manages to obtain sufficient (sometimes more than sufficient) protection.

It is obvious that in terms of market strategy, the granting of tariff protection to an investor in a new field means that the investor who is willing to make an industrial investment is rewarded with the effective exclusion of his competitors from the market they were formerly contending for on equal terms. The granting of tariff preference to Philips Industries (initially at 37½ per cent, raised subsequently to 50 per cent *ad valorem*) for the assembly of radios served to keep the Matsushita Electric Company of Japan's share down even though the latter's products were generally cheaper than the former's in the pre-tariff period. The problem that is important for us, though, is the gains to the economy as a result of granting such protection. To discuss this issue meaningfully, I will have to examine briefly the recently introduced concept of effective protection. I will then be in a position to discuss the significance of the various levels of protection afforded to various industries.

Recent studies on tariff protection have concluded that normal tariff rates on final products of an industry are inadequate and often misleading indicators of protection afforded to domestic producers.[15] This is for two reasons. First, in order to compare the level of protection between different industries, one must also take into account tariffs on inputs used in the industry, for a tariff on an industry's input will raise the costs of production and therefore reduce the protection received by the domestic producer. Secondly, it is argued that protection should be measured in relation to value added in the industry and not in relation to the total value of production. This is because from the point of view of (static) efficient resource allocation, it is the scarce factors (presumably skilled labour and capital) which should be offered protection, especially if it is assumed that the supply of other inputs (unskilled labour, raw materials, etc.), is highly elastic. Under certain assumptions (which are not too unreasonable in the Tanzania context) it is shown that the effective rate of protection is the percentage increase in value added made possible by the tariff structure relative to the situation whereby tariffs are absent but the same exchange rate obtains. More formally, let X_i represent the output of any industry and $\sum_j a_{ji} X_i$ its intermediate inputs, both valued at free-trade prices. Then,

$$V_i = X_i - \sum_j a_{ji} X_i \qquad (4.2)$$

is value added at free trade prices, and

$$V_i^* = V_i(1+T_i) = X_i(1+t_i) - \sum_j a_{ji}(1+t_j)X_i, \qquad (4.3)$$

is actual value added under protection, where t_i represents tariff rate on the ouput, t_j tariff rate on input j and T_i the total rate of protection of the ith industry. Equation (4.3) can be simplified as:

$$V_i(1+T_i) = V_i + t_i X_i - \sum_j a_{ji} t_j X_i \qquad (4.4)$$

or

$$T_i = \frac{V_i + t_i X_i - \sum a_{ji} t_j X_i}{V_i} - 1 = \frac{t_i - \sum a_{ji} t_j}{V_i / X_i} \qquad (4.5)$$

From equation (4.5) it is seen that the total rate of effective protection will be greater if its own particular rate of protection (t_i) is high, or, if,

---

[15] William M. Corden, 'The Structure of a Tariff System and the Effective Protection Rate', *The Journal of Political Economy*, vol. LXXIV, no. 3 (June 1966) pp. 221-37; Harry G. Johnson, 'Tariffs and Economic Development', *Journal of Development Studies* (October 1965); Giorgio Basevi, 'The United States Tariff Structure: Estimates of Effective Rates of Protection of United States Industries and Industrial Labour', *The Review of Economics and Statistics*, vol. XLVII, no. 2 (May 1966), pp. 147-60.

ceteris paribus, the particular rate of protection of its supplying industries t_j's are low, and/or, if the share of value added in total output is small.

Dudley Kessel, using the above measure for effective protection of a significant part of Tanzania's industries in 1966, resorted to Kenyan input-output data taken from the 1963 census of industrial production and Tanzania's tariff structure in 1966.[16] His use of Kenya input-output data was due to the unavailability of sufficiently detailed data on Tanzania with which to compute the effective rates of protection. To a large extent, this type of data is still unavailable in Tanzania. I will therefore present Kessel's results for the following other reasons. The computed value added for the industries on which I have specific data are close to those used by Kessel and because of the connectedness of the industrial structures of Kenya and Tanzania as mentioned before, I can assume (in using Kenyan value-added and input-output structures) that production functions as well as earnings of primary factors for different industries are similar for the two countries.

As shown in table 4.9, it is apparent that effective rates of protection rather than nominal tariff rates yields a somewhat different picture of the structure of protection of industry in Tanzania. For example, clothing, wattle bark extract, meat products, and soft drinks show a lower effective protection rate than the nominal rates. The tariffs on imports of wattle bark and meat products are not, however, relevant as measures of protection since the bulk of production in these industries is for exports. In most industries, the effective protective rates are considerably *greater* than the nominal rates. For the non-processing industries, this is mainly because in East Africa duties on most raw materials and other inputs are either zero or very low. Thus the level of protection of capital and labour used in Tanzania is much higher than is indicated by the nominal tariff rates, which exceed the 100 per cent range in tobacco, matches and beer.

Table 4.9 also reveals a few other interesting results. It shows that effective protection in Tanzania is generally *highest for import substitutes producing* non-durable *consumer goods*, though paints and bicycle tyres and tubes are two main exceptions which do not fall under such a classification. It is also worthy of note that tobacco, which is a luxury consumer good, has the highest effective protective rate.[17] Beer also

---

[16] Dudley Kessel, 'Effective Protection in Tanzania', ERB Paper 67.8 (mimeo.), published in *The East African Economic Review*, June 1968 (with minor revisions).
[17] The high effective rate is in the nature of excise tax on tobacco.

TABLE 4.9
Effective protection of Tanzanian industry, 1966

Industry	Value added	Nominal external tariff %	Nominal tax protection %	Effective protection %
(1)	(2)	(3)	(4)	(5)
1. Tobacco	0.4	314	234	528
2. Matches	0.433	174	87	395
3. Paints	0.314	37.5	37.5	394
4. Bicycle tyres and tubes	0.35	36	36	270
5. Textiles	0.35	73	73	269
6. Cosmetics	0.283	75	75	265
7. Dairy produce	0.231	37.5	37.5	216
8. Sugar refining	0.417	84	84	193
9. Beer	0.661	159	103	187
10. Canned fruit and veg.	0.3	37.5	37.5	184
11. Biscuits	0.3	37.5	28.0	166
12. Soap	0.341	40	27.5	151
13. Clothing	0.3	60	60	144
14. Tanning and leather	0.376	30	30	130
15. Footwear	0.4	43	43	123
16. Metal products	0.335	25	25	95
17. Radio assembly	0.55	50	50	95
18. Furniture and fixtures	0.447	30	30	58
19. Glass products	0.617	30	30	51
20. Groundnuts	—	0	7.5j	47
21. Coffee processing	—	30	40	42.5
22. Cotton seed oil	—	0	17j	34
23. Paper and paper products	0.421	12.5	12.5	26
24. Insecticides	0.283	0	1.7j	24
25. Cashew nut processing	—	0	10j	20
26. Cement	0.614	7.5	7.5	12.1
27. Groundnuts (edible)	—	0	1.5j	9.4
28. Castor seed oil	—	0	0.9j	7.2
29. Sisal cordage and rope	0.488	15	1.5j	1
30. Sisal and jute bags	0.488	0	1.5j	1
31. Pharmaceutical prod.	0.283	0	0	0
32. Printing and publishing	0.542	1	1	−1
33. Wattle bark extract	0.6	37.5	0	−2
34. Meat products	0.186	37.5	−3	−14
35. Soft drinks	0.4	34	16	−23

Notes and Sources (1) Kenya value added coefficients were obtained from Kenya, *Census of Industrial production*, 1963 (Nairobi, Ministry of Economic Planning and Development, 1965). Where a particular product in an industry is of special interest in Tanzania, it has been presented on its own, e.g. matches from 'other wood products', biscuits from 'bakery' industry, radio and TV. assembly from 'electrical machinery', insecticides and pharmaceuticals from 'chemical industry'.

(2) Nominal external tariffs for Tanzania in 1966 were taken from the *Customs and Excise Tariff Handbook* for 1966, published by East African Customs and Excise. When the tariff is specific, the unit cost of the import was calculated by dividing the value of imports by the volume of imports from figures in the *Annual Trade Report of Tanganyika, Uganda and Kenya, for the Year Ended 31st December, 1966*, published by the Commissioner of Customs and Excise in Mombasa. The tariff rate was then calculated by dividing specific tariff by the unit c.i.f. cost of the import.

(3) *Nominal tax protection* is the nominal protection given to the domestic producer from import duties, excise duties and export taxation on the final product. An excise tax paid by the domestic producer has the opposite effects of an import duty since it reduces the price received by the domestic producer. Where there is both an import duty and an excise tax nominal tax protection is given by the import duty less the excise duty. Export taxes on final products lower the price received by the producer and therefore have negative protection, i.e. they are a tax on the domestic producer. Export taxes on inputs, however, are a form of protection to domestic producers if we assume that they allow domestic producers to obtain domestically produced inputs at a lower price than foreign competitors. This applies particularly to industries processing primary products and the nominal protection is shown here as the percentage reduction in the price of the primary product (which accounts for a large share of the total inputs in most processing industries) as a result of an export tax. The use of this measure is indicated by superscript j.

(4) Effective protection which takes into account taxes on inputs as well as those on final products is measure by the following

$$T_i = \frac{t_i^{66} - \sum a_{ji} t_j^{66}}{V_i / X_i} \tag{4.6}$$

where T_i is the effective rate of protection of industry i

t_i^{66} is the 1966 Tanzania tariff rate (net of excise duty on the final produce)

t_j^{66} is the 1966 Tanzanian tariff rate on input j in industry i,

a_{ji} is the free trade input coefficient of input j in industry i derived as

$$a_{ji} = \frac{a^*_{ji}}{1 + t_j^{63}} \bigg/ \frac{1}{1 + t_i^{63}} \tag{4.7}$$

and V_i / X_i is the share of free trade value added for industry i, where V_i is obtained as in column (3).

In the case of industries (mainly processing of primary products) where the main input is a primary product which is subject to export tax, effective protection is given by

$$T_i = \frac{E_i a_{ji}}{V_i / X_i} \tag{4.8}$$

where E_i is the figure in column (4), i.e. the export tax as the percentage of the f.o.b. value of the input and a_{ji}'s are based on the assumption that primary inputs make between 70-90 per cent of total inputs.

ranks second on nominal tax protection though the effective rate of protection is diminished by the excise duties and the beer consumption taxes. These observations correspond to those made by Soligo and Stern in the Pakistan case.[18] There seems to be a tendency for consumer goods industries, and in particular the less durable and luxurious types, to be heavily protected.

[18] R. Soligo and J. J. Stern, 'Tariff Protection, Import Substitution and Investment Efficiency', *Pakistan Development Review*, V (Summer 1965).

Moreover, for the first seventeen industries, the effective protection rates are 95 per cent or higher. This implies, under static conditions, that labour and/or capital is receiving at least twice the remuneration they would have received under 'free trade' conditions.[19] Clearly firms in these categories should either be earning substantial profits or else they are operating inefficiently or at well below full capacity. In order to distinguish one or the other of the above possibilities, I present in table 4.10 below the profitability of the protected firms as calculated

TABLE 4.10

Profitability of some of the protected firms, 1966

Industry category		$\dfrac{Profit \ \& \ interest}{Gross \ output} \times 100$	$\dfrac{Profit}{Equity} \times 100$	Effective protection
Tobacco	firm 1	21.6 per cent [a]	22.8 per cent	528
Matches	firm 1	25.1 per cent [a]	39.2 per cent	395
Paints	firm 1	38.5 per cent [a]	159 per cent [b]	394
Textiles	firm 1	8.0 per cent [a]	16.5 per cent	269
	firm 2	8.7 per cent [a]	n.a.	269
	firm 3	23.8 per cent [a]	n.a.	269
Dairy produce	firm 1	−3.6 per cent	n.a.	216
Sugar refinery	firm 1	27.8 per cent	15.3 per cent	193
	firm 2	12.0 per cent	18.7 per cent	193
Beer	firm 1	52.4 per cent	n.a.	187
	firm 2	49.5 per cent	63 per cent	187
Canned fruits and vegetables	firm 1	4.1 per cent	n.a.	184
Clothing	firm 1	4.5 per cent	5.4 per cent	144
	firm 2	16.1 per cent	n.a.	144
	firm 3	8.0 per cent	n.a.	144
	firm 4	−0.5 per cent	n.a.	144
Footwear	firm 1	10.0 per cent	263 per cent [b]	123
Metal products	firm 1	18.1 per cent	27 per cent	95
Radio assembly	firm 1	2.9 per cent	10.4 per cent	95
Glass products	firm 1	−21.1 per cent	−8.5 per cent	51
Cement	firm 1	31.7 per cent	51.9 per cent	12.1
Sisal cordage	firm 1	28.8 per cent	25.2 per cent	1
	firm 2	2.9 per cent	n.a.	1
	firm 3	0.6 per cent	−2.7 per cent	1
	firm 4	5.5 per cent	7762 per cent [b]	1
Wattle extract	firm 1	7.0 per cent	111 per cent [b]	−2
Meat products	firm 1	8.1 per cent	22.1 per cent	−14

Source: Survey by the author.

Note (a) Calculation was based on profit income alone.
     (b) The rates of profit are exaggerated by the low equity capital of these firms, relative to total capital.

[19] Bella Balassa, 'Integration and Resource Allocation in Latin America'.

from the balance sheets and other data. The results obtained are rather mixed. First, in the cases of beer, paints and even matches, tobacco and sugar refining, the high protection would seem to serve the cushioning of high profit rates observed. Here it is safer to use the rate of return on turnover, since the rate of return on equity is largely influenced by the debt/equity ratio. The losses observed in the case of dairy produce, clothing firm no. 4, and glass products are explained by other factors. The particular dairy plant suffers from inadequacy of locally available raw materials (milk) and works considerably below capacity (about a third); the clothing firm no. 4 and the glass products firms have recently been established and were still suffering from teething troubles.

From the above table, if the firms with negative rates of return on turnover are eliminated (because of their specific characteristics already described) and the rates of return of the various firms per industry are averaged, it is found that the rate of return on turnover varies directly with the rate of effective protection. In fact, the Spearman correlation coefficient is 0.60. This result, subject to the qualification with respect to the nature of the data, would seem to suggest that the tariff structure, in general, tends to cause excessive profits. The results thus obtained are consistent with the expectations of tariff policy under the motivation to invest discussed in the last chapter.

CHAPTER FIVE

THE EMPIRICAL RESULTS OF THE PERVERSE CAPITALIST INDUSTRIAL DEVELOPMENT MODEL: THE CASE OF TANZANIA

This chapter is concerned with the testing of the hypotheses advanced at the end of chapter 3 in the case of Tanzania. The data are not always in sufficient detail to provide the rigorous tests that some of the hypotheses demand. Nevertheless, I believe meaningful conclusions can be derived from the results that have been obtained subject to the constraints of data that I have pointed out in each case.

Hypothesis 1
A part of the profits of large oligopolistic foreign firms in the ex-colonial countries are not shown in the accounting records of the ex-colonial countries but instead are realized through over-invoicing of equipment, parts, raw materials etc.

Both economic theory and industrial experience would suggest that the critical variables of an industry—prices, costs, levels of output, profit levels, and rates—are strongly influenced by the nature of the prevailing market structure. While the traditional concepts of monopoly and pure competition have been found to be wanting in several respects, it is still generally believed that performance is fundamentally related to market structure. Of course, monopoly and competition imply an array of distinct issues: buyer concentration, seller concentration, conditions of entry, extent of product differentiation, market power, etc., and performance can be characterized by different indices, e.g. productive efficiency, output levels and rates of growth, price-cost relations, profit levels and rates, speed and character of technological change, resource conservation, etc. However, in most empirical work, seller concentration has attained prominence, largely because concentration data are easily available and easily computed, and concentration has come to serve as a proxy term for the degree of oligopoly.[1]

[1] See for example, Tibor Scitovsky, 'Economic Theory and theMeasure ment of Concentration', *Business Concentration and Price Policy* (Princeton, Princeton

Thus, concentration will be taken as a measure of oligopoly and the hypothesis will be tested by relating some measure of concentration with another measure of performance. These measures will be derived from a consideration of economic theory.

Given the cost structure of the firm, and the market demand, economic theory assures us that prices will be higher and price-cost margins wider under conditions of monopoly (and oligopoly) than under conditions of competition. If I therefore approximate a measure of monopoly (or oligopoly) to a set of concentration ratios, I can hypothesize that *ceteris paribus* (i.e. cost and demand conditions) the average profit rate of firms in highly concentrated industries will tend to be significantly larger than that of firms in less concentrated ones. There are several aspects of this hypothesis which should now be examined. In the first place, the hypothesis assumes identical demand and cost conditions. This raises two problems. If current costs are identical, but capital costs differ, then the observed relations of the concentration-profit share will tend to reflect differences in capitalization. It is therefore necessary either to include capital costs in the total cost variable or to introduce capital as a separate explanatory variable. The second problem relates to assumptions regarding demand. Since under monopoly the marginal/price-cost ratios are functions of elasticity, I must either assume that the elasticity of final market demand is the same, or that there is no relationship between the elasticity of market demand and the concentration ratio. This is because, at least for horizontal average variable marginal cost functions, the greater the elasticity of market demand, the less the percentage margin between price and average cost. In the following section, I have assumed, for no demontrable reason other than expediency, that demand conditions are not substantially different among the industries in each grouping and that industry demand functions are equally elastic within the relevant range.

Data and Variables
My independent variable is the rate of surplus which is calculated as follows. From the gross value of output, I deducted goods sold in the

University Press, 1955); Joe S. Bain, 'Relation of Profit Rate to Industry Concentration: American Manufacturing, 1936–1940', *Quarterly Journal of Economics*, LXV, no. 3 (August 1951); Norman R. Collins and Lee L. Preston, *Concentration and Price-Cost Margins in Manufacturing Industries* (Berkeley and Los Angeles, University of California Press, 1968).

same condition as purchased, in order to obtain what, for want of a better term, is called gross industrial output. Taking gross industrial output, I deducted all the contractual costs including all the labour costs, total material and energy costs and work given out, leaving out what I have called the surplus. This surplus component differs from profit in several ways: it contains interest payment on short-term and long-term debt, it also includes depreciation charges. I have included depreciation charges because I could not assess the fraction of such costs that represented wear and tear. It is believed that depreciation charges are forms of hidden profits, that in some cases they may be fictitious, as in the case when an already written-off (fully depreciated) equipment is bought, installed and depreciated again, and it is influenced by the incentive structure of the country as the latter affects differentially various industrial categories. The depreciation data would also depend upon the vintage of the machinery, newly-established industrial categories would tend to have greater depreciation charges and hence less gross margin per unit of output than old industries. As shown in the cost data in appendix III, this would be particularly serious as depreciation cost comprises between 0.2 per cent to 6 per cent of total unit cost. Moreover, my gross surplus value suffers from other biases stemming from the inclusion of interest charges. This is due to variations in leverage, the debt/equity ratio among firms, since high leverage industries would tend, *ceteris paribus*, to have large interest rate charges and hence would display smaller 'net' surplus margins than those with smaller leverage. This might not be so serious in cases where interest payment is due to 'fictitious debt'.[2] Since it is unlikely that such practices vary to any significant regularity with the degree of concentration, I have assumed that the errors resulting from the inclusion of interest rates, other than the certified leverage ratio, should not be too serious.

There are, as well, other biases in the value of gross surplus as adopted. One of these errors is in 'other costs of production', which includes cost of common services. While for national firms this component might include genuine costs of administering a multi-plant enterprise, for subsidiaries of foreign companies this might represent hidden profits in the form of 'intra-company fees for services rendered'.

---

[2] A certain firm in Arusha converted part of its equity capital into loan which was provided by its directors, who at the end of the year claimed a 25 per cent rate of interest on the loan. The year-end balance sheet showed a book loss, and the company was not only exempted from paying taxes for the year, it was allowed to carry its fictitious debt forward!

Another, more serious, error lies in the major costs of capital equipment and other variable costs. Over-invoicing equipment costs has sometimes been mentioned as a practice of some of the international firms in transferring profits to their home base. So, too, is the over-invoicing of imported raw materials, and spare parts and components. Other forms of monopoly may be hidden in fringe benefits and salaries enjoyed by the expatriate executives. In order to obtain a feel for the magnitudes these biases lead to, it is interesting to report on a study made by Constantin Vaitsos on the 'transfer of resource and preservation of monopoly rents' in Colombia.[3] Defining over-pricing as

$$\frac{\text{(Price paid by Colombia)} - \text{(FOB prices quoted in different markets of the world)}}{\text{(FOB prices quoted on different markets of the world)}} \times 100$$

he found that 'the weighted average of overpricing (not the prices paid) of the seventeen firms selected amounted to 155 per cent for 1968'.[4] Individual firm over-pricing ranged from 1 per cent to 483 per cent! He adds:

> In 1968, the dollar value of the above overpricing amounted to close to U.S. $.3 million. About 50 per cent of this would have been taxed by the Colombian Government if it were declared as profits at the subsidiary level, and of the remaining, the largest percentage, perhaps as high as 70 per cent or higher would legally also have remained in the host country since the companies would have reached the limit of permissible repatriated profits with only a small part of the amount paid through overpricing.[5]

For all these reasons, there is reason to expect the more concentrated industries, especially if they are the large ones, to have the greatest incentives and ability to adopt practices that would tend to minimize the value of gross surplus as I have computed it.

The rate of surplus was obtained by dividing the surplus by gross industrial output. This is the variable that will be used as the dependent variable. Turning now to the independent variable, I have defined concentration (seller concentration that is) by the percentage share of the largest *three* firms. The basic statistical data from which measures of industrial concentration have been developed for each ISIC two-digit category, consist of two tables of frequency distributions for each-digit ISIC category which show (a) the number of establishments in each category, in each of a series of size classes, where size is measured

[3] Constantin Vaitsos, 'Transfer of Resources and Preservation of Monopoly Rents' (mimeo., 1970).
[4] Vaitsos, ibid., p. 35.
[5] Vaitsos, ibid., p. 35.

by the number of employees in the establishment, and (b) the share of gross output in each category, for every class size per ISIC category as defined above. This being the case, it is obvious that some of the concentration ratios are approximate only. An example may suffice to suggest the problem involved. In the beverage industries category (ISIC 21), 63 per cent of gross output was produced by establishments employing between 100 to 499 persons per establishment, and 29 per cent by those employing between 50 and 99 persons. Since I know from the table that relates the number of establishments by size and industrial activity that there were three establishments in beverages employing 100-400 people, I concluded that the concentration ratio for the beverage industry was 63 per cent. In the textile industry, however, where there are 1 and 5 establishments respectively in the same size categories as above contributing 27 and 38 per cent, I assume that the concentration ratio for the latter categories is $27 + 38/5 \times 2$ per cent $= 42$ per cent. In other words, I assume that the contribution of each of the five firms in the 50-99 size range contribute an equal share of gross output. This results in a downward bias of some of the concentration indexes.

There is one further issue to be discussed which is related to the short-run variation of the dependent variable. While this has not been a particularly important issue in the data presented in the previous chapter, the behaviour of the rate of surplus deserves some comment. As is well known, the rate of surplus is one of the most volatile elements among the critical variables of an industry. Consequently, a one-period observation is insufficient to support or verify the above hypothesis. I have tried to meet this objection by using the survey data of the 36 firms, which ran for a period of three years. This, however, may not be quite satisfactory to meet the objection raised above. It is difficult to believe, though, that the bias due to short-run fluctuations in the value of the rate of surplus is systematically related to the market structure of the industry. Granted, differences in rates of surplus variation may be due to the initial stages of competitive adjustment rather than stable monopoly profits. In that case, only a classification that took such factors into consideration would eliminate this error. In what follows, I have assumed that such errors are either small or uniformly distributed over the industrial structure.

The Empirical Results

A regression on rate of surplus (Y) and the concentration ratio (X_1)

gave the following results:

$$Y = 0.9574 + 0.8113 X_1, R^2 = 0.069 \qquad (5.1)$$
$$S_0 = 0.561 \quad S_1 = 0.0822 \quad F = 1.12$$
$$t_0 = 1.707 \quad t_1 = 1.059 \quad df = 15$$

where df = degrees of freedom,

S_0, S_1 refer to standard errors of appropriate coefficients

t_0, t_1 refer to t-ratios of appropriate coefficients.

These results show that the rate of surplus (Y) is *not* significantly related to the degree of concentration, since the degree of fit (R^2) is very low and the t ratio is also low for the given degrees of freedom. This result may be due to at least two factors. Either, though Y varies with X_1, it does not vary with it continuously, i.e. variations between Y and X_1 may be in the nature of a step function or the relationship may not be linear. I tried to distinguish the most concentrated industries from those that were less concentrated, but found, even before doing any regression, no systematic relationship. I therefore tried the logarithmic transformation of the variables Y and X_1, and the results were not significant.

At this stage, I introduced the data of the 36 firms which were averaged over the three-year period (1965-7). These data were presumed superior to the previous ones used for the following reasons.

Instead of the rate of surplus, I had a rate of return on equity capital before tax. I also used the available leverage data as well as the size data to eliminate some of the errors in the variables I had mentioned in connection with the earlier equations. The results, as depicted in equation (5.2) were as follows:

$$R = -1.756 + 33.344 S - 0.10887 L \qquad (5.2)$$
$$+ 0.0024 X_1,$$
$$R^2 = 0.1876$$
$$s_0 = 1.35 \quad s_1 = 20.2 \quad s_2 = 0.1074 \quad s_3 = 0.0046 \quad F = 1.23$$
$$t_0 = -1.3 \quad t_1 = 1.65 \quad t_2 = -1.0107 \quad t_3 = 0.531 \quad df = 16$$

where R = rate of return over capital

S = measure of size, i.e., 1/log (assets)

L = equity/total capital

X_1 = concentration ratio

From the values of R^2, F, s, and t, it is seen that the relationship between R and X_1 is such that it could have occurred through chance. In other words, the results so far do support the hypothesis that concentration is not statistically related to performance.

This result raises one issue: the lack of an observed relationship as would be predicted by economic theory and experience in the advanced countries. With respect to this problem, I believe that the data on surplus suffer from errors in variables. A few aspects are considered here. First, even if I had the balance sheet profit data (as used in equation 5.2), there is reason to believe that I would have obtained a non-positive relationship between profit rates and the degree of concentration. This would not imply that there are no monopoly profits or, more correctly perhaps, monopoly rents being earned. It only suggests that the variable taken as representative of such profits is the least representative in fact. And from studies of other countries and to the extent that the large enterprises are foreign, it is postulated that such monopoly rents as accrue to the firms will be concealed in the 'over-invoicing' or 'overpricing' of raw materials, components, parts, machinery, inter-branch fees for services rendered, etc. They will invariably be under-reported for several reasons. On the one hand, high declared profits might invite competitors to share the booty, and fear of competition was the *raison d'être* for establishing the plant. The stock-holders would not complain since they would share the booty. On the other hand, correct reporting of profits, especially if they are 'embarrassingly high', might lead the government to take away tariff protection. Moreover, there is always the problem of repatriating 'excess' profits even in the most generous recipient countries. Finally, because of a high degree of risk leading to high leverages (debt/equity ratios) income transfers will be taken in the form of interest rather than profits. For all these reasons, I think it is fair to claim that while the full validity of the hypothesis will depend on the availability of data from other countries with similar *ab initio* conditions, the analysis above increases the degree of belief in its validity.

Hypothesis 2
Foreign-owned firms tend to be more capital-intensive than locally-owned enterprises.

The hypothesis to be tested here is that foreign-owned and operated firms, especially subsidiaries of large multi-national corporations, tend to use similar techniques of production as in the developed countries (techniques that have a capital-using bias). In other words, they tend to be more capital-intensive. The verification of the hypothesis requires that one has information on ownership per industry. This would be the only way to safeguard comparability. Unfortunately, I do not have sufficient evidence to satisfy the above condition. I do have data, however, that may at least point to certain conclusions regarding the hypothesis. My data consist of thirty-six firms which can be classified under twelve industrial categories, of which only half are both locally and foreign-owned. The other six categories are, strictly speaking, incomparable on that basis, but I have included them because they reflect the dual nature of the technological basis of Tanzanian industry as well as the limitations of demand. For example, beverage, tobacco, petroleum and radio assembly are all foreign-owned, and in most cases consist of single-firm industries because of the size of the market. On the other hand, those industries in which only local firms participate (at least from my observed sample) include wood products and suitcase manufacturing. The distribution of the sample of firms with respect to ownership and classification is given in table 5.1.

TABLE 5.1
Distribution sample of 36 firms by ownership and industry

| Industry | Number of firms | | |
	Foreign-owned	Locally-owned	Total
Food manufacturing	4	1	5
Textiles and cordage, rope and twine	2	3	5
Clothing and footwear	1	6	7
Chemicals	2	1	3
Non-metal products	1	2	3
Metal products	2	1	3
Beverages	2	—	2
Tobacco, including cigarettes ..	1	—	1
Radio assembly	1	—	1
Wood products	—	3	3
Petroleum refinery	1	—	1
Miscellaneous	—	2	2
Total	17	19	36

Despite the inadequacy of available data, I have tried, using the techniques of regression analysis, to explore the hypothesis above. The dependent variable is the logarithm of operatives for any firm. The independent variable is the logarithm of value added, the logarithm of capital engaged and a dummy variable for ownership. The value added variable is used as a control on the size of the firm, for it would be expected that the degree of capital intensity varies with the size of the firm.

More formally, let

Y_i = logarithm of labour, $i = 1, 2, \ldots 36$,
X_{1i} = logarithm of value added, $i = 1, 2, \ldots 36$,
X_{2i} = logarithm of capital, $i = 1, 2, \ldots 36$,
$X_{3i} = \begin{cases} 1 \text{ if } i \text{ is foreign-owned} \\ 0 \text{ otherwise.} \end{cases}$

Then I estimated

$$Y_i = a + b X_{1i} + c X_{2i} + d X_{3i} + u_i$$

where a, b, c, d are constant coefficients and u_i is the unobservable random term.

The results obtained were as follows:

$Y_i = 4.195 + 0.469 X_1 + 0.189 X_2$ (5.3)
$- 0.694 X_3$,
$R^2 = 0.62$
$s_0 = 1.44 \quad s_1 = 0.2227 \quad s_2 = 0.1804 \quad s_3 = 0.2816$
$F = 17.32$
$t_0 = -2.907 \quad t_1 = 2.107 \quad t_2 = 1.048 \quad t_3 = -2.466 \quad df = 32$

From the values of t, it is found that X_1 and X_3 are statistically significant at a 5 per cent level of significance. X_2 is, however, not statistically significant at a reasonable level. This suggests that a percentage increase in capital engaged does not significantly affect the number of people employed. On the other hand, the statistical significance of X_3 implies that ownership patterns significantly affect labour employment. In particular, the above equation (5.3) reveals that foreign-owned firms have a tendency to employ less labour, for a given value added and capital, or in other words, that they are relatively more capital-intensive.

Equation (5.3) is certainly not enough to show that there is a systematic bias against the employment of labour using techniques, since such a conclusion can be drawn if data relating to identical industries are available in a number of countries. It is possible, as Professor Hirschman argues, that foreign firms invest in those branches which are entirely outside the technological and capital capabilities of the local handicraft and small workshop industrialists. And as I have already pointed out, such industries as petroleum refinery, cement, radios, etc., which Professor Hirschman considers to be beyond local capability, are owned and operated by foreign firms.

Nevertheless, regardless of the local capability aspects, probably in spite of it, the end result is that foreign technology appears unsuitable to the employment and income needs of the ex-colonial countries. The restriction of employment has had momentous effects on the development, or rather lack of development, of a proletariat class in these countries, apart from the more serious issue of breeding unemployment. Secondly, the adoption of these techniques invariably means that labour income is not as high as it would be under different techniques of production, a factor that constrains the growth of the domestic market.

I attempted to determine the effect of foreign firms on factor shares by using the following regression equation. Let

Y_i = logarithm of wage bill of firm i, i = 1, ... 36

X_{1i} = logarithm of value added of firm i, i = 1, ... 36

X_{2i} = logarithm of capital of firm i, i = 1, ... 36

X_{3i} = dummy foreign s.t. $\begin{cases} 1 \text{ if i is foreign-owned} \\ 0 \text{ otherwise.} \end{cases}$

Then estimating

$Y_i = a + bX_{1i} + cX_{3i} + dX_{3i} + U_i$, where a, b, c, d are constant coefficients and u_i is a random term. I found that

$Y = 2.318 + 0.66X_1 + 0.125X_2 - 0.259X_3$, $R_2 = 0.84$ (5.4)

$s_0 = 1.05$ $s_1 = 0.1619$ $s_2 = 0.1312$ $s_3 = 0.2048$ F = 57.91

$t_0 = 2.21$ $t_1 = 4.083$ $t_2 = 0.957$ $t_3 = -1.26$ df = 32

The degree of fit of (5.4) is quite good. The independent variables explain 84 per cent of the variation in wage bill. However, X_2 (capital) and X_3 (ownership) do not appear to be statistically significant. The fact that the size of the firm in terms of value added is a significant determinant of wage bill, while the level of capital engaged is not, may be due to the high degree of collinearity between the two variables. The statistical insignificance of X_3 is rather unexpected, though it should be noted that it has at least the right sign.

Hypothesis 3
Foreign firms, though capital-intensive, are not necessarily total factor productive.

It could be argued that the bias in favour of capital-using techniques by the foreign firms is, in the long run, beneficial to the national economies of the ex-colonial countries, if it could be shown that these techniques were in fact total factor productive. This is the aspect of **hypothesis 2** that I would like to examine here.

The measurement of total factor productivity requires, ideally, a computation of the shadow prices of the factors of production.

From the data available, I have not been able to derive such shadow prices. I have, however, again used the regression model to estimate the effect of foreign ownership on total factor productivity. The regression is based on an assumption that all the firms in the sample operate on the same production function. Using the logarithm of value added as the dependent variable and the logarithm of capital and labour respectively as the independent variable together with a foreign dummy variable, I attempted to measure the impact of foreign ownership on value added.[6] Thus, letting

Y_i = logarithm of value added of firm i, i = 1, 2 36
X_{1i} = logarithm of labour of firm i, i = 1, 2 36
X_{2i} = logarithm of capital of firm i, i = 1, 2 36
X_{3i} = dummy foreign $\begin{cases} 1 \text{ if i is foreign-owned} \\ 0 \text{ otherwise.} \end{cases}$

I obtained,

$$Y = 4.443 + 0.2597X_1 + 0.5845X_2 + 0.1305X_3, \quad (5.5)$$
$$R^2 = 0.89$$

$s_0 = 0.917 \quad s_1 = 0.123 \quad s_2 = 0.089 \quad s_3 = 0.227 \quad F = 85.73$
$t_0 = 4.847 \quad t_1 = 2.107 \quad t_2 = 6.554 \quad t_3 = 0.57 \quad df = 32$

The degree of fit equation (5.5) is quite reasonable and X_i and X_2 are statistically significant at least at the five per cent level of significance. X_3 is statistically significant only at the 60 per cent level of significance. This result would tend to suggest that there is very little evidence to indicate that foreign firms, though capital-intensive, are necessarily more productive. Incidentally, if these results are interpreted in a neo-classical framework, with equation (5.5) appearing as a Cobb-Douglas production function, it is observed that there are non-increasing returns to scale, and labour's share is particularly small as compared with other countries where it is about 0.75.

The tentative conclusions derived from equation (5.5) would tend to be collaborated by evidence supplied by Zofia Dorbska.[7] In her study of five representative firms of Tanzanian manufacturing industry, she found out that in those cases of mixed local-foreign-owned ventures, the local share of value added was relatively higher

[6] The measurement of labour by number of workers leaves labour skills unaccounted for as a factor of production (human capital). Assuming these are greater in foreign-controlled enterprises, one would expect *ceteris paribus* that foreign controlled enterprises should show higher productivity by the regression above.
[7] Zofia Dorbska, 'Criteria for Evaluation of Investment Projects in Manufacturing Industry' (Economic Research Bureau, Dar es Salaam, 1968, mimeo.).

than the share of local capital. She explained her result, noting that the local component of wage fund was always higher than the foreign one. She also discovered that although her results might tend to suggest that the most effective use of local resources was to associate them with foreign capital, this was not necessarily the case, for in her analysis she realized that the addition of foreign capital does not appreciably change the productivity of the local one. Her finding is illustrated in table 5.2. As shown, the difference between the local capital-output ratio of the enterprise in no. 1, wholly locally-owned, and enterprise no. 4, in which local participation is not more than 12 per cent in magnitude, is certainly not very substantial. Also the effectiveness of local capital is higher in enterprise no. 2 than in enterprise no. 3, although the latter benefited from foreign support twice as large in magnitude. Nor does the large foreign capital investment in enterprise no. 5 present a very unfavourable local capital-output ratio.

TABLE 5.2

Ownership and capital effectiveness in five firms

Enterprise				Local capital/ local value added ratio	Share of local capital in total capital (per cent)
1	..	..	..	1.8	100
2	..	..	..	1.5	51
3	..	..	..	1.6	25
4	..	..	..	1.4	12
5	..	..	..	5.4	25

Source: Zofia Dorbska, 'Criteria for Evaluation of Investment Projects in Manufacturing Industries' (Economic Research Bureau, Dar es Salaam, 1968, mimeo.).

As Professor Hirschman has observed, the crux of the matter lies in the fact that enterprises which are wholly or mainly locally-owned concentrate on those branches of production where capital outlays are small relative to production effects. It is just because some branches of production necessitate huge capital expenditures that foreign participation is looked for, the more so, the larger the capital expenditures involved. But this is not the whole story, for it must be remembered also that foreign capital itself is especially interested in ventures requiring large quantities of foreign-made equipment. This consideration is true whether foreign investment is in partnership with local private entrepreneurs or with publicly-owned corporations. As such, it will bear on the policy issues to be discussed in part III.

Hypothesis 4
Linkage effects of the industrial structure of the ex-colonial countries are limited and there is a high dependence on imports.

In trying to examine the above hypothesis, one is confronted with a host of theoretical and empirical problems. I will first deal with the theoretical aspects of linkage effects. Then I will explore the problem of measuring such links.

With the extension of the static notions of external economies, and technical complementaries to the dynamic contexts of growth and development, structural interdependence among the various sectors of an economy has provided the analytical basis for some of the most significant propositions in this otherwise sterile branch of the dismal science.[8] Given a fixed final demand pattern, the linkage effects theory, which is one of the approaches to investment dependence, seeks to trace out those sectors with high technological linkages which are able to induce the expansion of other sectors and sometimes even help in the initiation of new industries.[9] It is thus contended that a pattern of pressures and incentives can be worked out by investing in those sectors initially which have higher technological linkages. It is obvious that the theory purports to maximize private investments as it relies on inducements and incentives rather than on comprehensive, centralized planning. Nevertheless, if the theory is shorn of its *laissez-faire* underpinnings, such as the incentive mechanisms, it can be useful even to centralized economies. This becomes more apparent when one regards the linkage theory to be advocating a sequential pattern of growth, the purpose being to select the most efficient sequence which would accelerate the growth process through technological interrelationship.

Two types of structural linkage effects have been noted in the literature: the first type results whenever an industry provides inputs to other firms or industries and in so doing, either through the cheapening of its products or through greater availabilities, stimulates the setting up of, or increasing the output levels of the output absorbing

---

[8] See for example Tibor Scitovsky, 'Two Concepts of External Economies', *Journal of Political Economy*, LXII, no. 2 (April 1954), pp. 143-51; Albert O. Hirschman, *The Strategy*, op. cit., especially chapters 4 and 6; Hollis B. Chenery, 'The Interdependence of Investment Decisions', in Bernard F. Haley (ed.), *The Allocation of Resources* (Stanford, Stanford University Press, 1959).
[9] Another school of thought, largely inspired by Keynesianism, analyses the interdependence of investment arising from the consumption side. See especially Simon Kuznets, *Modern Economic Growth: Rate, Structure and Spread* (New Haven and London, Yale University Press, 1966).

industries. These have been called the 'forward linkage' effects by Professor Hirschman.[10] The second type occurs as a result of an efficient industry absorbing inputs from others, and as such, whenever it operates on a positive output level, provides stimulus for the expansion or initiation of production of the input-providing industries. These have been termed the 'backward linkage' effects.

The above propositions can be considered against the theory of production. Whereas, however, the theory of production assumes (especially neo-classical theory) equilibrium in factor and product markets, nationally integrated and flexible economies capable of self-generated and sustained growth, as well as full employment of available resources leading to only marginal changes in factor use as a result of exogenous increment in output demand (due to augmentation of real capital, also exogenously given); the linkage effects theory asserts that in a typical underdeveloped economy, the industrial structure is in disequilibrium (and incomplete?). Therefore, assuming high supply elasticities of primary factors relative to factor prices (and hence output), exogenous increment in output demand in the latter situation will lead to tensions and pressures to either expand the capacity of the supplying factors, or to establish such capacities locally as soon as the cumulative demand of such factors attains optimum economic size. Such backward linkage tensions will be the greater if (a) thanks to the establishment of capacity of such supplying industries, some part of the otherwise idle capacity of existing industries (e.g., electric power, transport, etc.) is used, and (b) when they induce an increase in the production of local raw materials.

Forward linkage effects, on the other hand, emerge largely as a result of the intervention of external economies within a given industry (in the case of pure competition); or due to increasing returns arising from indivisibilities in production methods or in factor inputs in a given industry; or from the fact that one of the above features is present at some 'earlier' stage of production. In other words, the forward linkage effects are largely conditioned by the price effects and this should be borne in mind when pricing the output of those industries that could potentially produce forward linkage effects.

Some problems arise on how to measure these linkage effects. The input-output matrix of the Leontief-type has been suggested as an empirical tool to quantify the linkages, as it brings out in detail

---

[10] Hirschman, *The Strategy*, op. cit., p. 100.

the production relations prevalent at a point of time in the economy. Professors Chenery and Watanabe, in their study of international production structure, suggested that a statistical measure for estimating backward linkage effects might be the ratio of purchased inputs (X_{ij}) to the value of total production of the jth industry, or

$$b_j = \frac{\sum\limits_{i=1}^{n} X_{ij}}{X_j} \qquad j = 1, 2, \ldots n \qquad (5.6)$$

A large b_j would imply that a large proportion of industry j's output was made up of intermediate purchases, provided by other producing industries so that the value added by the j industry itself would account for but a small portion of its total output.[11] In other words, b_j indicates the extent to which industry j uses as inputs, the outputs of other industries as compared to the direct use of capital and labour. Similarly, such a measure considers only direct purchases, although it takes into account the magnitude of the transactions. Similarly,

$$f_i = \frac{\sum\limits_{j=1}^{n} X_{ij}}{X_j} \qquad i = 1, 2 \ldots n \qquad (5.7)$$

measures the degree of forward linkage effects. A large f_i means that industry i is important as a supplier of materials and semi-finished goods rather than as a supplier of final goods. It is to be noted that from (5.6) a higher backward linkage effect might come about because of heavier reliance on purchased inputs or sometimes because of the sheer inefficient utilization of inputs which inflates the input requirements per unit of output. Thus, a large-scale manufacturing activity operating with an efficient technology might show up an equivalent backward linkage to that of a more inefficient activity operating on a small scale. The reliance on marketed inputs which gives higher backward linkage of the former as compared to the latter might be countervailed by the higher inefficiency of input utilization of the former. Furthermore, equations (5.6) and (5.7) do not distinguish between sectors which have a highly skewed input or deliveries pattern and those whose structural relations might be more evenly characterized. Also, as discussed above, since the equations are based

[11] Hollis B. Chenery and Tsunehiko Watanabe, 'International Comparison of the Structure of Production', *Econometrica*, XXVI, no. 4 (October 1958), pp. 487-521.

upon direct input requirements, the indirect and secondary repercussions of the input requirements are not included in the estimate.

Table 5.3 gives the linkage effects as measured by equation (5.6). From column (2) of table 5.3, it is observed that activities with below-average backward linkage effects consist of services (i.e. services proper, which in this case include commerce, public and private services, maintenance and repair), agriculture and mining (the so-called primary sectors) and miscellaneous manufacturing; textiles; petroleum products; paper, printing and publishing; and metal industries and metal products. The low backward linkage effects in the tertiary and primary sectors (if mining and public utilities are included in the primary sectors) need little comment as studies of other countries (developed and underdeveloped) reveal that these sectors tend to have relatively low linkage effects.[12] What needs to be explained is the relative low

TABLE 5.3
Backward linkage effects as measured by equation 5.6

Industrial Classification	Import content (1)	Tanzania (2)	Japan-U.S. –Italy* (3)
Alcoholic beverages	12.1	65	
Manufactured tobacco	5.7	60	
Manufacture of food and soft drinks	3.4	73	89
Clothing and footwear	60.7	54	69
Textiles	61.2	14	69
Paper, printing and publishing ..	49.8	35	53
Chemicals and products	56.2	45	60
Petroleum products	72.7	21	65
Cordage, rope and twine ..	8.1	71	
Leather and rubber	0.5	57	58
Wood and products	4.3	50	61
Non-metal and products	4.0	48	47
Metal and products	65.4	27	51
Processing for exports	3.0	79	
Maintenance and repair	20.5	6	43
Miscellaneous manufacturing ..	15.6		
Agriculture		27	31
Mining		13	17
Building and construction ..		60	
Public utilities		53	27
Services		7	18
Average		42	45

* Chenery and Watanabe, 'International Comparisons', op. cit., p. 493.

[12] Chenery and Watanabe, 'International Comparisons'; Colin Clark (ed.), *The Conditions of Economic Progress* (London, Macmillan, 1957).

degree of backward linkage effects observed in the industries normally categorized as the 'secondary sector'. Petroleum products, paper, printing and publishing, textiles, which form the bulk of 'intermediate manufacture' of an economy are normally expected to have above-average backward (as well as forward, see below) linkage effects. Miscellaneous manufacture and metal products grouped under 'final manufacture' by Chenery and Watanabe have normally relatively above-average backward linkage effects, though their forward linkage effects are generally weak. One way of accounting for the difference is to note that all these industries with relatively low linkage effects have a very high import content as revealed in column (1) of the table. Secondly, these industries have been set up recently, and to the extent they are 'enclave import industries', they have not yet induced significant linkages. In other words, the low degree of backward linkage effects of these industries reflects both the manner of industrialization in Tanzania (i.e. import-substituting industrialization beginning with the 'final touches') and the early stage of the industrialization process.

For the fifteen sectors for which comparable data are available, it can be seen from column (3) of table 5.3 that, except for public utilities and non-metal products, the backward linkage effects are relatively higher in the more developed countries (Japan-Italy-U.S.) than in Tanzania.[13] The divergence between the two sets of figures is largely explained by the import content and the stage of import substituting industrialization, and the difference may be taken as a measure of the backward linkage effects accruing overseas and yet to be realized in Tanzania. To the extent that demand patterns of various countries are assumed to be broadly similar, the above-noted differentials may be taken as a measure of the strength of the linkages yet to be induced. In other words, industries with higher absolute differences will tend to be developed relatively faster than others as income grows. Under this interpretation, textiles, petroleum products, metal industries and metal products and miscellaneous manufacturing can be expected to grow (not only in the value of output but more significantly, in the roundaboutness of the production process) in order to take advantage of existing idle capacity of already existing activities, especially power generation and the utilization of local raw materials.

[13] These comparisons must be read with extreme caution as the differences in product mix of the various industrial categories necessarily imply differences in linkage effects.

There is reason to believe that the above interpretation accords with the recent pattern of industrial growth in Tanzania. As pointed out in the preceding chapter, the textile industry had lagged behind the technological threshold. The earlier textile establishments, such as Tasini Textiles, tended to use imported raw materials (in 1966, import content of its raw materials was over 80 per cent) rather than using local ones. However, since then, the newly established textile mills (Friendship Textile Mill, Kilimanjaro Textile Mill Ltd., Mwanza Textile Mill) have been designed to use relatively more local materials, and to integrate the production process from spinning to printing. Obviously, this development will reduce import dependence of the industry and raise its backward linkage effects. In the case of petroleum, there are fewer opportunities for expansion, given the existing demand and resources, but the fact that ENI has been granted prospecting rights for petroleum around the Tanzanian coast is certainly a very significant indication of the future possibilities. As for the metal industries and metal products, the newly established Steel Rolling Mill will obviously raise backward linkage effects, though the contribution of this industry will depend upon the development of the iron and coal resources of the country.

It is interesting to note that with the exception of textiles, these industries generally have very high growth elasticities. In the study of industrial patterns, Professor Chenery found that machinery and petroleum products had growth elasticities of 2.80 and 2.22 respectively, as compared to the average for all manufacturing which is 1.44. Here the growth elasticity is taken as a percentage rate of change of *per capita* value added due to a percentage rate of change of *per capita* income.[14] In a more disaggregated study, Chenery and Taylor show that these industries, together with paper, printing and publishing, grow relatively faster than *per capita* income growth even for small primary-oriented countries.[15]

Turning now to the forward linkage effects, it is noted in table 5.4 that apart from public utilities, large forward linkage effects are associated with industries that provide packing materials: wood products (wooden crates, cases, chests, etc.), paper printing and publishing (cartons, bags, boxes, labels, etc.), metal products (con-

[14] Chenery, 'Patterns of Industrial Growth', op. cit.
[15] Hollis B. Chenery and Lance Taylor, 'Development Patterns: Among Countries and Over Time', *Review of Economics and Statistics* (November 1968), pp. 391-416.

tainers, tins, hoops, etc.), and textiles (bags, cloth). This is indicative of the already observed symptoms of import-substituting industrialization where only final touches are added to the product in the earlier phases. The relatively high linkage effects of alcoholic beverages is purely a statistical freak, since it is the recorded transactions of Tanzanian brewery's output to its bottling plant in Moshi.

TABLE 5.4
Forward linkage effects as measured by equation 5.7

Industrial Classification				Tanzania	Japan-U.S-Italy*
Alcoholic beverages	..	..	..	35	
Manufactured tobacco ..	..	..	..	3	
Food and soft drinks ..	..	..	..	4	42
Clothing and footwear ..	..	..	..	0	12
Textiles	..	..	..	28	57
Paper, printing, publishing	..	..	..	50	62
Chemical	..	..	..	34	69
Petroleum products	..	..	..	9	68
Cordage, rope and twine	..	..	..	0	
Leather and rubber products	..	..	4	42
Wood and products	..	..	..	78	38
Non-metal products	..	..	..	2	30
Metal products	..	..	..	32	
Processing for exports	..	..	21	
Maintenance and repair	..	..	50	
Miscellaneous manufacturing	..	..	2	
Agriculture	..	..	..	44	72
Mining	..	..	..	20	52
Building and construction	..	..	21	
Public utilities ..	..	..	..	72	59
Services	..	..	..	20	17
Average	..	..	..	25	43

* Chenery and Watanabe, 'International Comparisons', op. cit., p. 493.

Final manufactures have, as would be expected, below average linkage effects. The same is true of services (though not of maintenance and repair). Primary production shows no consistent pattern. Agriculture has a high forward linkage effect as would be expected, but mining's coefficient is very low due probably to the fact that most mining is non-metallic and is exported. The low linkage effects associated with the export industries confirm the generally observed fact that the export structure of Tanzania forms an enclave. This view, however, fails to consider the significant backward linkage effects of these industries noted above.

When the two linkage effects are placed side by side, a certain industrial pattern begins to emerge. Final manufacture industries (beverages, tobacco, food, clothing and footwear) all have relatively above-average backward linkage effects and below-average forward linkage effects. This is in conformity with the findings of Chenery and Watanabe and can be taken to characterize these industries. Most of the intermediate manufacturing industries have relatively above-average backward and forward linkages. This includes chemicals, wood products and paper products. Textiles, metal products, non-metal products and petroleum products depart considerably from this pattern largely because they are in their incipient stages of formation. The data that are available therefore support the view that the little industrialization that has taken place is characterized by limited linkage effects, though one must distinguish backward from forward linkage effects.

So far, however, the above analysis has been based on direct purchases and sales, the indirect and secondary repercusions of the input requirements having been disregarded. To the extent that the average measures do not distinguish between sectors with a highly skewed input deliveries pattern and those whose structural relations might be characterized more evenly, there is the danger of drawing inferences which may merely reflect the structural properties of the identified industries as such but with little meaningful policy options. For this reason, I turn to devise a more refined measure of these linkages as suggested by Rasmussen.[16] This measure deals with magnitudes contained in the inverse of the Leontief matrix, and to the extent that it is being devised for the purpose of checking the accuracy of the above measures, it is only necessary to consider the backward linkage effects.

The inverse matrix, it will be recalled, contains the general solution for direct and indirect requirements per unit of final demand in a given sector. The average value of coefficients in a given row or column relative to the average value of all coefficients in the inverse matrix therefore gives a comparative picture of economic interdependence for each sector of the economy.

The backward linkage from a given industry's final demand to the total economic effect of that demand may be determined by studying the columns of the inverse matrix. Rasmussen's method of calculation normalizes to a value of 1.0 for a typically linked industry,

[16] P. Rasmussen, *Studies in Intersectoral Relations* (Amsterdam, North-Holland Publishing Company, 1956).

with the highest values showing the greatest interdependence. Rasmussen defines the 'power of dispersion', analogous to the backward linkage effect, as

$$U_j = \frac{\dfrac{1}{n} r_j}{\dfrac{1}{n^2} \sum\limits_j r_j} \qquad (5.8)$$

where

$$r_j = \sum_{i=1}^{n} r_{ij} = \text{element of } (I-A)^{-1}$$

and A is the matrix of technical coefficients.

U_j measures the relative extent to which an increase in final demand for the product of industry j is dispersed throughout the system of industries. If $U_j > 1$ for given industry j, this implies that an industry chosen at random will need a comparatively large production increase in the final demand for the products of an industry j. In other words, U_j expresses the fact that industry j draws heavily (i.e. relative to other industries in general) on the system of industries—and vice versa for $U_j < 1$. U_j thus measures backward linkage effects normalized to a value of 1.0 for a typically linked sector, with the highest values showing the greatest interdependence.

A better perspective is obtained by carrying out the same operations with the effect of within-sector transactions eliminated. This alternative is defined as

$$U_j^* = \frac{\dfrac{1}{n-1}\left(\sum\limits_{i=1}^{n} r_{ij} - r_{ii} \right)}{\dfrac{1}{(n-1)^2}\left(\sum\limits_i^n \sum\limits_j^n r_{ij} \sum\limits_i r_{ii} \right)} \qquad (5.9)$$

Table 5.5 presents the three measures of backward linkage effects according to equations (5.6), (5.8) and (5.9). It is clear from table 5.5 that the three measures appear to give closely similar rankings of backward linkage effects. In fact, the rank correlation between b_j and u_j is 0.98, that between b_j and u^*_j is 0.94, and that between u_j and u_j^* is 0.91. These results imply that the conclusions drawn from the results of b_j and f_i remain largely unaltered by using more refined methods.

TABLE 5.5

Backward linkage effects as measured by equations (5.6), (5.8), and (5.9)

Industrial Classification			b_j	u_j	u^*_j
Alcoholic beverages	..	..	65	1.35	1.41
Manufactured tobacco			60	1.16	1.70
Food and soft drinks		..	73	1.30	2.14
Clothing and footwear	..	..	54	1.05	1.49
Textiles	..	..	14	0.78	0.11
Paper and printing	..	..	35	1.00	0.40
Chemicals	..	..	45	1.11	0.65
Petroleum products	..	..	21	0.82	0.51
Cordage, rope and twine	..	..	71	1.28	2.25
Leather and rubber products	..	..	57	1.15	1.69
Wood products	..	..	50	1.00	0.98
Non-metal products	..	..	48	1.12	1.57
Metal products	..	..	27	0.90	0.15
Processing for exports	..	..	79	1.35	2.34
Maintenance and repair	..	..	6	0.71	0.14
Miscellaneous manufacturing	..	..	6	0.70	0.13
Agriculture ..	..	..	27	0.88	0.52
Mining	..	..	13	0.76	0.28
Building and construction	..	..	60	1.20	1.85
Public utilities	..	..	53	1.10	1.50
Services	..	..	7	0.73	0.16

Hypothesis 5
Modern industries of the ex-colonial economies are located in the export enclaves.

Two aspects of this hypothesis will be tested, namely, the validity of
the assumption that the industrialization that has taken place in
Tanzania has been largely concentrated in the export enclaves, and
that such a pattern can be explained by the *modus operandi* of the
private enterprise system. The first aspect leads us to the search for
the measures of location and concentration, to which I now turn.

In order to measure the locational structure of industry for making
certain structural comparisons among the various economic zones
of Tanzania, one has to find some statistical measures which can aid
in answering such questions as: where, if at all, is an industry concentrated and to what degree; and secondly, what industries, taking the
country as a whole, are concentrated or not and to what degree?
It will be shown presently that some aspects of these questions can
be answered by the location quotient and the coefficient of localization

as developed by Regional Science.[17]

The *location quotient* shows the relative share of a specified industry belonging to a given region. It measures the degree to which those occupied in any industry, in any place, are more or less numerous than would be expected if industries were evenly distributed among the population of each area as a whole. For example, from Tanzania's *Survey of Industrial Production, 1966*, Dar es Salaam is shown to have had 18 per cent of its working population in the food manufacturing industries, though in the same year 27 per cent of the working population of the whole of Tanzania was so employed. Relative to the country as a whole, Dar es Salaam can be said not to specialize in the food manufacturing industry and the industry is therefore not localized in Dar es Salaam. The precise degree of this specialization (or lack of it) of any one community or locality in any one region is therefore what is measured by the location quotient—the percentage employed in a given industry (e.g. food manufacturing) of all the given region's workers (e.g. Dar es Salaam) divided by the corresponding national percentage: $18/27 = 0.67$. Where the quotient is less than unity, as in this particular case, the region is said to have less than its 'fair share' of the industrial activity in question, and where above unity, it has more than its fair share. By measuring where an industry localizes, if at all, the quotient throws light on the causes of localization.

Table 5.6 shows the various location quotients computed for Dar es Salaam, Tanga, Arusha, and Moshi in combination and the rest of Tanzania. These quotients indicate that Dar es Salaam has attracted more than its 'fair' share of paper, rubber and metal products, the assembly of transport equipment, non-metallic mineral products, furniture and fixtures. It also shows that Dar es Salaam has acquired less than its fair share of food manufacture, wood products, assembly and repair of electrical products, textiles and chemicals and petroleum products. On the other hand, the rest of Tanzania has less than its fair share in beverages, footwear and wearing apparel, furniture and fixtures, printing and publishing, rubber products, non-metallic mineral products, metal products, repair of non-electrical machinery, assembly of transport equipment and miscellaneous manufacture.

It is pertinent to point out at this stage that although localization is popularly thought to mean the concentration of some industry in

---

[17] Walter Isard, *Methods of Regional Analysis* (New York, John Wiley and Sons, 1960) and Sargant P. Florence, *Investment, Location and Size of Plant* (London, Cambridge University Press.)

TABLE 5.6

Locational quotients of Tanzania's manufacturing industry

Industry	Industry, 1966 (Establishments)		
	Dar es Salaam	Tanga-Arusha-Moshi	Other
Food	0.74	0.93	1.39
Beverage	1.32	1.48	0.13
Tobacco	1.42	0	1.48
Textiles	0.95	0.22	1.84
Footwear	1.42	1.32	0.16
Wood	0.39	1.97	0.77
Furniture	1.95	0.35	0.48
Paper	2.63	0	0
Printing	1.95	0.39	0.45
Leather	1.18	0.58	1.19
Rubber	2.63	0	0
Chemicals	0.92	1.03	1.06
Non-metals	1.97	0.32	0.48
Metals	2.37	0.03	0.29
Non-electricals ..	1.26	1.58	0.10
Electricals	0	1.64	1.58
Transport	2.42	0.26	0
Miscellaneous	1.13	1.55	0.29

Source: Survey of Industrial Production, 1966.

one particular place, i.e. as a relation between an industry and a geographical area; this is not what economists generally mean and is not particularly significant.[18] What is important is the relation between an industry and the distribution of the population as a whole. Thus, the statistical index of localization should then measure the local concentration of that industry compared with the distribution of industries as a whole. A coefficient of localization can thus be worked out from the *Survey of Industrial Production, 1966,* by the following formula—when workers are partitioned off regionally as percentages of the total in all regions, the coefficient is the sum, divided by 100 of the plus deviations of the regional percentage of workers in the particular industry from the corresponding regional percentages of workers in all industry.[19] It is a measure of the local concentration

[18] D. H. Robertson, *The Control of Industry* (London, Cambridge University Press, 1960), chapter III. Alfred Marshall, *Principles of Economics* (London, Macmillan, 1961), book IV, chapter XI, part II.

[19] It should be noted that the total of plus deviations is identical with the total of minus deviations. This follows from the fact that the various columns of figures whose deviations are measured by being percentages, must both add up to one hundred. Coefficients could thus be obtained equally by adding all the minus deviations.

Underdevelopment and Industrialization in Tanzania

of a particular industry compared with the distribution of industry as a whole. The value of the coefficient varies from zero to one. A coefficient of zero means that the distribution of workers in that particular industry coincides completely with the distribution of industrial workers in general (i.e. dispersion). On the other hand, a coefficient of unity indicates extreme differentiation (i.e. workers in the particular industry are all concentrated in one region).

The computed coefficients for the localization of manufacturing as a whole, given in table 5.7, show a relatively heavy locational concentration in furniture and fixtures, paper products, printing and publishing, rubber products, non-metallic mineral products, metal products, assembly and repair of electrical machinery and assembly of transport equipment.

TABLE 5.7

Coefficients of localization of Tanzania's manufacturing industry, 1966

Industrial classification	No. of establish-ments	Employment coefficients I*	Employment coefficients II**	Establishment coefficient
Food	120	0.13	0.08	0.12
Beverage	11	0.31	0.31	0.27
Tobacco	3	0.24	0.11	0.31
Textiles	50	0.22	0.22	0.26
Footwear and apparel	26	0.30	0.30	0.26
Wood, excluding furniture	53	0.37	0.11	0.30
Furniture	28	0.33	0.20	0.36
Paper	3	0.59	0.35	0.62
Printing	30	0.33	0.21	0.36
Leather	10	0.06	0.02	0.13
Rubber	4	0.59	0.35	0.62
Chemicals, petroleum	30	0.08	0.02	0.03
Non-metallic minerals	13	0.34	0.20	0.37
Metal products	19	0.32	0.26	0.52
Non-electrical machinery	10	0.49	0.32	0.18
Electrical machinery	3	0.41	0.14	0.38
Transport	11	0.51	0.35	0.54
Miscellaneous manufacturing	14	0.26	0.26	0.22

* Employment is partitioned into Dar es Salaam, 3 other major towns (Tanga, Arusha, Moshi) and the rest of Tanzania.
**Employment is partitioned into major urban areas (Dar es Salaam, Tanga, Moshi, Arusha) and the rest of Tanzania.

Source: *Survey of Industrial Production, 1966.*

162

This pattern can be compared with examples from other countries. Bohr shows that industries with below-average coefficients of localization (in the case of those U.S. industries that are comparable to Tanzanian industries) are beverage industries, food industries and non-metallic products.[20] On the other hand, those very much above average (0.43 and over) include furniture, cordage, rope and twine, rubber products, leather products, footwear and apparel, petroleum products, textiles and metal products. There is a considerable similarity of industrial structure—a fact which may be due to the greater degree of aggregation employed in the statistical data used—but this is perhaps largely determined by the similarity of the investors' behaviour and motivation.

It is clear from the results of the above calculations that a relatively disproportionate concentration of manufacturing exists in Dar es Salaam and a few other enclaves. This conclusion remains largely true despite the drawbacks of the method used. A most likely drawback are the possible variations in the values of location quotients and the coefficients of localization resulting from degrees of aerial sub-divisions and according to the choice of the base. Moreover, concentration is particularly strong in a wide range of intermediate goods other than simple chemical products. These results lead to an examination of the factors responsible for this locational pattern.

Determinants of Locational Patterns

The most significant factors that explain locational patterns under a private enterprise system are the relative costs of transporting the inputs and outputs of a given establishment; the size and other characteristics of the market and the occurrence and magnitude of external economies or diseconomies to the individual establishment because of location (i.e. the so-called localization and urbanization economies.)[21]

To the extent that sources of raw materials attract industrial activities, one should expect an inverse correlation between the location quotient and the share of raw material cost in the value of output. Table 5.8

[20] Kenneth A. Bohr, 'Investment Criteria for Manufacturing Industries in Underdeveloped Countries', *Review of Economics and Statistics*, XXVI (May 1954), pp. 157-66. The data referred to above are found in table 6, 'Selected Industries in Order of Coefficient of Localization, U.S., 1939'.
[21] See E. A. G. Robinson, *The Structure of Competitive Industry* (rev. ed. Cambridge University Press, 1968), pp. 143-55; Edgar M. Hoover, *The Location of Economic Activity* (New York, McGraw Hill, 1948); Melvin L. Greehut, *Plant Location in Theory and Practice* (Chapel Hill, University of North Carolina Press, 1956); and Alfred Weber, *Theory of Location of Industries* (Chicago, University of Chicago Press, 1929).

below shows that such a relationship is in fact observable, the rank correlation being −0.28. Of course, the degree of attraction exercised by materials varies widely according to the raw materials themselves, the processes that use them and the techniques available in distribution

TABLE 5.8

Relationship between location quotient and the share of raw material cost in gross output

Industrial classification	Location quotient (Dar)	Share of raw materials cost in gross output %
Food	0.74	61.8
Beverage	1.32	43.7
Tobacco	1.42	28.4
Textiles	0.95	77.1
Footwear	1.42	68.6
Wood	0.39	28.0
Furniture	1.95	35.4
Paper	2.63	60.7
Printing	1.95	42.4
Leather	1.18	92.4
Rubber	2.63	31.6
Chemicals	0.92	68.9
Non-metallic mineral products	1.97	57.9
Metal products	2.37	66.6
Non-electrical machinery	1.26	30.3
Electrical	0	76.2
Assembly of transport	2.42	38.5
Miscellaneous manufacturing	1.13	56.8

Source: *Survey of Industrial Production, 1966.*

and utilization.[22] For example, industries which use raw materials that lose greatly in weight or bulk in manufacture will tend to be located at the source of the raw materials. This may explain why cordage, rope and twine industries (part of the textiles) are not concentrated in Dar es Salaam but are *rooted* in areas with the requisite raw materials. The notable exception is the location of Tanganyika Packers, a meat canning and packing plant that is located in Dar es Salaam instead of the cattle-raising areas in the hinterland. But as Mrs. Dorbska observes, this locational choice must be regarded as 'a major mistake. It is undoubtedly one of the chief reasons limiting its expansion possibilities. It must

---

[22] Gunnar Alexandersson, *Geography of Manufacturing* (New Jersey, Prentice-Hall, 1967); R. C. Estall and R. Ogilvie Buchanan, *Industrial Activity and Economic Geography* (New York, John Wiley and Sons, 1967).

also have an appreciable influence on the processing costs of the factory and on the price received by the cattle producers.'[23] Correspondingly, the cattle-linked industries, e.g. leather products, have tended to congregate in Dar es Salaam.

The degree of perishability of the raw materials is also of importance in assessing the strength of the raw material's attraction for manufacturing industries. Dairy produce (part of the food industries) will tend to be found near the sources of supply, as will the processing of primary products such as coffee, cashew nuts, tea, etc., where the difficulties of bulk, waste content and perishability are an important consideration. The instant coffee factory in Bukoba, tea factories in Iringa, cashew nut processing in Mtwara and Dar es Salaam, pyrethrum in Iringa and saw milling in Tanga are good examples.

A significant number of industries, however, are not supply-based. They may be oriented towards the general personal consumer markets (e.g. apparel, footwear, tobacco) or to the producer markets (e.g. fabricated metals, machinery). Among these, industries for which an increase in weight, bulk or fragility is added to the product (e.g. the addition of water to the product) will normally lead industrial location to the consumer market. This in part explains the concentration of beverage plants in the four major towns. The concentration of metal products (especially metal containers), barrels (part of wood products), and bakeries in the few urban centres would be similarly explained.

Industries for which localization and urbanization economies are very important have found Dar es Salaam a congenial place to locate. Localization economies, as will be recalled, accrue to all firms in a single industry, in a single location. They depend on accessibility to buyers, a full utilization of diverse, specialized facilities, markets for by-products or opportunities for waste disposal, etc. Urbanization economies, on the other hand, accrue to all firms in *all* the industries at a single location. They result from the greater use of infrastructural facilities, finer articulation of economic activities usually found in urban structures, and social welfare gains. The relatively high *per capita* income of Dar es Salaam (sh. 4,152/- as compared to the national average of sh. 478/-), the range of its industrial skills, and access to the non-farm industrial materials (especially imports) and inter-industrial links (especially contact between producer and consumer) seem to have been responsible for the disproportionate concentration of

[23] Zofia Dorbska, 'Criteria for Public Investment in Manufacturing: Five Tanzanian Case Studies' (Economic Research Bureau No. 68.7, 1968, mimeo.).

the following industries in Dar es Salaam: maintenance services, especially the repair of machinery and servicing of transport equipment; tailoring and footwear and the intermediate industrial activities (rubber products, chemicals, petroleum products and paper products).

Thus, it is reasonable to conclude from the foregoing discussion that the locational pattern of Tanzania's manufacturing is fundamentally consistent with the operating economic forces and existing relationships. The effect of these forces leads to a concern about (a) the direct cost of moving inputs and outputs given the geographical distribution of the local raw materials and of the markets for industrial output; (b) the regularities and market characteristics in the purchase of inputs and the shipment of products; (c) conditions of transportation and hence the direct and indirect costs involved; (d) the least costly access to imported raw materials; and (e) the emerging conditions of the so-called agglomeration economies. The concentration of manufacturing firms in the export enclaves is but the natural outcome of past conditions and expectations which have led the individual firm to search for the 'optimum location' of their plants (with minor exceptions such as Tanganyika Packers). This finding, as will be shown in part III, bears seriously on any deliberate government effort to influence the locational pattern of industry in Tanzania, given the nature of the existing forces and inter-relationships.

Hypothesis 6
The system of industrial production of the ex-colonial countries is characterized by a low percentage share of capital goods, and a high percentage share of luxury consumer goods relative to the world average, for a given income and population.

In testing this hypothesis, there emerges a difficult problem of classification in order to match the ISIC data that I have available. In doing so, the following definitions have been adopted. Consumer goods industries are those that produce commodities which when finished are used by households or the state for non-productive purposes. Capital goods industries are defined as those that produce machines (i.e. metal working or machine-building industries), excluding metal fabrication but including electrical machinery and transport equipment. These two categories do not exhaust industrial output unambiguously. I have, therefore, distinguished three further categories: (a) building materials, which although ultimately serving ends not unlike the products of the capital goods group, are differentiated because of the direct importance from the consumers' point of view of residential housing, and in our circumstances the extent of sumptuary housing, (b) producers' supplies, e.g., fuels, containers, paints, etc., and (c) other, mostly services and intermediate products that do not fit into any of the above categories.

Appendix V indicates the distribution of the various industries to the above classifications. Since I was interested in examining the distribution of value added and employment among the above sectors, I was able to use the more disaggregated data in three-digit and sometimes four-digit ISIC classification. However, the 1966 *Survey* does not often disaggregate the industries as shown in appendix V. For example, it does not break down ISIC 319, which includes soap, pharmaceuticals, other chemical products, insecticides, matches, and pyrethrum processing. In cases like this, I have supplemented the *Survey* with data I obtained from a sample survey I made in July-August 1969. In this way I was able to make the disaggregation indicated in appendix V.

Table 5.9 shows the distribution of value added and employment (in percentage of the total manufacturing industry) among the five

TABLE 5.9
Tanzania: sectoral distribution of value added and employment, 1966
(in percentage of total manufacturing industry)

Sector				Value added	Employment
(a) Consumer goods industries	..	..		75.8	75.0
(b) Capital goods industries	..	..	..	0	0
(c) Building materials industries	..	..		12.5	15.8
(d) Producers' supplies	..	..	..	10.1	7.6
(e) Other	..	..	..	..	1.6	1.6
Total	..	..	..	..	100.0	100.0

TABLE 5.10
Comparative sectoral distribution of value added in manufacturing industry

	Tanzania (1966)	Kenya (1963)	Africa (1963)	World (1963)	LDC* (1963)
Consumer goods industries	70.5	46.60	45.09	29.02	48.01
Building materials industries	10.3	10.06	10.42	9.18	9.53
Intermediate goods industries	11.2	11.30	22.79	22.74	23.30
Capital goods industries	7.1	30.90	19.14	35.20	16.53
Other	0.9	1.14	2.56	3.86	2.64
Total	100.0	100.0	100.0	100.0	100.0

*underdeveloped countries

Source: United Nations, *The Growth of World Industry, 1967 Edition*, vol. I (New York, United Nations, 1969), for Kenya, Africa, World and the less developed countries. *Survey of Industrial Production, 1966*, for Tanzania.

identified sectors. It is obvious from the table that manufacturing value added and employment is concentrated in the consumer goods sector. While 75 per cent of industrial output in consumer goods is not atypical of many low-income countries, it is important to note that there is no capital goods capacity in Tanzania. What is atypical of Tanzania's industrial structure, in other words, is not the high ratio of consumer goods output in total industrial output, but rather the conspicuous absence of any capital goods output. This is what is reflective of the deformed structure of Tanzanian industry.

These observations come into full relief when Tanzania's sectoral distribution of output is compared with other countries on a two-digit level as shown in table 5.10. The aggregation of this table differs from that of table 5.9 in several respects. Food, beverage, tobacco, textiles, footwear and wearing apparel, printing and publishing, leather products, are defined as consumer goods industries, wood products (excluding furniture and fixtures), and non-metal products comprise the building materials industries. Intermediate goods industries are made up of paper products, chemicals (including petroleum products), rubber products and basic metals. 'Other' includes miscellaneous manufacturing, and capital goods include only metal products. In the case of Tanzania, basic metals and metal products are aggregated together and the figure 7.1 is made up mostly of the servicing of machinery and the assembly of transport equipment. Yet, even when the capital goods sector is treated in this way, the Tanzanian manufacturing sector appears to differ quite significantly from all other countries or regions to which it has been compared.

There are several possible reasons to explain the absence of a capital goods industry in the Tanzanian industrial structure. As pointed out earlier, industrialization in East Africa was centralized in Kenya so that the few basic industries that were established in the region were located in Kenya. When Tanzania, after attaining independence, began demanding her 'fair' share of the industrial output induced by the common market arrangements, it was the consumer goods industries (and the cement industry) which got shifted to Tanzania. As for the new establishments, and mainly because they were established by investors with export interests, they tended to concentrate in the consumer goods sector where the market is easily accessible, products are standardized, and the risks of gestation period are minimal.

Secondly, the motivation to invest that I explored earlier contributes to the bias of investment in the economy against the development of the capital goods industry. The exporter of capital goods does not feel threatened in the same way as the exporter of consumer goods, because his products are more specialized and normally subject to low duties, which eliminates the threat that motivates other types of foreign investment. The low duties on capital goods are partly due to the historical necessity of lowering the costs of the planters, as discussed in part I, and as a means of encouraging the importation of capital equipment. Moreover, the tariff structure tends to reinforce the bias of investment decisions against the capital goods sector in so far as the already protected industries (the consumer goods industries) resist the protection of the input-supplying industries (the capital goods industries).

In order to indicate that the sectoral distribution of investment, as shown above, is due to the system described in the theoretical chapter, and not simply due to the lack of an adequate technical capacity, I present table 5.11, which shows that high capital-labour ratios are not characteristic of capital goods industries. In fact,

TABLE 5.11
Japan's machinery production

Industry	Direct capital/ Labour ratio
Petroleum products	1.200
Coal products	0.682
Non-ferrous metals	0.363
Chemicals	0.338
Iron and steel	0.337
Non-metallic mineral products ..	0.298
Non-metallic minerals	0.298
Processed foods	0.193
Grain mill products	0.193
Ship building	0.174
*Transport equipment	0.174
Metal mining	0.172
Fishing	0.170
*Machinery and electrical equipment	0.161
Apparel	0.132
Textiles	0.131
Paper	0.120
Rubber	0.119
Lumber and wood	0.111
Printing	0.093
Leather	0.068

*Capital goods industries.

Source: Institute for Social and Economic Research (Osaka University, mimeo.).

TABLE 5.12

Capital-labour ratio and capital-output of 36 firms, Tanzania

Industrial classification	Number of establish-ments	Capital/ Output ratio	Capital/ Labour ratio (shs.)
Petroleum	1	4.3	310,606
Food processing	5	5.1	99,822
Discretionary consumer goods	3	1.6	84,245
Construction materials	8	2.5	43,793
Intermediate exportables	5	1.7	34,669
Other intermediate	1	1.2	18,052
Consumer exportables	2	1.3	12,645
Other necessities (excluding textiles) ..	7	1.2	9,070
Textiles	4	1.4	8,563

petroleum products, chemicals, non-metallic mineral products, processed foods and grain mill products—industries which have been established in Tanzania (even though the output mix is obviously different)—have relatively higher capital/labour ratios than machinery and electrical equipment and transport equipment which, according to the definition adopted above, constitute capital goods industries. The survey of the thirty-six firms I made indicates a similar ranking of industries with respect to the direct capital/output ratios as do the Japanese data, and this suggests that the capital goods industries would fall in a similar position in Tanzania as in Japan.

It is obvious from the lack of a capital goods industry that industry's contribution to agricultural productivity and the development of transport networks has been negligible. For, in general, inputs that would greatly enhance agricultural productivity include fertilizers, insecticides, simple farm implements (hoes, ploughs, tractors), agricultural machinery, and parts and servicing. By 1966, however, there was no fertilizer plant, although one is being constructed; there were three small-scale insecticide plants, including Sapa Chemical Industries and Fisons (T) Ltd., with a total value added share in total manufacturing output of less than 0.3 per cent. There was no farm implements factory, although a small plant has been set up in Dar es Salaam (an area with a minimum concentration of agricultural activities). The same can be said of the transport industry. So far, a tyre-retreading plant has been set up, a bicycle assembly plant (in partnership with Raleigh Industries of England) and a bicycle tyre and tube plant (in partnership with General Tyres, Ltd.) are projects currently being considered by the National Development Corporation. These projects, however, do not greatly widen the transport capacity of the economy. Importation which has been relied upon both in the case of agricultural machinery and transport equipment, results in the use of numerous non-standardized models which definitely forestall the establishment of such industries, or even those geared to produce spare parts, for a considerable period.

It may be argued that these capital goods can be imported, that the export proceeds of agriculture and possibly industry should help the importation of the agricultural and transport machinery requirements. However, the domestic production of these goods is deemed essential for the following reasons. First, is the list of advantages to accrue to the economy as a result of producing capital goods domestically as discussed in the introductory chapter to this part. Secondly, agricultural machinery and techniques are very specific to climate and soil conditions, let alone the type of crops being produced. The proper specifications of these types of machines would seem to be well adapted to local production. Moreover, demand for these goods is likely to rise once the efficiency of the local products is demonstrated. In many countries, agricultural machinery has been a basis for a metallurgical industry. Finally, as long as these goods are not produced locally, few agricultural workers are likely to know how to repair them. There have been numerous instances where the inability to repair imported equipment has resulted in unnecessary waste of resources. It is likely that if the import costs of these agricultural machines were to be evaluated in such a way as to include the servicing costs, their appropriateness, etc., the domestic production of these machines is likely to be much cheaper if an appropriate time horizon is allowed.

Turning now to the question of the luxury bias of the industrial goods, there is a serious problem of definition. Definitions of luxury goods are never value free. I have defined luxury goods as those enjoyed by the high income group of society because of the price paid for the good (relative to its utility) and the embodiment of tastes that are not typical of the general level of the population. The following industries have been therefore classified as luxury-good industries: breweries, tobacco, tea processing, coffee curing, cashew nut processing, and miscellaneous manufacturing. My defence for including these is as follows. Breweries produce 'European' beer (consumed mainly by the high income people) in competition with 'local' beer. The same applies to cigarettes. Miscellaneous manufacture is included because its output mix is made up of meerschaum smoking pipes, goldsmiths, foam mattresses etc., outputs which are consumed by the well-to-do and cannot be regarded as 'necessities' in any meaningful sense. Beverage industries (tea, coffee) and cashew nuts are included for similar reasons.

A significant proportion of the consumer goods industries is exported and the proportion of exportables is not the same between luxury and non-luxury consumer goods. In order to obtain comparable estimates of the contribution of these two categories to domestic final demand, I

TABLE 5.13

Structure of non-exportable consumer goods industry: value added and employment as a per cent of total industry

Classification	Value Added	Employment
(1) Non-exportable consumer goods, total	44.1	32.5
(2) Non-exportable luxury consumer goods	12.8	6.7
(3) (2) as a per cent of (1)	29.0	20.6

eliminated all the exportables from the consumer goods. When these items are excluded (essentially ISIC sections 201, 2091, 2093, 2094, 2095, 2097, 2311, 399), I obtain the above table relating non-exportable luxury consumer goods industries' value added and employment as a per cent of total consumer goods industries. In this table, it is clear that luxury consumer goods make up about three-tenths of the total value added of the consumer goods industries and only a fifth of the employment. It is likely that luxury consumer goods in the public sector were established at the initiation and to the benefit of the more well-to-do who also hold important positions in government. A survey of middle grade civil servants showed that 7 per cent of their total expenditure (an average of sh. 732/-) was spent on alcoholic beverages, as compared to 1 per cent of the lower paid civil servants (sh. 126/-). One implication that can be drawn from this table is that the benefits of industrial development have been unevenly shared. The wage-employees earning over sh. 200/- per month, whom I can assume enjoy these luxury goods, are about 200,000 out of a total population of 12 million.

A second implication of the above table is that non-exportable luxury consumer goods industries are relatively less labour-using industries. Moreover, from the survey data, the luxury goods sample tends to have a higher average wage per worker. These aspects of the luxury goods industries imply not only a concentration of income and wealth in a selected few, but also suggest that such a pattern is likely to be perpetuated.

PART THREE

Towards a socialist industrialization strategy

...Africa now has an opportunity to build an ethic appropriate to the development of a good and stable society or allow one to develop which contains the seeds of future strife and confusion...

J. K. Nyerere,
Freedom and Unity,
introduction, p. 20

CHAPTER SIX

TOWARDS A SOCIALIST
INDUSTRIALIZATION STRATEGY

6.1 PRELIMINARY CONSIDERATIONS

In part I, I outlined both the *historical necessity* and the Tanzanian leadership's *resolve* (as in the Arusha Declaration and subsequent pronouncements) to establish a socialist society. In part II, I explored how and why the pattern of industrialization that was taking place in Tanzania was deepening its underdevelopment. In this chapter I endeavour to explore, though briefly, to what extent the pursuance of a socialist industrialization strategy might eliminate underdevelopment and establish the economy on a self-sustaining basis. This is done in several stages: section 6.2 examines the nature of Tanzanian socialist goals and in section 6.3 the nature of planning relations and their implications for socialist resource allocation is discussed. Section 6.4 concludes with an exploration of socialist production relations.

I should point out at the very outset that some of the discussion which follows is speculative. The science of the political economy of socialism is relatively young and the experience of the post-capitalist societies, even when available in print, is not always unambiguous. I must therefore disclaim any pretension to specialist knowledge. The areas of ignorance and uncertainty on this subject remain distressingly large. In what follows, I have simply tried to fit available scraps of information into a coherent theoretical framework, but this framework must, of course, be regarded as tentative and subject to revision as and when further information becomes available.

6.2 TANZANIA'S SOCIALIST GOALS

As the discussion of socialist goals and objectives (and *a fortiori* the theory of socialist economy) is marked by a great lack of precision and of definition of even the most fundamental concepts, with the result that even the goals of society mean different objectives to different people, it is appropriate to specify that in the following section socialism is taken to mean the domination by the immediate producers over their conditions of existence and, therefore, in the first instance, over their means of production and products.[1] Politically, socialism implies *power* to the working class (i.e. industrial workers and peasants) whereas economically socialist development necessitates *collective ownership of the means of production*, that is, the end of exploitation. Under socialist conditions, the development of society becomes purposeful and conscious and the organized social activity of man is directed to achieving the effective realization of definite purposes— this is expressed by the *planning* of economic and social development.

But the domination of workers over their conditions of work means more than this; it signifies a new type of relationship among men, a new order of priorities, a new mode of life and culture. If it does not include all this socialism loses its meaning and appeal. This meaning, to define it concretely, is the subordination of production to needs, as much of *what* is produced as of *how* it is produced.

This defines the *ultimate* relations of production that can be identified with the *existence* of a socialist society. We do not at the present moment have such a society. Our immediate problem is, therefore, how to plan to attain this particular socialist society. In other words, we have to discuss the nature of our *immediate* objectives, that is, those of the *period of transition*, in order to specify the means that will increasingly approximate the ultimate attainment of socialism as formulated above.

The immediate goals of Tanzanian development, if it is to attain socialism, are clear enough. First and foremost it is necessary to eliminate Tanzania's present underdevelopment in order to establish an internally integrated and self-reliant economy.

Secondly, it is necessary to establish the foundation for the emergence of socialist man. Moreover, these two objectives are to be attained simultaneously rather than sequentially.

Briefly, underdevelopment can be cured only if the dependency relationships created by the colonial and post-colonial division of labour, namely the dependency on the centre's markets; technological dependency and dependency on foreign (metropolitan, private) entrepreneurs (relationships that necessarily lead to perverse capitalist development and a significant lack of changes in modes of production and production relations) are eliminated, so that the economy of

[1] Charles Bettleheim, 'More on the Society of Transition', *Monthly Review*, vol. XXII, no. 7 (December 1970) p. 2.

Tanzania becomes internally integrated and self-reliant. On the other hand, the foundations for the emergence of socialist man can be said to exist if appropriate mechanisms and institutions are created to guarantee the socialist relations of production described above. Specifically, attempts must be made to eliminate (though by no means abolish, at least during the period of transition) alienating and exploiting relations of production.

However, the struggle against exploitation (and to some extent alienation) does not take its full meaning until it becomes a conscious struggle against false priorities, a battle against the waste and deprivation that capitalism imposes on society (developed or underdeveloped). To struggle against the exploitation (and alienation) of labour is necessarily also to struggle against the *purpose* for which labour is exploited. Thus the proximate goals of Tanzanian socialism during the period of transition reduce to the acquisition of *collective ownership of the major means of production* and the *ability to plan* in such a way as to liquidate underdevelopment. This interpretation implies an initial bias towards concentrating on measures of expanding productive forces as well as altering the structure of the economy rather than concentrating on a process of creating new production relations and new norms of distribution. This is inevitable, in view of the low level of productive forces from which we start. Nevertheless, this should not obscure the fact that what distinguishes socialism as a system and gives its appeal is the nature of its production relations.

It is now appropriate to indicate how the socialist pattern of development *can* liquidate underdevelopment. It will be recalled that the major cause of 'perverse capitalist industrial development'—a significant component of underdevelopment—was traced to the following dependency relationships: dependency on the centre's markets (for exports) as well as technological dependency and dependency on foreign (metropolitan, private) entrepreneurs. Technological dependency and dependency on the centre's markets is due to the lack of symmetry between the structure of production and the structure of consumption, and consequently the absence of capital goods industries, especially those geared to raising the labour productivity of the agricultural sector. Moreover, the dependency on foreign (private) entrepreneurs reinforces the above dependency relationships in so far as foreigners' investment decisions are merely an extension of their home countries' demand. To the extent then, that socialist development requires collective ownership of the major means of production, it necessarily weakens the foreign and private content of investment decisions and *a fortiori* enables the society to orient its investment decisions in accordance with its real needs. Collective ownership of the basic means of production achieved through nationalization measures therefore sets the basis for fundamental changes.

Once one of the basic foundations of socialism has been laid (i.e. nationalization), as it has in the case of Tanzania, the major concern turns to the nature of socialist planning, that is, to the specification of priorities in such a way as to ensure growth and balanced development. This raises a host of important questions including, among others, the objectives of planning; planning methodology and implementation; resource allocation and production relations. It is to these issues that we now turn.

6.3 PLANNING RELATIONS AND RESOURCE ALLOCATION

Economic planning, or more precisely the planning of economic development, is an essential feature of socialism. It belies the fact that a socialist economy does not develop in a spontaneous manner but that its growth is guided and directed by the conscious will of organized society. Considering the low level of material forces from which we start, the major task of planning must be to develop our productive forces, particularly the industrialization of the country and the modernization of agriculture. Planning techniques and methodology will therefore be dominated by this fundamental problem: to ensure a sustained rate of economic growth through accumulation. But planning must be geared towards establishing socialist production relations and as such it must be elaborated and set in operation on the basis of the initiatives of the masses, so that it concentrates and co-ordinates the experiences and the projects of the masses. However, this consideration raises the issue of centralization-decentralization which will be discussed in due course.

Two problems arise immediately with regard to planning as formulated above. *First*, what is the *scope*, i.e. the activities in the economy that have to be planned? And secondly, what are the *methods* of ensuring the realization of the plan?

First, let us consider the scope of national planning which depends on the ownership structure. In the case of Tanzania we have the nationalized sector, the co-operative sector and the private sector.

In order to plan effectively it is necessary that state ownership become the *key* form of social ownership in the process of constructing socialism. For only in this way is it possible to construct an economy serving the needs of the whole society.

Secondly, socialist planning and effective direction of the development of the national economy does *not* require that every activity of society should be planned. Only two major decisions must be incorporated in the plan: the division of the national income into consumption and investment, and the allocation of investments to different sectors of the economy. The first determines the general rate of economic growth, the second the direction of economic development. Of course, the plan must ensure that technical and general economic requirements are fulfilled. For example, the plan must observe the general equilibrium conditions affecting the proportions necessary in the process of production and reproduction. These are, however, merely technical aspects while the above decisions are really of a political character.

The problem of allocating resources between consumption and investment is one of the most difficult to resolve unambiguously. On the one hand, a high proportion of investment leads to high rates of growth but implies low consumption levels. However, one of the principal productive forces in building socialism is the productive power of an increasingly skilled and conscious individual. Consequently, improvements of such manpower, through increases in the rates of consumption at the early period of transition, should be regarded as one of the most productive investments. On the other hand, the relations between proportions of consumption and investment depend on the *planning horizon* and, *a fortiori*, on the *expected length of the period of transition*. For in the short run, for example four to five years, maximizing the growth rate of income is incompatible with increasing consumption. But for longer periods, this incompatibility can be eliminated. It is thus necessary to have some idea of the expected length of the period of transition. The choice of the time period in which the optimization of consumption is compatible with optimization of output expansion is therefore an important theoretical problem.

On the basis of available evidence (i.e. on the historical performance of the existing post-capitalist societies) it is reasonable to assume a fairly long period of transition. This empirical recommendation is also fortified by the following consideration: the *ab initio* conditions of Tanzania are such as to expect economic decolonization and development to be agonizingly slow *even* with efficient policy formulation and execution, as well as the most favourable external relations.[2] To the extent that a long period of transition is acceptable, the plan period can be determined by maximizing the growth of the national income and subject to a minimum level of consumption being attained, and increased, every year. The level of consumption and its rate will be partly determined by the structure of the basic goods, to be discussed below.

With respect to the sectoral distribution of investments, we encounter even more fundamental difficulties. As already pointed out, the allocation of investments to the different sectors of the economy determines the direction of economic development. The problem is: what should be the criteria for making such a choice? More fundamentally, we must establish a criterion that will ensure that provided we are pursuing 'non-perverse growth', the goods being produced at any given time are really those which at a given stage of technological evolution allow for the best and most rational satisfaction (at the least cost in terms of money, time and trouble) of a given need.

To begin with, the fundamental needs of man are not predetermined once and for all by human nature. They are conditioned by the development of the means available for their satisfaction, the development techniques of production (i.e. the nature and conditions of work) and by the changes which the development of production techniques bring about in the natural environment. Indeed, as Marx points out:

> Production furnishes consumption not only with its object. It gives consumption its definition, its character, its finish .... The object is not an object as such, but a specific object, which must be consumed in a specific way, a way which is again determined by production itself. Hunger is hunger, but the kind of hunger that is satisfied with cooked meat eaten with a fork and knife is different from the hunger which bolts down raw meat with hand, tooth and nail. Therefore production produces not only the object of consumption but also the manner of consumption, not only objectively but also subjectively. Production thus creates the consumer. Production not only furnishes the object of a need, but it also furnishes the need for an object.[3]

Nevertheless in our present circumstances a broad categorization of our fundamental needs can be made. It can safely be asserted, for

[2] Reginald H. Green, 'Political Independence and the National Economy: An Essay on the Political Economy of Decolonization' in C. H. Allen, and R. W. Johnson (eds.), *African Perspectives* (London, Cambridge University Press, 1970), p. 286.
[3] Karl Marx, *A Contribution to the Critique of Political Economy* (Moscow, Progress Publishers, 1970), p. 197.

example, that production should be geared to producing *basic goods*, basic in the sense that they are used in the production, directly or indirectly, of all the other goods.[4] These basic goods consist essentially of *wage goods* and the *means of production* that establishes the foundation of a self-sustaining economy, and *a fortiori* guarantees the reproduction and expansion of wage goods. It is the first category of basic goods that has often been given attention, even though wage goods have sometimes been confused with consumption goods. The former do not include luxuries *ex definitione* since luxuries are not used either as instruments of production or as articles of subsistence in the production of others. Wage goods can be subdivided into primarily private consumption wage goods and collective consumption wage goods, although this latter distinction is not easy to define precisely.

The instruments of production necessary for guaranteeing the reproduction and expansion of basic wage goods have often been given scant attention in our development plans. But these are the *only* goods that can transform our economy from a dependency relationship to one of economic independence. They include both raw materials and capital goods, i.e. machines to produce machines. As pointed out in part II these capital goods have certain properties that have important implications for the growth process. The major argument against the introduction of capital goods and important raw materials is the lack of economic capacity to do so, in particular, the inability of the underdeveloped countries to take advantage of economies of scale, which are assumed to characterize modern industrial production. Let us review the nature of the economies of scale argument.

Ordinarily economies of scale denote the existence of an inverse relationship between monetary cost of production and the level of output. This has normally been taken to indicate the existence of an optimum level of output, i.e. a single level of output at which unit costs are lower than at any other level. But as the studies by Bain and Jewkes indicate, the notion of an optimum level of output is not supported by available evidence.[5] Moreover, as Brewster and Thomas cogently point out, the debate on economies of scale has failed to take notice of the well-known Marshallian distinction between levels of cost curves

---

[4] Pierro Sraffa, *Production of Commodities by Means of Commodities* (London, Cambridge University Press, 1960), p. 7.
[5] J. S. Bain, *Barriers to New Competition* (Cambridge, Mass., Harvard University Press, 1956); J. Jewkes, 'Are Economies of Scale Unlimited?' in E. A. G. Robinson (ed.), *Economic Consequences of the Size of Nations* (New York, St. Martin's Press, 1960).

and movements along cost curves. If this distinction is made, it is possible for economies of scale to be a characteristic of different situations where at any given level of output the absolute levels of unit cost may vary. Moreover, economies of scale should be interpreted as the existence of an inverse relationship between the *physical* input/output ratio and the level of physical output.[6]

In the literature on economies of scale, the major source of purely physical unit cost savings as output is increased derives from the phenomenon of cubic dimensions and avoidance of 'short runs'.[7] There are, however, other factors which introduce variation in unit cost and level of output but not in an inverse way. These are primarily pecuniary factors including factor prices, the level of labour productivity, the size of external economies or diseconomies and exchange rates. In view of these factors it is clear that monetary economies of scale do not necessarily establish the case for attaining a certain minimum level of output that can be regarded as optimal. In other words, it is possible for the same absolute levels of unit cost to prevail in different industries or firms even though they are producing at widely different levels of output. Indeed, as Brewster and Thomas point out:

.... a sufficient volume of empirical documentation has been built up to permit us to conclude fairly confidently that when there is an inverse relation between unit cost and output, the rate of the inversion tends to vary along the cost curves.[8]

This suggests two important policy implications.

In the first place, since the inverse relationship is often a varying one, it is possible that the attainment of the optimum level of production may not be the variable to be considered. Rather, attention must be given to 'critical minimum' levels of output, which in the case of steel, for example, may be as low as a quarter of the generally accepted least cost volume of output.[9] However, this does not mean that Tanzania can establish any industry. Indeed, the argument calls for stronger

[6]Havelock Brewster and Clive Y. Thomas, 'An Organic Theory of Economic Integration (University of Guyana, 1971, mimeo.)

[7] For a discussion of 'cubic dimension', see Hollis B. Chenery, 'Engineering Production Functions' in W. W. Leontief and others, *Studies in the Structure of the American Economy* (New York, Oxford University Press, 1953).

[8] Brewster and Thomas, op. cit., p. 59.

[9] Brewster and Thomas indicate that from the evidence they have drawn from case studies in specific developing countries, an increase in production of finished steel from 50,000 tons to 250,000 tons reduces the unit cost of production by 36 per cent, whereas it calls for a further increase of as much as 750,000 tons to lower the unit cost by only 25 per cent; see Brewster and Thomas, op. cit., p. 60.

measures towards regional integration. But the above is intended to dispel the common fallacy that even in such a grouping, such as the East African Community, the production of basic goods is 'uneconomic'. While we are on the topic of regional integration it should be noted that the enlargement of the market (partly to reap the benefits of economies of scale) has the principal effect of bringing a greater range of resources and consumption requirements into the orbit of a single economic system. The potential advantages of this are that resource combinations which would have been unlikely under autarky now become possible, resulting in greater scope for the use of regional resources and their by-products. Furthermore, with a wider variety of consumption weights in the expanded market, it becomes easier to create an economic system which displays a reasonable symmetry between the structure of production and the structure of consumption.[10]

Secondly, in view of the differences in inter-firm, inter-country comparisons of different levels of unit cost at different levels of output, it may be preferable to be guided by import prices in designing investment projects. However, the use of import data is constrained by the pervasity of 'dumping'.[11]

To the extent that boundaries ascribed to an industry may vary and, when defined, industries have different critical and optimum sizes of output, these magnitudes themselves varying in the same industry, from country to country, firm to firm and from time to time, there is no reason why Tanzania in the framework of the East African Community should not endeavour to establish some of the means of production industries. In view of resource constraints, Tanzania should concentrate on the production of iron and steel, and chemicals, in her first efforts towards a self-sustaining economy. The choice of iron and steel is because of there being resources for such an industry, and it is one with the highest level of 'technological convergence'.[12]

Although the change in the factor bias of technical progress was one of the aspects stressed when discussing the technical foundations of

[10] Brewster and Thomas, op. cit., p. 29.
[11] The existence of dumping owes its theoretical explanation to differential pricing under monopolistic competition. Its pervasive nature in international trade is shown by H. W. de Jong, 'The Significance of Dumping in International Trade', *Journal of World Trade Law*, vol. 2, no. 2 (March-April 1968), where it is shown that steel, textiles, synthetic rubber, non ferrous-metals, chemicals, refined sugar, household appliances, footwear, etc. are subject to dumping.
[12] E. Ames and Yan Chiou-Shuang, 'Economic Interrelatedness', *Review of Economic Studies* (October 1965). See also, Simpson and Tsukui, 'The Fundamental Structure of Input Output Table, An International Comparison', *Review of Economics and Studies* (November 1965).

development, there is another aspect that deserves our attention. The source of gains from technical progress has often been understated in the literature on development, in relation to the gains from accumulation. Empirical studies in the advanced countries have indicated, using the residual method, that a significant increase in the growth of output is due to increases in the rate of technical progress rather than increases in the rate of accumulation and labour.[13] However, a controversy has raged on regarding the residual method, and doubts have been expressed about the validity of attributing to technological progress an increase in output, a phenomenon which is supposed to occur irrespective of increases in the rate of accumulation and labour. Yet, there can be little doubt that the results obtained by Abramovitz, Solow, Lave, Fellner, Nelson, etc. are not significantly different from what we would expect. Marx showed over a century ago that constant technical progress exists within a capitalist economy of necessity. A capital owner who did not introduce it not only denied himself surplus profit but was liable to be eventually excluded from the production process. As a competitor introduced technical improvements into his production plant and lowered the costs of production, the price of the given article fell to a level equal to the sum of the new lowered cost of production plus an average rate of profit. Bankruptcy threatened capital owners who did not carry out innovations in their plant because the price which they could obtain on the market would be lower than the costs of their own production.[14] It was this compulsion to achieve technical progress within the capitalist system which carried with it the compulsion to accumulate, the inevitability of the centralization of capital and the continual upsurge of the reserve army of the unemployed. A theoretical issue which has not yet received the attention it deserves is whether this accelerated tempo of technical

---

[13] Solow, for example, fitting a Cobb-Douglas production function to data on the U.S. for the period 1909-49, attributes 90 per cent of the rise in GNP per man hour to technical progress, see Robert Solow, 'Technical Change and the Aggregate Production Function', *Review of Economics and Statistics* (August 1957).

[14] For example, Marx in *Hired Labour and Capital* says: 'By applying new and better means of production, the capital owner will be able to sell his goods at a price exceeding the actual cost of production . . . . However, our capitalist's privilege will not last long; other capitalists in rivalry with him will introduce the same machinery and the same division of labour . . . . Such is the law which again and again forces capitalists to put strain on the productive force of labour since capital has previously created this tension; it is a law which gives the capitalists no rest, and continually whispers: forward! forward!' Quoted by O. Lange, *Papers on Economics and Sociology* (New York, Pergamon Press, 1970).

progress is possible under a socialist regime.[15]

An important aspect of this unique role of technical progress is its 'embodiment' in capital goods. Of course, progress is necessarily 'disembodied' in the sense that new ideas must always be put into effect in relation to the initially given resources. This is an essential constraint under which all economies operate. Improved production methods working on the initially given resources then lead to more and better capital goods. However, the chances of substantial and *continued* improvement are undoubtedly greater if the processes used on the initial resources are rich in changeable properties, i.e. in what Fellner called the 'dimensions of improvement'—than if these processes offer improvement possibilities in a few directions.[16] The use of a large variety of instruments of production opens up a large number of dimensions of potential improvement. Indeed, Fellner found out that the results of 'learning by doing' are significantly influenced by differences in the available number of dimensions of improvement. Hence physical capital formation helps in the improvement process if for no other reason than it increases the number of directions in which improvement can proceed. The link between capital goods industries and technical change is also provided by 'vintage models' developed by Solow, Johansen, Kaldor and Mirrlees.[17] Their production function becomes a 'choice of design function', i.e. new technology is 'embodied' in new capital goods. Once a machine is constructed factor proportions determine output per unit of labour, since each machine requires a fixed amount of labour, i.e. there is no possibility of *ex post* capital labour substitution. Finally there is the close relationship between technology producers and users which facilitates the flow of knowledge between them thus enhancing the embodiment of technical progress in capital goods.

There are many theoretical considerations related to the problem

---

[15] There is some doubt expressed by Ota Sik, among others, that the socialist countries are capable of leading the capitalist countries technologically. This is one reason for Ota Sik's recommendation of introducing market socialism. See his book, *Plan and Market Under Socialism* (White Plains, New York, International Arts & Sciences Press, 1968).

[16] W. Fellner, 'Trends in the Activities Generating Technological Progress', *American Economic Review* (March 1970).

[17] R. Solow, 'Investment and Technical Progress' in K. Arrow, S. Karlin and P. Supper (eds.), *Mathematical Methods in the Social Science* (Stanford, Stanford University Press, 1960), pp. 89-104; L. Johansen, 'Substitution Versus Fixed Production Coefficients in the Theory of Economic Growth: A Synthesis', *Econometrica* (April 1959), pp. 157-76; N. Kaldor and J. Mirrlees, 'A New Model of Economic Growth', *Review of Economic Studies* (1962), 29 (3), 80, pp. 174-92.

of technical change which will require the immediate attention of theorists: what, for example, determines the stock of knowledge of a society, how and when does part of that knowledge take the form of innovations, which industries are likely to initiate adoption of the new techniques, and what are the characteristics of the transmission mechanism that underlie the diffusion of new techniques throughout the economy? While awaiting answers to such questions there are immediate policy implications of singling out the role of technical change in development.

First, the plan should establish indigenous industries for machine tools, machine building and repair, material and component manufacture. These industries are not large establishments, they are, contrary to what is often believed, labour intensive industries. They accelerate the process of technical change through their intimate contacts with the technology users. Their familiarity with the environment ensures that technical developments are practical and economical in their local setting. Building up such industries in the Tanzanian context means starting on the ground floor and at a relatively low technical level in some cases. By a combination of imaginative *improvisation* and *adaptation*, the absorption of scientific knowledge from abroad, an emphasis on technical training, tolerance of initial imperfections by the customers, and accumulated experience and confidence emanating from self-achievement, Tanzania is capable of establishing a strong and healthy technology-producing sector over the next ten to fifteen years. The Soviet Union, Japan, Eastern European countries and China have demonstrated in this century that the transition from a largely imitative to an innovatory role can be accomplished in this way.[18]

Secondly, Tanzania, together with the other partner states, must, in the context of the East African Community, set up documentation and information centres to keep track of past and current technological developments throughout the world.[19] These would establish a close liaison with international and other national advisory services for the

[18] A. Maddison, *Economic Growth in Japan and the USSR* (London, George Allen and Unwin, 1969).
[19] Scientific and technological centres have played an important part in Japanese and Soviet economic development. In 1963 about 210,000 abstracts of foreign scientific papers were made by the Japan Information Centre for Science and Technology. In the Soviet Union the All-Union Institute of Scientific and Technical Information has an abstracting service which digests 400,000 scientific papers a year. See, K. Marsden, 'Progress Technologies for Developing Countries', *International Labour Review*, vol. 101, no. 5 (May 1970), pp. 475-502.

selection of equipment. They must pool their research resources because the existing research and technical skills are not available in sufficient quality, and a lack of centralization leads to unnecessary duplication and spreads the existing resources too thinly.

Thirdly, the government must institute incentive rewards schemes for inventions, as well as patent protection for local adaptations of foreign designs. The issue of incentives will be discussed separately below. Moreover, there must be a campaign to stimulate people to write down their innovations, inventions, etc. which will be distributed throughout the country. Apart from instructions to farmers during the planting season and dissemination of planned research findings, some of the radio time must be reserved for craftsmen and farmers who may have innovations and inventions to offer.

Another major dimension of the allocation of investments between various branches of the economy is the division of labour between the state and the co-operative sectors. All the large, basic means of production, as well as consumer goods industries, must be under the management of the state sector. There is, however, room for participation by the co-operative sector in some of the industries. The co-operative sector has the basic task of mobilizing the social initiatives of the working class. It is a form of economic management which activates certain special economic incentives and in that way develops certain special methods of economic administration. These economic incentives result from the collective nature of ownership and from the fact that it is a form of socialist ownership which is nearer to private ownership than is ownership by society as a whole. As such, the co-operative sector is ideally suited to developing small scale production, performing the task of socialist transformation at this level of operation, by providing efficient, cheap and democratic management which may favourably influence the state sector by attracting personal savings as a contribution to the process of socialist accumulation.[20]

The major areas of co-operative endeavour include the traditional types of small-scale undertakings (manufacture of household utensils, processing of foodstuffs, manufacture of some agricultural implements, carpentry, pottery, smithery, basketry, shoemaking and repair); artistic goods industries, e.g. carpet weaving, embroidery, etc.; small scale repair services, and 'subcontracting' work.

There are several advantages to having small-scale industries.

[20] O. Lange, *Papers on Economics and Sociology*, op. cit., pp. 443-56.

Being small projects, they can be widely dispersed throughout the country, thus enabling the process of industrialization to start in rural areas and smaller centres where large industries will not be established for a long time. They create new employment opportunities locally and serve as a check on migration to towns. They establish a learning process to an understanding of a commodity economy. They offer opportunities for efficient use of ploughs, tractors, engines, power machinery, etc. through servicing and repair. They can accommodate changing demands more flexibly than can large industries and they can also complement the activities of large industries by producing components for the latter and process the semi-finished products of large industries as well as of agriculture.[21]

There is no doubt that the dispersal of production in small units in villages or small towns would be particularly suited to the social and economic conditions and needs of Tanzania at the present time; it would at least be consistent with the policy of ujamaa socialism. Tanzania has many geographical, linguistic and ethnic regions with large differences in climate, food habits and social customs. Small-scale industries would be ideally suited to taking advantage of such a diversified demand pattern. Moreover, if mechanized industrial occupations can be established in the countryside, many of the workers would stay in or near villages which would ensure an adequate supply of agricultural labour at peak periods. This suggests that the establishment of small industries must be co-ordinated with the agricultural and large industrial sectors. Furthermore, such a policy of dispersal would have political advantages as well. It would tend to create a large number of small-scale enterprises which would be organized on a socialist co-operative basis, providing a sound foundation for a socialist society based on ujamaa.

Two other aspects of resource allocation need emphasizing. One is that the allocation of investments between the various branches must be guided by the need to establish symmetry between the structure of consumption and the structure of production. This is, of course, why we have concentrated attention on the capital goods industries. At the present time when Tanzania imports almost all her capital requirements, it is essential to establish such industries. Probably about 40 per cent of the investments must be geared to this sector; at least the proportion of investments geared to the production of

[21] ILO, *Services for Small-Scale Industries* (Geneva, 1961).

the basic means of production must be large enough to overcome the threshold below which gradual change dissipates without tangible results. Such an approach would result in a new qualitative situation where economic development becomes a self-generating process. The *product-mix* of the capital goods sector must, however, reflect the pattern of wage goods as specified below.

The pattern of wage goods must reflect the socialist orientations of the country, which in broad terms imply that the development of productive forces should be done only within the context of the development of human beings and of encouraging them to realize fully their manifold creative powers in such a way that everyone rises together. In the introduction to his *Freedom and Unity*, for example, President Nyerere says:

> Underlying everything must be a consciousness that the very purpose of society—its reason for existence—is and must be the individual man, his growth, his health, his security, his dignity and therefore his happiness.[22]

These considerations imply that investment in *education* occupies a key role in the development process. There are several reasons for this emphasis on education. On the one hand, education of *all* the people is seen as the foundation for the development of the individual, and this in turn increases his usefulness to society and thus makes for the development of the country. In other words, the mobilization of human resources is regarded as the touchstone for the mobilization of economic resources. On the other hand, since in a socialist society the status and opportunities of individuals are not largely determined by their ownership of capital or land, but are controlled by their occupational status which in part depends on the level of education acquired (and the skills hopefully ensuing from that education), it becomes necessary to provide education for all in order to ensure egalitarianism. Of course, the nature of education under socialism must be such as to lead to greater productivity while encouraging selflessness, active participation, etc. Such an emphasis on education implies investments in such backward linkage industries as paper, printing and publishing, etc.

Secondly, the goals of the Tanzanian society imply an improvement of life in the *rural areas*. The rationale for the priority of the rural sector was advanced in part I and will not be repeated here. The

[22] J. K. Nyerere, *Freedom and Unity* (Dar es Salaam, Oxford University Press, 1966), p. 7.

investment implications are the need to increase the production of farm implements and to explore other investment choices, e.g. fertilizer use, improvements of seed varieties, control of insects and diseases, etc.

A third industry which is related to the development of the rural sector but which needs treatment in its own right is the transport industry, which remains one of the bottlenecks of development in Tanzania. Part of the reason is that transport networks were undertaken to carry colonial produce to the sea where it could be shipped to the metropolitan centres. Occasionally, they were established to ease administration. But there was little attempt to bring transport networks to bear on the expansion of the domestic market. The rural population requires improvements in roads and increases in bus and truck services. This implies greater production of buses, trucks, cement, lime and bitumen. The latter products can be produced domestically and by a careful study of local moisture conditions in soils, it should be possible to reduce design thicknesses of roads, thus making savings in construction costs.

For the urban population, a different problem has emerged. The absence of good, reliable public transportation in the past resulted in a rising car import bill.[23] The earlier instruments for regulating motor vehicle imports were import duties. In late 1971 car imports were virtually banned. But neither of these two policies solve the basic problem, which is that of providing an alternate transport mechanism. Given the structure of society at the present time, such policies as have been followed can only lead to further segmentation of society. Moreover, it is important to establish correct policies in this sector because the longer an incorrect policy is followed, the harder it is to change both politically and economically.

The fourth area of emphasis is *health*. A socialist government must aim at providing free health and medical care. This requires an increase in medical personnel, hospitals and equipment. More fundamental, however, is the approach to socialist medicine which, especially in the conditions of rural Tanzania, must be mainly concerned with *preventing* illness for all the people, no matter where they live or how low their

---

[23] The total number of licensed private motor vehicles rose from in 17,461 1960-2 to 29,784 in 1969, indicating an annual growth rate of 7.9 per cent over the period. The automobile import bill rose from sh. 28 million in 1964 to sh. 36 million in 1966, slackened after the early months of the Arusha Declaration to its 1964 level in 1967, but thereafter continued to accelerate attaining a level of sh. 35 million by 1969. The United Republic of Tanzania, *The Economic Survey and Annual Plan, 1970-1971* (Dar es Salaam, Government Printer, 1970).

incomes.[24] Closely related to health is the provision of better and more adequate water supplies and food, and the establishment of an indigenous pharmaceutical industry. Greater research should be allocated to tapping the potential of traditional medicine.

A fifth priority is *housing*. The provision of decent housing to all is a very important policy goal of any socialist government. The construction of these houses, whether communally-owned as in ujamaa villages or through a national agency such as the National Housing Corporation, requires the availability of such basic imports as cement, bricks, tiles, corrugated iron sheets, wooden furniture and fixtures, etc.

The last priority area is *rural electrification*, the effects of which can be extended to the social, agricultural and industrial spheres. Electricity helps to improve the services of hospitals by making it possible to use modern equipment, and in education by giving facilities for evening classes, etc. It can also be used in irrigation work, in processing and in large manufacturing plants.

These six areas then: education, rural development, transport, health (including water supplies), housing and electricity, provide the focus around which industrial activities must be generated. The industrial activities, in the form of instruments of production (i.e. raw materials and capital goods) and whose limited output is a constraint to the attainment of the above wage goods, constitute the core activities of industrial policy. They symbolize the establishment of strategy in the sense that their presence can set the economy in motion.

A final aspect of resource allocation relates to the division of labour between the centre and the regions. We know that on the whole the socialist economy is and must be centrally directed. Without this, it would develop haphazardly, and the conscious shaping of economic development would be impossible. Thus centralism in the planning of such an economy is essential. However, we also know that a certain degree of decentralization in everyday management is necessary, if only to ensure flexibility in the operation of the economy. In the case of Tanzania decentralization must be an important policy measure in order to encourage people's initiatives in establishing their order of priorities. The important questions are, however, how much decentralization? and What should be the scope of decentralization? Fortunately, the new science of cybernetics provides us with an important approximation to the above questions. For it says that

[24] Leo Huberman and P. M. Sweezy, *Socialism in Cuba* (New York, Monthly Review Press, 1969).

decentralization is necessary where the time needed for the flow of information from the outfield to the centre, for the information received at the centre to be made into a decision, and for the transmission of the decision from the centre back to the outfield is so long that certain irreversible changes may have meanwhile taken place in the outfield, thus rendering the decision inoperative.[25] Thus cybernetics gives us two crucial variables to consider: the *time* taken for the information and its attendant answer to be relayed and the *capacity* of the centre to transform information into decisions. It will be readily evident that both variables imply a high degree of decentralization in the Tanzanian context.

6.4 SOCIALIST PRODUCTION RELATIONS

Turning now to the problem of production relations, we note first that the ownership of the means of production provides the workers in those enterprises with *opportunities* to restore their dignity in the work process. For it is now generally recognized that the dignity of the worker cannot be maintained unless the work process allows autonomy, responsibility and self-fulfilment.[26] These in turn can only be attained if (i) there is no separation of worker from ownership of the means of production, (ii) workers are able to influence general managerial decisions and (iii) workers are able to control their immediate work process as well as their conditions of employment. Obviously, as has been suggested above, these relations of production are not automatically guaranteed by the act of nationalization, even though the latter provides the material basis for initiating the necessary changes. In what follows, I shall endeavour to outline briefly the framework within which the major aspects of production relations must be carried out, i.e. worker participation and incentive structure, if the workers will *eventually* attain autonomy, responsibility and self-fulfilment in their work activities.

First, the workers in every production unit must acquire skills not only in the individual aspects of the work process which they

25 O. Lange, *Papers on Economics and Sociology*, op. cit., p. 515.
26 F. G. West, 'The Political Economy of Alienation: Karl Marx and Adam Smith', *Oxford University Papers* (N.S) vol. 21 (1969), pp. 21-3; R. Blauner, *Alienation and Freedom* (Chicago, University of Chicago Press, 1967); and F. Pappenheim, *The Alienation of Modern Man* (New York, Monthly Review Press, 1959).

have either been working on or are expected to work on, but in the mechanism of the entire production unit as well. They must also understand the relationship between their productive unit and society at large, they must be aware of the significance of their productive efforts in raising the standard of living of the country. Workers must gradually recognize the forces of society as their *forces propres*; that is, they must identify their interest with the increase of social rather than of private wealth and their pride with collective rather than with individual achievement. This was effectively expressed by the *Nationalist* in its editorial of 20 October 1970 when it pointed out on the occasion of the establishment of the Workers' Council at the Ubungo Farm Implements Factory that

> . . . . what is now required is an intensification of the workers' education programme to include not only reading and writing, but trade skills and management of people's industries. NUTA through its workers' education programme must concentrate on these subjects so that no chance is given to the enemies of socialism who will be quick at pointing out the shortcomings or failure of workers' management. In taking over management, the workers must all the time bear in mind that the industries belong not only to the workers but to their compatriots, the peasants as well. In the majority of cases, it will help the peasants who will be supplying the raw materials or buying the finished products. Thus, in considering the needs of the factory workers, the new management will also have to con-sider the needs of the peasants outside the factory.

It is from such an educational base that other reforms can be meaning-fully implemented.

Secondly, the work process must be rationalized in such a way as to allow for greater participation of the majority of workers in decision-making. Increased participation will lead to more interest and commitment to the job; it may generate genuinely helpful sugges-tions from the shopfloor worker which frequently outpace those of the more remote management. Moreover, worker participation may promote better and quicker communication of ideas between workers and management to ensure the rapid heading off of potential conflict. The results of the above may be real and immediate benefits from the workers' interest in their jobs as well as an important learning process. Certainly workers' participation must be seen as a prerequisite for workers' control. It is a period during which it is hoped that the worker will begin to feel more interest in matters about which he is properly informed, to have more responsibility for decisions in which he has participated and an enhanced sense of satisfaction and commitment in his work because, whatever his job, his ideas merit consideration and his decision may, even in some small way, influence his working life.

It must be pointed out, however, that the *right* to manage the enterprise in which he works is one thing for the worker; the *effective exercise* of his right is something else. The latter is often obstructed by survivals of the past, as for example a lack of skills, a lack of consciousness and the socio-economic reality of the transitional period with its attendant paucity of information and scarcity of manpower. It is at the present moment in Tanzania also blocked by a lack of a *sense of responsibility* on the part of the majority of workers; the failure to realize that rights go with duties and responsibilities.

The above suggestions concerning worker participation imply a significant change in the orientation of the workers' movement, NUTA, which must be made to appreciate its role in the socialist context, namely that the improvement of the workers' welfare consists not only in enlarging their private consumption but in expanding collective consumption and in improving the other conditions of work (i.e. maximizing the non-alienating aspects of the work process). Through its educational programmes, NUTA should anticipate management decisions (especially during this period of 'contractual' management), it should try to influence them even before they are made. It should endeavour to place the workers in an offensive rather than a defensive position. It should aid the workers to specify their goals (and their responsibilities), which should be aimed at a strategic and programme orientated outlook.

Government, too, must appreciate the fact that NUTA cannot play this role without a *high degree of autonomy*. This is so because the permanent role of the labour union must be to express and articulate the workers' real needs and to work towards their satisfaction. The role of the national plan, on the other hand, in whose formulation the union must have every interest in participating, must be to organize the means for the satisfaction of those needs. *The tension between the needs and the means to satisfy them must be accepted by the leadership as the driving force of economic planning and of democracy in the period of transition towards socialism.*

Another policy implication of worker participation centres on the relationship between enterprise and the parastatal, and between the parastatal and government ministries. The pattern of worker participation described above assumes a specific relation between them, namely a degree of autonomy on decisions made by the workers. Enterprises must be given a certain amount of autonomy in carrying out their investment projects. For example, they must be allowed to determine their output assortment (i.e. the plan should not dictate whether Bora Shoes should produce so many ladies shoes, or so many black shoes, etc., but only the level of total shoe production). Enterprises must also have the financial flexibility to cater for unforeseen repairs and to initiate technical improvements to augment production. The financial resources of these enterprises must consist partly of a depreciation fund and some bank credit allocated to them.

A final aspect of production peripherally related to worker participation hinges on the choice of techniques. This has often been discussed in terms of factor combinations and factor input relations (especially the factor-price frontier). Given fixed factors, it is argued that a given technique will be chosen if its factor price configuration is such as to minimize total cost or conversely to maximize total surplus. In other words, to the extent that there is abundance of labour and shortage of capital, then a labour-intensive (capital saving) technique will be chosen, provided of course that there exists no market imperfections. If market imperfections exist, then it is conceivable that a capital-intensive technique may be chosen, though it will be 'inefficient'. Conversely, under the above conditions, the choice of a capital-intensive technique implies market imperfections, or discontinuity in the factor intensities of those techniques.

It is quite obvious that the 'imperfect market' as well as the 'technique discontinuity' arguments assume that the demanders of capital equipment operate in the same market configuration as the producers of that equipment. For if they do not, as is certainly the case in underdeveloped countries, the argument has very little explanatory value. For even if these problems were overcome by establishing an indigenous capital goods industry in the underdeveloped countries, it may not always be appropriate to have labour intensive techniques if their production potential per unit of output is very low. Furthermore, labour-intensive techniques may not be applicable in certain industries.

It would seem to me, however, that the most important consideration for a society tending towards socialism is that choice of techniques should not be concerned with the factor-price frontier (the law of value problem!) but should be geared to satisfying socialist relations of production. Techniques should be chosen with the intention to minimize alienation, to improve co-operation in the work force and to encourage the dignity of work, etc. Here is a whole area of research that has hardly received attention.

With respect to the *incentive structure*, we should note that the plan is a logical elaboration, an aspect which cannot be said of its management. The plan has to be applied by men, by millions of men who have to be interested in the execution of the plan. It is thus necessary to introduce into the national economy a system of incentives which will induce individuals and various organizations to act in the directions outlined in the plan. This must be taken as an important policy issue since effective systems of incentives tap enormous reservoirs of creative energy which might otherwise be wasted. By governing *behaviour*, incentives directly affect the rate of economic growth and by governing *consciousness*, they indirectly accelerate or retard the emergence of socialist man.

It is important to pay special attention to the behavioural implications of incentives in so far as they affect economic growth. Once the means of production become owned by the whole society (i.e. state ownership), the ownership principle of distribution ceases to operate and *during the period of transition* to socialism is replaced by the *principle of distribution according to work* (i.e. quantity and quality of work done). This is an important point to keep in mind because the period of transition is still in the realm of 'necessity' rather than in the realm of 'freedom'. Given this fact, it is important that we change our wage and salary structure to reflect the operation of the principle of distribution according to work done. At the present time this is not so, for the administration takes the upper hand. For example innovative engineers and doctors cannot expect to be rewarded according to their achievements unless they become administrators! This not only results in dissipation of scarce skills but is unjust as well.

Consideration must also be given to the level of consciousness needed to create incentives. For example, incentives that increase productivity by improving the technical level and organization of labour ultimately give far better results than those obtained by techniques of increasing individual productivity. And such incentives call for little use of individual material incentives. They are best furthered by collective *bonuses*, or by sharing in the supplementary results of an enterprise. Such types of incentives have the advantage of favouring the cohesion and internal solidarity of the working class, but this can only be realized if parochialism in enterprise is resolutely combated.

Thus, although the problem of incentives has normally been discussed in the framework of 'material' versus 'moral' incentives, it may be preferable to discuss it in terms of 'private' versus 'collective' incentives in the period of transition. Moral incentives, i.e. the devotion of the masses to the revolution, their conscious participation in building socialism, depend crucially on the historical circumstances of the working classes. In a situation of initial poverty, moral incentives are difficult to sustain because of the masses' time preference and pre-capitalist work habits. Consequently, emphasis on moral incentives may tend, during the crucial period of transition, to be reduced to mere voluntarist exhortations with less and less effect on productive effort. Private incentives therefore should be the predominant ones during the early part of the period of transition, and these should be governed by the principle of distribution according to work done. They should be supplemented, however, by collective incentives in the form of expanding collective goods and should be governed according to *need*.

The above discussion reveals the elements of socialist planning. Some of the steps have already been taken by Tanzania. It should be pointed out, however, that when implementing the measures of reconstructing the economy various problems will be encountered. Some of these arise from the historical heritage of capitalism and underdevelopment and are continually intensified by the processes of ideological and political infiltrations from the imperialist countries. Others will result from the *very* process of building socialism. Finally, other difficulties will arise from the fact that the development of a socialist society is also subject to the laws of dialectics. For socialism does not mean the absence of contradictions in social and economic development. In other words, the differences between socialism and earlier social systems does not consist in the absence of contradictions in the former, but in their different nature and in the way of overcoming them.[27] In our present conditions, moreover, the above three types of contradictions and difficulties are entangled. They should be perceived and scientifically analysed no matter whether they are inherited from the past or are peculiar to the period of transition, or whether they arise from the inner dialectics of current and developing socialist institutions. At the moment only the first type is widely acknowledged; this stems from the heritages of the past, which are still predominant, although the ease of shifting responsibility

[27] O. Lange, *Papers on Economics and Sociology*, op. cit. pp. 418-21.

to 'sabotage' may also be a factor. The danger of not seeing the nature of problems in their proper perspective is to build up the illusion among the people that all these shortcomings will automatically disappear with the progress of socialist reconstruction.

More significant, however, is the following consideration. The intermediate goals and the structural changes that have been briefly outlined above constitute a strategy and an economic structure which when it emerges will escape reabsorption into capitalism (albeit state capitalism). This can happen *only* if they are presented from the beginning as successive approximations and stages towards a socialist society which is their meaning. If the overall perspective is lacking (and in the absence of any idea about the length of the transition, this will be most likely), then the sum total of the changes that have already been undertaken, and those I have suggested, however advanced they may be, will at best degenerate into perverse capitalist development in which the power of capital and alienated labour will survive and underdevelopment will persist.

APPENDIX I

SOURCES OF DATA

Most of the data used in chapters 4 and 5 is taken from the *Survey of Industrial Production, 1966* (hereafter referred to as the *Survey*).[1] This is the latest industrial survey available and it is the second most comprehensive one. Earlier surveys of industrial production were carried out by the East African Statistical Department for 1954, 1956 and 1958 and by the Central Statistical Bureau for 1961 and 1963. Due to the incompleteness of the returns, poor response rate, differences in concepts, coverage and definitions used, the result of these surveys makes them incomparable and unusable for most of our purposes. This leaves the surveys of industrial production for 1965 and 1966, which are generally comparable except that the former includes sisal decortication and processing activities (other than into baler twine, cordage and rope) while the latter does not, and also the 1966 survey includes establishments which were set up after 1965, especially the cement factory, the oil refinery, the match factory at Moshi, the diamond cutting factory at Iringa and the sisal cordage, rope and twine factory at Tanga. Since I was not particularly interested in sisal decortication and the two surveys obviously could not form a basis for any time series analysis, I have used the 1966 survey for a significant part of the following analysis.

Surveys of industrial production use an establishment, i.e. an individual factory or workshop engaged in the production of a homogeneous group of goods and services, as its basic unit. Only establishments engaging ten persons or more are included in the surveys. This means that small-scale establishments and cottage industries are excluded from the data presented. The lack of information on small-scale establishments is unfortunate since it might have enabled us to study the possibility of encouraging such enterprises (on the basis of co-operatives, for example). Coverage of the large-scale establishments by the 1966 survey is quite adequate. Out of about 500 questionnaires sent (apart from close-downs, etc.), there were 438 usable returns which form the basis of this study.

[1] United Republic of Tanzania, *Survey of Industries, 1966* (Central Statistical Bureau, Ministry of Economic Affairs and Development Planning, 1969).

There are considerable statistical problems with the data presented in the *Survey*. First, most information is available at a two-digit level of the SIC classification. As is well known the two-digit industry groups are composed of many diverse component industries, and the groups differ in the degree of internal diversity as well as in size, age, pattern of technological and market history, and so on. This raises many problems of aggregation which we need not enter into now but which are very serious especially when international comparisons are attempted. Ideally one would have liked to establish one's own standards of industry definition so that the terms 'industry' and 'market' would correspond, and then to cross-classify these ideal industries on the basis of full information about their potentially important characteristics. This procedure is difficult to follow, however, even when some information is available of some sub-sample of the industry because of the intractability of data and the inadequacy of our basic information and concepts. We are therefore forced to rely to a very great extent on the SIC system and on survey data compiled on that basis, with minor adjustments to be introduced from time to time. These adjustments originate from a small survey I carried out in 1969 of some 36 firms, largely in an attempt to supplement the information contained in the *Survey*. The list of the firms was extracted from the Directory of Industries, 1967. The choice of the firms examined was dictated by size (in terms of employment) and availability of information. Only the largest firms were chosen (representing about 70 per cent of industrial value added). Furthermore, these firms were located in Dar es Salaam, Tanga, Arusha and Moshi, areas I was able to visit during the months of July and August 1969.

Secondly, the *Survey* data contains no information on fixed assets and capital structure. Nor is there any indication of utilization of plant. The datum on surplus, which is supposed to be interpreted as gross margin, is biased downward for at least two reasons. On the one hand it is *net* of depreciation. To the extent that this rate is fixed by special regulations relating to tax deductions, it permits the writing off of a large part of the value of fixed assets during the first years of plant operation. This practice was introduced as an additional incentive for investors, who are thus enabled to avoid taxation of a part of their profits, assumed to represent depreciation charges. The latter do not therefore represent the real wear and tear of fixed assets but contain some sort of 'hidden profits'. On the other hand the surplus is obtained after deducting as part of the cost a term called 'other costs of production', which includes, apart from transport (a genuine deductable expense), common services, maintenance costs of capital assets and advertising costs. While some of these costs accord with conventional accounting principles, they are sometimes (especially with respect to foreign firms) allocated in a way that tends to inflate expenses, thus reducing the book value of surplus.[2] Mention should also be made of the failure to include 'monopolistic profits' accruing to some of the larger firms because of the written down excessive unit costs of imported materials and components.

Thirdly, the *Survey* data is likely to be biased downwards in the computed values of labour productivity in cases of those enterprises which are established during the year. This is because it does not correct industrial output for days worked. The output of the refinery which began production in July is recorded as annual output. This discrepancy has been corrected where information was available, especially in comparing labour productivities internationally, though errors due to lack of information certainly remain.

Fourthly, it must be noted that to the extent the age, record of technological change, level and pattern of change of demand and inter-industry position of each group of establishments are unique, they are not comparable among industries even ordinally. However, many of these industrial characteristics, often difficult to describe in general terms, are apt to be more similar among industries closely related in terms of products, technology or specific sources of demand (as classified under SIC) than among industries selected at random from the entire population.

Finally, there remains one important statistical problem which requires some extensive clarification—my constant use of cross-section data. One obvious reason for my resorting to cross-section data is due to the unavailability of comparable time-series data on industrial structure. There is, however, a more fundamental reason that justifies my use of cross-section data. As is well known, the manufacturing process may be studied in several ways. For instance, changes in manufacturing activity may be indicated by a comparison of output during successive periods, i.e. time serially. This method of analysis which has been adopted by many economists in their inquiry of the structure of

[2] For instance one shoe firm reported sh. 2.5 million as 'other costs' when total gross output for the year was sh. 7.8 million. This is a firm with no burdening rental and transportation costs. Clearly a significant portion of 'other costs' is another form of hidden profits.

manufacturing industry usually gives acceptable measures of the varying success of the manufacturing process but tells little about the manufacturing process itself.[3] In other words, it does not indicate, for example, the relative importance of the various types of manufacturing activity, nor does it reveal the relative proportions in which productive resources are employed in the manufacture of different types of goods. For a study of 'endogenous' structural change—the type of change embedded in the manufacturing process itself, we must turn to cross-section data.[4]

A cross-section picture of manufacturing is intended to describe manufacturing operations at some given time. Accordingly, a cross-section study is essentially descriptive and in form suggests a 'static' analysis of an admittedly dynamic economy. Artificial in certain respects as such a study must be, it nevertheless can yield fruitful information. For if our interest lies in the changes that mark the development of an evolving economic system, the first step is our appraisal in the light of the circumstances of some particular time. Every researcher of the varying composition of manufacturing output, for example, or of the changing characteristics of manufacturing operations, must have some bench-mark for his findings.

However, since any cross-sectional study must pertain to some specific period, its findings will reflect circumstances peculiar to the time of observation—the combination of forces tending to continue relationships of a prior period and forces making for change. The fact that, for example, the government took a majority shareholding in some of the large manufacturing establishments in 1967 might be construed as an indication of a substantial shift in industrial structure which would invalidate the significance of the present study. Yet without denying the significance of the nationalization measures, I wish to reaffirm the view presented in chapter 2 that the above

[3] See for example Z. Griliches, 'Production Functions in Manufacturing: Some Preliminary Results' in *The Theory and Empirical Analysis of Production*, M. Brown (ed.) (New York, Columbia University Press for National Bureau of Economic Research, 1967), pp. 277-322; G. H. Hildebrand and T. C. Liu, *Manufacturing Production Function in the U.S., 1957* (Cornell Studies in Industrial and Labour Relations no. 15, Ithaca, New York, 1965); J. R. Maroney, 'Cobb-Douglas Production Functions and Returns to Scale in U.S. Manufacturing Industry', *Western Economic Journal* (December 1967), pp. 39-51 and Marc Nerlove, 'Recent Empirical Studies of the CES and Related Production Functions' in *The Theory and Empirical Analysis of Production*, M. Brown (ed.).
[4] Charles A. Bliss, *The Structure of Manufacturing Production: A Cross-Section View* (New York, National Bureau of Economic Research, 1939), pp. 3-8.

measures have as yet involved insignificant structural changes. The acquisition of majority shareholding by the government, though very important in the long run, has not yet (and will not in the short run) affected sectoral distribution, choice of techniques, inter-industry relations, location or even management. Nevertheless, it remains true, of course, that any given year presents an admixture of continuous, i.e. permanent, relationships and transitory elements. As this admixture is likely to vary in the different relations to be studied, some of the conclusions to be derived subsequently must keep these issues in mind.

APPENDIX II

TABLE A2.1

Number of factories registered as of
31 December 1964, by industry and employment

Code	Industry	Number of factories		Total	Employment
		With power	No power		
20	Food manufacturing				
	Bacon manufacturing	1	—	1	3
	Bread and flour confectionery	31	59	90	653
	Coffee curing	9	—	9	899
	Coffee manufacture	1	—	1	16
	Coffee pulping	141	24	165	1,886
	Copra drying	3	2	5	66
	Dairy produce	6	3	9	102
	Edible oil refining	5	—	5	33
	Fish curing	—	1	1	78
	Flour milling	1,986	20	2,006	7,859
	Food manufacture	6	2	8	65
	Food canning	6	—	6	1,522
	Fruit cordial manufacture	3	—	3	35
	Honey processing	1	—	1	21
	Jaggery manufacture	62	—	62	813
	Ice manufacture	7	—	7	55
	Milk pasteurizing	11	3	14	163
	Nuts processing (cashew)	3	1	4	534
	Rice mills and hulleries	150	1	151	1,532
	Salt manufacture	1	—	1	9

	Seafood processing	1	—	1	12
	Sugar confectionery	8	2	10	157
	Sugar manufacture	6	—	6	924
	Tea manufacture	23	—	23	1,262
21	Beverage industries				
	Aerated water manufacture	39	23	62	560
	Bottling of wines and spirits	1	—	1	16
	Breweries	3	—	3	455
22	Tobacco manufacture				
	Tobacco processing	34	60	94	3,771
23	Manufacture of textiles				
	Coir fibre processing	6	—	6	461
	Cotton ginning	43	—	43	5,034
	Cotton weaving	3	—	3	333
	Cotton-wool products	1	—	1	30
	Kapok ginning	13	—	13	201
	Sisal decortication	243	—	243	25,243
	Sisal ropes and twine	2	—	2	202
	Textile dyeing and bleaching	5	—	5	707

Code	Industry	Number of factories			Employment
		With power	*No power*	*Total*	
24	Footwear and apparel				
	Blanket manufacture	1	—	1	314
	Clothing manufacture	1	—	1	400
	Footwear manufacture	9	129	138	519
	Tailoring and dressmaking	44	937	981	2,485
25	Manufacture of wood except furniture				
	Saw milling	111	1	112	3,266
	Wood working, general	355	75	430	4,378
27-28	Manufacture of paper products				
	Printing and publishing				
	Letterpress printing	41	5	46	1,079
	Paper conversion (paper bags)	3	—	3	51
29	Manufacture of leather products				
	Hides, skins processing and baling	3	35	38	457
	Tanneries	2	—	2	76
30	Rubber products				
	Rubber processing	2	2	4	54
	Tyre retreading	7	—	7	58
31	Manufacture of chemical and products				
	Chemical products manufacture	6	—	6	143
	Essential oil extraction	3	—	3	24
	Industrial gas manufacture	1	—	1	24
	Paint manufacture	3	—	3	80
	Papain manufacture	14	6	20	49

	(1)	(2)	(3)	(4)
Pyrethrum drying	20	21	41	
Soap manufacture	42	17	59	498
Vegetable oil extraction	80	1	81	1,286
33 Non-metallic mineral products				
Brick and tile manufacture	12	8	20	609
Cement processing	1	—	1	10
Mica cutting and grading	1	2	3	108
Pre-cast concrete works	6	2	8	95
Stone grading and crushing	17	1	18	203
34–35 Metals and metal products	2	—	2	26
Aluminium manufacturing	1	—	1	166
Aluminium rolling mills	2	—	2	372
Can manufacture	1	—	1	65
Enamelling	1	—	1	130
Galvanizing metalware	1	—	1	10
Nail manufacture	1	—	1	30
Razor blades manufacture	1	—	1	26
Scrap metal processing	3	1	4	16
Screw manufacture	1	—	1	
Sheet metalwork	10	15	25	140
Wrought iron works	5	—	5	20
36–37 Manufacture and repair of machinery	27	2	29	198
Agricultural plant, maintenance, repair	2	1	3	11
Assembly and repair	29	4	33	238
Electrical repairs	1	—		2
Electro plating				
Engineering, general	154	11	165	2,850
Light engineering, assembly	1	—	1	9
Typewriter and other repair	2	2	4	14

Code	Industry	Number of factories		Total	Employment
		With power	*No power*		
38	Manufacture and assembly of transport equipment				
	Aircraft maintenance	2	1	3	36
	Bicycle assembly and repair	1	30	31	72
	Boat building and repair	2	1	3	263
	Dock equipment repairs	6	1	7	73
	Locomotive and rolling stock repairs	13	—	13	2,057
	Marine engineering	2	1	3	49
	Motor vehicle repairing	293	51	344	4,780
39	Miscellaneous manufacture				
	Gunsmith—gun repairing	1	—	1	3
	Jewellers and goldsmiths	3	26	29	121
	Mattress manufacture	1	—	1	8
	Meerschaum pipe manufacture	1	—	1	200
	Neon sign manufacture	1	—	1	5
	Photographic development and printing	14	3	17	77
	Plastic manufacture	3	—	3	165
	Sign writing	—	1	1	4
	Watch repairing	1	7	8	13

Source: Labour Division, Ministry of Labour.

APPENDIX III

STATIC CHARACTERISTICS OF TANZANIAN INDUSTRY

As pointed out in appendix I, sometimes great importance is to be attached to an examination of the system in its static cross-sectional aspects in order to underscore the interrelationships that define a system at a specific time period. This is done in this appendix partly in order to explain further some of the data used in chapter 5. The discussion is largely confined to two topics: (a) cost structure and inter-industry relations, and (b) efficiency and factor productivity.

I.I COST STRUCTURE AND INTER-INDUSTRY RELATIONS

In classical and neo-classical theory, cost of production determines not only the commodity's supply price, it simultaneously determines the total of distributive payments to the factors utilized in the production process. In the latter form, the cost structure indicates the relative significance of various inputs used in the production process and hence the extent to which a given productive activity depends on other activities of the economic system, including the primary factors of production. The cost structure of manufacturing activities can therefore be used to study the various aspects of inter-sectoral relations. In this appendix I will be primarily concerned with examining the efficiency of the industrial structure and the degree of dependence between the various material and service-supplying sectors, in particular the extent to which the manufacturing industry depends on imports and the degree of the industrial base. Much of the emphasis will be placed on those measurable aspects of cost that have relevance to the theoretical framework indicated in chapter 3.

Any examination of cost-output or cost-input relations faces the problem of availability and accuracy of data demanded. Thus in the study of comparative cost efficiency at industrial level, one assumes that one possesses comparable data on establishments of various industrial origin and scale. These plants or establishments are assumed to

TABLE A3.1

The structure of costs in Tanzanian manufacturing industry, 1966

(a) Variable costs (in per cent of unit cost)

Code	Industrial group	Materials	Energy	Wage bill	Services	Total
20	Food manufacturing industries	65.0	2.0	5.5	0	72.5
21	Beverage industries	45.5	2.3	4.7	0	52.5
22	Tobacco manufactures	35.5	0.6	7.9	0	44.0
23	Manufacture of textiles	75.2	1.1	4.3	0	80.6
24	Footwear and wearing apparel	69.4	0.6	8.1	0	78.1
25	Wood products except furniture	29.0	4.2	17.1	0.5	50.8
26	Furniture and fixtures	41.7	1.7	20.2	0.3	63.9
27	Paper products	60.7	0.4	4.3	0	65.4
28	Printing and publishing	49.7	1.4	24.3	0	75.4
29	Leather products	92.4	0.1	1.4	0	93.9
30	Rubber products	32.4	2.7	9.1	0	44.2
31-32	Chemicals, chemical products, petroleum	71.1	3.0	4.5	0	78.6
33	Non-metallic mineral products	58.4	4.4	8.8	0	72.0
34-35	Basic metal industries and products	68.1	2.1	6.9	0	77.1
36	Repair of non-electrical machinery	32.0	5.6	14.0	0	51.6
37	Assembly and repair of electrical machinery	80.1	0.2	5.8	0	86.1
38	Assembly of transport equipment	40.7	1.1	17.4	0	59.2
39	Miscellaneous manufacturing	57.7	1.8	16.6	0.1	76.2
2-3	All manufacturing	64.9	1.8	6.6	0	71.3

(b) *Fixed Costs and Surplus (in per cent of unit cost)*

Code	Industrial Group	Salary bill	Depreciation	Other costs	Total fixed	Surplus
20	Food manufacturing	3.8	4.2	9.6	17.6	9.9
21	Beverage industries	4.5	5.1	22.5	32.1	15.4
22	Tobacco manufacture	5.4	5.7	25.2	36.3	19.7
23	Textiles	2.3	2.3	4.7	9.3	10.1
24	Footwear and apparel	4.5	4.8	11.0	20.3	1.6
25	Wood products except furniture	6.2	5.9	20.9	33.0	16.2
26	Furniture and fixtures	6.6	5.2	5.9	14.7	21.4
27	Paper products	3.7	2.7	13.8	20.2	14.4
28	Printing and publishing	13.1	3.3	6.7	23.1	1.5
29	Leather products	1.7	0.2	3.5	5.4	0.7
30	Rubber products	7.9	4.5	7.5	19.9	35.9
31-32	Chemicals, chemical products, petroleum	6.8	3.3	7.5	17.6	3.8
33	Non-metallic mineral product	3.1	6.6	6.9	16.6	11.8
34-35	Basic metal industries and products	5.2	4.5	6.9	16.6	6.3
36	Repair of non-electrical machinery	14.1	3.8	8.4	26.3	22.1
37	Assembly and repair of electrical machinery	3.6	2.2	4.6	10.4	3.5
38	Assembly of transport equipment	8.0	2.8	7.5	18.3	22.5
39	Miscellaneous manufacturing	10.1	6.4	13.4	29.9	-6.1
2-3	All manufacturing	4.3	3.7	9.3	17.3	9.4

Source: Survey of Industrial Production, 1966.

buy and sell their input factors and product in the same or similar markets so that they are confronted with the same prices. Likewise it is assumed that each plant in any industrial classification produces and utilizes homogeneous output and factor inputs respectively.

It is obvious that the information I have available—the two-digit (SIC) standard industrial classification—does not satisfy the above assumptions. Apart from the cost aggregation problems, there are a great many ambiguities due to the lack of uniform accounting methods in the various enterprises. Furthermore the survey report that I have used has not separated types of categories of cost that are pertinent to my analysis. For example, administration, transport, rental and cost of repair and maintenance are all reported in one catch-all category of 'other costs'. In spite of these difficulties and problems of data, I have thought it imperative to resort to the structure of unit cost on an industry average in an attempt to get some insight into the above-mentioned issues, given the attributes of the various cost components and perhaps to identify some of the major cost items on which attention must be concentrated in any economizing effort. I have pointed out some of the problems underlying the data I use in this appendix not because it necessarily invalidates the analysis but only as a warning to the acceptance and to the interpretation of the results. And, despite the limitations of the data, one may be able to learn how the imperfect data and the theoretical data can be reconciled so that one may interpret the results accordingly.

From the obtained value of output per industrial classification, I have computed the unit cost of materials (including packing materials and chemicals), depreciation, energy (i.e. electricity, fuels, lubricants and water) and services from other activities (work given out). As for labour costs, other costs of production and surplus, I adopted the following techniques. Whereas the wages bill and the salary bill are given separately, fringe benefits (i.e. provident funds, pension funds and benefits in kind) were not divided between wage earners and salary earners. By assuming that fringe benefits depend upon income earned, I computed the 'imputed' share of wage earners in total wage and salary bill and applied that ratio on fringe benefits in order to obtain the value of fringe benefits to be imputed to the wage earners. Then these benefits were added to the total wage bill. By subtracting wage earners-imputed fringe benefits from total fringe benefits, I obtained the salary-earned fringe benefits which I added to the total salary bill. The data relating to wage and salary bills therefore *include* the imputed fringe benefits component. These benefits average 11 per cent of the total labour cost.

Other costs include transport costs (both the cost of operating own transport and transport costs paid to other firms), cost of maintenance and repair, rental and administrative costs. In order to partition total cost into variable and fixed costs, I would have liked to have had a breakdown of these costs into the above components. With the available data, however, I was not able to do so. I have therefore assumed that the component 'other costs' is dominated by administrative expenses and treated it as a fixed cost. Even if I had more disaggregated data, the transportation cost component would have been difficult to allocate since I would have required more detailed information at the industry level as to whether transport costs vary with output. In the given circumstances, I have assumed that though transport costs are not tightly linked to output changes, they are in the nature of the 'quasi-fixed' component and thus classifiable with administrative cost under fixed cost.

Among the variable costs, I have included material cost, energy cost, wage cost and services from other activities. All these costs are assumed to vary with the level of output, though no doubt small proportions of electricity and water may be invariant to variations in output. As for fixed costs, I have included depreciation, salary cost and other costs as defined above. Surplus per unit of output is obtained by subtracting value unit output from cost per unit of total variable and fixed costs.

After making this long, though necessary, digression, let me now turn to some of the implications of this table. In the first instance, table A3.1 indicates that over 70 per cent of the unit cost on an industrial average is represented by variable costs. In some industries (textiles, assembly and repair of electrical machinery) the proportion is 80 per cent, and in the case of leather products, variable costs account for over 90 per cent of unit cost. There are, however, a number of industries (beverages, tobacco, wood products, rubber, repair and assembly of non-electrical machinery) where variable cost per unit cost is very low, at least when compared with the overall economy. From such a structure of unit cost, and given the fact that the salary cost is very low, one can infer that the industrial structure is dualistic (see table A3.1). On the one hand, there are some industries with a very high variable cost structure whose degree of capitalization should be taken as low. Many of these industries would be dominated by small firms and a good proportion of them would be locally-owned. On the other hand, there are some industries with a low variable cost, and fairly high capitalization. These industries are likely to be foreign-owned. These observations must not be taken very strictly since, as I pointed out before, the allocation of cost between fixed and variable costs is far from perfect. They should rather be taken in a tentative manner.

Secondly, there is considerable variability among industrial groups in the composition of variable costs. For industry as a whole, materials account for 65 per cent of total unit cost. In some industries, e.g. wood, tobacco, repair and assembly of non-electrical machinery, transport equipment and rubber products, the proportion is much less, which indicates that these industries are generally not supply-based. Other industries such as leather products, assembly and repair of electrical machinery and textiles, exhibit contrary tendencies. These considerations have a great significance when one is interested in stimulating incentives for changing the industrial location.

The data on energy costs (electricity, fuels, lubricants and water) indicate that to date Tanzania has not yet developed an energy-intensive manufacturing sector. The energy component constitutes on the average 1.8 per cent of unit cost. This compares with 3.27 for Uganda and 2.6 for Kenya. The rather low energy cost per unit output arises from, or at least reflects, the fact that most of Tanzania's industries are close to final demand. Amann has found out that activities that add 'final touches' only are generally not energy-intensive.[1] The exception is non-metallic mineral products where cement is a large consumer of energy inputs, and non-electrical machinery where repair services consume considerable quantities of fuel and electricity. It should be pointed out, too, that the energy data include only purchases from energy supplying firms. This is especially true of the electricity data. Electricity supplied by individual establishments themselves is not recorded in the survey data. Therefore, and to the extent that such establishments are not uniformly spread over the various industrial categories, the energy data contains downward biases in certain industries. Note should be taken, however, of the low energy cost coefficients in industrial categories such as chemicals, metal products, electrical machinery which, as shown by Amann, reflect inadequate development in these fields relative to other countries. This limited development is exemplified by the composition of their output. In more developed economies, simple metal products such as cans, nails and screws,

[1] Hans Amann, *Energy Supply and Economic Development in East Africa* (Munich Weltforum Publishing House, 1969), p. 79.

constitute 6 per cent of the metal products industry whereas in Tanzania these constitute 100 per cent of the industry.[2] The same can be said of other industries.

The wage bill component is very low, 6.6 per cent on the average, as compared to, say, Greece with 11.9 per cent of unit cost and the United States with 21 per cent.[3] It is above the average in wood, furniture and fixtures, printing, assembly, and repair of transport equipment and miscellaneous manufacturing. It is quite obvious from labour's small share in total cost that it is *not* the decisive factor in the cost of production. This may be due to a low employment coefficient, that is, the existence of capital intensity, or due to low remuneration per labour unit due, presumably, to the unskilled character of the labour force, or both. The identification of the cause of low labour cost was discussed in chapter 5.

The column of work given out (see 'services', table A3.1) shows that inter-industry co-operation is still weak. This may be due to the lack of facilities to process by-products or a lack of research facilities to determine new uses for such by-products. The zero entries in the services sector denote the rather meagre economies of agglomeration. It is probable that Tanzanian firms send their by-products either to Kenya or abroad for further processsing.[4]

Salary cost is also low in unit cost, in comparison with other countries, though its relative size *vis-à-vis* wage unit cost is very high when compared with the industrialized economies. This reflects the high cost of management in these firms, the members of which probably receive higher salaries than they would receive elsewhere. Other costs are also high, reflecting either inefficiencies in management, expensive transportation facilities, or both.

The considerations of the structure of cost have important implications for policy. These were treated in part III. Before I turn to the problems of factor productivity, I must briefly discuss the industrial base and origin of industrial inputs.

The value added content indicates the extent to which intra-industry productive differentiation has proceeded. A relatively high ratio of value added implies low material content in the value of output and hence a

---

[2] Cy Cukor, 'The Growth of Engineering Industries in the Developing Countries', *Acta Oeconomica*, 3 (1968), p. 189.
[3] George Coutsoumaris, *The Morphology of Greek Industry* (Athens, Center for Economic Research, 1963).
[4] At Arusha Chini (sugar refining) the manager told me that as there were no facilities to process molasses, he was forced to ship the by-product abroad.

greater demand for primary factors and *vice versa*. The high material cost I have noted above means that the value added share in gross output is fairly small. This observation is, of course, consistent with the statement I made earlier to the effect that the cost structure reflects the fact that industry is for the most part limited to the very few final stages (last touches) of the manufacturing process. A comparison with corresponding data of other countries shows that Tanzania's share of manufacturing value added is small.

TABLE A3.2

Tanzania: value added per person engaged, in U.S. dollars (1966)

	10–19	20–49	50–99	100–499	500+	Total
20	2,382	1,571	1,002	1,125	2,238	1,388
21	812	1,844	9,219	2,584	—	3,051
22	—	828	—	—	2,467	2,426
23	1,365	526	884	1,151	904	1,056
24	519	522	635	653	704	667
25	1,037	955	942	597	—	767
26	712	1,781	786	1,382	—	1,134
27	1,793	2,821	—	—	—	2,413
28	853	1,229	972	1,193	—	1,124
29	47	850	1,741	—	—	910
30	4,448	2,480	—	—	—	2,750
31–32	1,504	1,926	3,716	1,764	172	1,581
33	154	—	913	1,196	—	1,016
34–35	1,050	1,810	7,596	1,345	—	1,814
36	2,854	1,982	1,473	—	—	1,880
37	594	1,390	—	—	—	1,293
38	1,392	1,193	1,789	—	—	1,503
39	1,482	739	356	657	—	664
Total	22,998	24,447	31,924	13,647	6,485	
Average	(1,353)	(1,438)	(2,280)	(1,240)	(1,297)	

Source: Survey of Industries, 1966.

Turning now to the origin of the manufacturing inputs in order to trace the degree of dependence of the industrial groups or the various supplying sectors, including imports, I note that such a task requires the construction of an input-output table. Since tracing linkage effects also required the same type of data, I decided to construct, from the scantily available data, an input-output table for the Tanzanian economy for the year 1966, giving prominence to the manufacturing sector. Appendix IV deals with some of the conceptual and methodological problems encountered in its construction and the way in which I approached them.

Table A4.1 presents a twenty-one sector input-output scheme (sixteen of which are manufacturing subdivisions) for Tanzania in 1966. Reading across gives a picture of the sales to the sector listed in a given row to each of the other sectors as well as sales to ultimate customers in the form of consumption investment and exports. These components of final demand are not differentiated because of the lack of data. All entries are in thousands of shillings and may be conceptualized either as shilling flows or as physical quantities, for which the unit of measure is 'a thousand shillings worth'. Thus the table reflects the pattern of commodity flows and structure of prices existing in Tanzania in 1966.

If the table is seen in shilling terms, one must add the elements in a sector's column to find the amount of total outlays for raw materials. The difference between the value of total output and the sum of material purchases is the 'value added' created in the production process. The shilling amount of value added is also a function of the price structure in the economy in 1966, or if one were to state values in the prices of another year, the magnitude of the value added residual would be altered.

Tables A4.2 and A4.3 give the inter-industry technical coefficients and the inverse matrix (or table of total requirements) respectively. These results were used in chapter 5 to aid the discussion on the inter-relatedness between industries.

The input-output table presented does not immediately reveal the degree of dependence of the manufacturing industry on the various supplying sectors because of the way it was constructed, explained in appendix IV. It is possible, however, to reconstruct the given information in that table in order to arrive at some meaningful measure of the manufacturing industry's relationship with other sectors. In table A3.4 I present the structure of manufacturing inputs by industrial origin. What I have done essentially is to consider the inputs (both primary and secondary) used to produce domestic output. I have neglected imports to the industry other than those used in the production process. I have then computed the contribution of primary production (agriculture and mining), services (commerce and public utilities), imports, labour, capital and other manufacturing activities. The degree of reliability varies from one industrial classification to another in the above sources of inputs. Let me discuss some of these relations briefly.

Industries that are dependent upon domestic primary sectors include food and soft drinks, cordage, rope and twine, leather and rubber products, non-metal products and processed export crops. It is obvious, of course, that processed export products, including cordage, rope and twine must depend to a large measure upon the domestic primary sectors. The non-metal products sector is influenced by building materials whose inputs are mineral products. These industries tend to have a fairly small share of wage bill in total product, which suggests that the processes involved are simple and require unskilled labour.

The contribution of inputs from other domestic manufacturing enterprises shows the extent of the industrial base. Table A3.4 indicates that, as one would expect, the industrial base for the Tanzanian economy is very narrow.[5] The production process is therefore incomplete. It is,

TABLE A3.3

Value added as per cent of gross output

Industry	Tanzania (1966)	Finland (1959)	Yugoslavia (1962)
Food manufacturing	0.22	0.32	0.46
Beverage industries	0.28	0.52	0.50
Tobacco manufacture	0.31	0.77	0.62
Textiles	0.19	0.77	0.37
Footwear and clothing	0.18	0.52	0.33
Wood except furniture	0.44	0.34	n.a.
Furniture and fixtures	0.43	0.54	n.a.
Paper products	0.25	0.30	0.32
Printing and publishing	0.36	0.52	0.57
Leather products	0.04	0.58	n.a.
Rubber products	0.56	0.72	0.47
Chemicals and petroleum	0.18	0.66	0.32
Non-metallic mineral products	0.30	0.57	0.48
Metal industries and products	0.22	0.40	n.a.
Non-electrical machinery	0.54	0.71	n.a.
Electrical machinery	0.14	0.65	0.42
Transport equipment	0.48	0.74	n.a.
Miscellaneous manufacturing	0.26	0.71	n.a.

Source: for Tanzania, *Survey of Industrial Production, 1966*. For Finland and Yugoslavia, United Nations, *Studies in Inter-industrial Relations* (New York, 1967).

[5] Although this might tend to suggest greater possibilities for backward linkage (5), these possibilities are limited by the nature of foreign investment as discussed earlier.

TABLE A3.4

Tanzania: the structure of manufacturing inputs by industrial origin, 1966 (per cent of total row)

Sector	From primary sectors (1)	From other manufacturing (2)	From imports (3)	From primary factors labour (4)	From primary factors capital (5)	From services (6)
Alcoholic beverages	0	46.7	12.1	12.8	25.0	4.4
Tobacco	29.0	26.2	5.7	13.4	25.3	0.3
Food and soft drinks	55.6	13.8	3.4	8.4	12.7	2.7
Foot wear and clothing	0	17.6	60.7	13.5	6.7	1.4
Textiles*	2.4	7.3	61.2	18.8	8.2	2.0
Paper and products**	0	8.4	49.8	32.3	6.8	2.7
Chemicals	14.4	11.0	56.2	9.7	6.6	2.1
Petroleum products	0	5.3	72.1	19.0	3.0	0
Cordage, rope and twine	50.5	10.5	8.1	12.6	15.9	2.4
Leather and rubber	84.3	4.0	0.5	4.2	4.3	2.7
Wood and furniture	10.5	18.3	4.3	24.2	22.3	11.6
Non-metal products	55.0	8.8	4.0	11.7	18.2	2.3
Metal products†	0	7.6	65.4	12.1	10.7	4.2
Processing for exports†	68.2	7.3	3.0	5.8	15.0	0.7
Maintenance and repair††	0	2.7	20.5	20.9	20.6	35.4
Miscellaneous manufacturing	0	0.2	15.6	26.3	0.3	57.6

Note: Because of the differences between earlier tables and the above, notation is given.

*Textiles excludes cotton ginning and cordage, rope and twine which has its own row.

**Paper and products includes printing and publishing and allied products.

†Processing for exports includes coffee, cashew nuts, cotton ginning and tea processing.

††Maintenance and repair includes what we called 'other costs' in the structure of cost table.

TABLE A3.5

Average labour productivity by sector, 1966

Sector	Product per man in the sector (*in shillings*)
Estate agriculture	2,750
Mining	55,340
Manufacturing	9,460
Construction	4,590
Public utilities	9,050
Commerce	36,600
Transport	8,960
Services	7,420

Source: United Republic of Tanzania, *Background to the Budget; An Economic Survey, 1968-69* (Dar es Salaam, 1968).

TABLE A3.6

Value added per person employed in selected countries (in U.S. dollars), in manufacturing industry

Country	Year	Average labour productivity
Tanzania	1966	1351
Zambia	1965	2470
Yugoslavia	1963	3712
Poland	1963	3129
USA	1966	13900

Source: For Tanzania, see above table (4.18). For other countries, United Nations, *The Growth of World Industry* (1967 edition), volume 1. *General Industrial Statistics, 1953-1966* (New York, United Nations, 1969).

however, supplemented by the foreign sector and so a considerable dependence of the manufacturing industry on imports can be discerned. The import column should be viewed as the lower limit, since my estimates have included only those categories of cost I was definitely certain were imports. It is shown in table A3.4 that industries which significantly depend upon imports for their inputs are footwear, clothing, textiles, paper, printing and publishing, chemicals, petroleum products and metal products. It is notable that these are industries with a relatively high wage bill and low margins. It should not be forgotten, though, that the import dependence that is being considered here, refers only to the flow variables; it does not consider capital dependence.

The many implications of the various aspects of import dependence for policy purposes were discussed in part III. Let me therefore turn to the discussion of factor productivity in Tanzania's manufacturing industry.

I.2 EFFICIENCY AND COMPARATIVE FACTOR PRODUCTIVITY

A quantitative approach to questions of productive efficiency, given the limited information I have available about the industrial structure of Tanzanian manufacturing industry, is not an easy task. Nevertheless, the main forces bearing upon efficiency need to be explored, and hence some measurement of these factors is indispensable. The possible observations I will make are only approximate, but are useful when comparing the use of resources and the state of technology in different industries, and in determining the distributive shares of the factors as well as indicating the possible effects of existing imperfections arising out of government policy, or investors' interests in the efficiency with which resources are utilized. With these considerations in mind, my attempt in this section will be to explore the productivity conditions in Tanzanian industry and the efficiency with which resources employed in it are utilized so that areas of potential improvement in productivity can be isolated.

Manufacturing output per man (that is in terms of value added) in 1966 amounted to shs. 9,460/-. This was over three times that of the estates agricultural labour productivity, but a sixth of the mining labour productivity and a quarter of the commercial labour productivity, as shown in table A3.5. This high labour productivity in the mining sector is due to the heavy capitalization of the Mwadui Diamond Mines (which contributes over 90 per cent of that sector). However, the average labour productivity of manufacturing is still very low, given its capitalization, especially in relation to the commercial sector. This is revealed by the inter-country comparison of manufacturing labour productivity in table A3.6. As shown, the labour productivity of Tanzanian manufacturing is very low in comparison with other countries.

However, these comparisons must be done with the understanding that despite the United Nations' attempt to standardize units of measurement, the individual country data still contain differences in accounting procedures, and other institutional differences such as the treatment of advertising costs, etc. It is also true that comparisons of this type normally assume that all firms in the various countries under consider-

TABLE A3.7

Comparative average labour productivity by industry (U.S. dollars)

Industry	Tanzania (1966)	India (1961)	Japan (1962)	U.K. (1958)	USA (1963)
Meat	1,432	n.a.	2,154	2,636	n.a.
Fruit and vegetables	475	438	1,305	2,584	10,666
Dairy products	629	1,066	2,472	4,033	12,400
Grain milling	1,518	793	3,929	5,199	16,652
Bakery	759	1,087	2,144	2,296	10,818
Sugar	1,517	899	7,846	2,532	18,460
Edible oils	788	1,664	5,361	n.a.	19,576
Breweries	2,663	3,376	3,563	5,533	20,598
Soft drinks	2,344	1,216	n.a.	n.a.	14,092
Tobacco manufacture	2,036	1,908	n.a.	5,354	26,702
Spinning (cotton)	652	676	1,034	1,532	5,924
Knitting mills	548	517	1,534	2,037	6,331
Cordage, rope and twine	1,072	485	1,349	2,095	6,459
Footwear	2,946	781	1,294	1,958	6,032

Wearing apparel	582	302		n.a.	5,999
Sawmilling and plywood	536	325	1,430	2,421	6,480
Wood products	1,333	n.a.	1,407	n.a.	5,630
Paper products	2,177	1,211	n.a.	3,602	10,612
Printing, publishing	1,035	696	n.a.	n.a.	9,909
Tanneries, leather	866	504	n.a.	2,511	8,692
Basic industrial chemicals	784	1,351	n.a.	3,778	22,450
Petroleum refinery	6,730	9,798	12,168	5,014	26,122
Paints	4,189	1,248	4,060	4,029	18,144
Matches	957	795	n.a.	n.a.	8,320
Cement	3,959	1,466	9,423	5,666	22,536
Aluminium rolling	3,175	n.a.	3,183	n.a.	n.a.
Metal containers	1,082	1,103	2,542	2,365	14,903
Radio assembly	1,282	1,120	4,947	n.a.	10,963

Source: H. B. Lary, *Imports of Manufactures from Less Developed Countries* (New York, Columbia University Press for the National Bureau of Economic Research, 1968).

ation operate on the same neo-classical production function so that differences in labour productivity among the various countries should reflect differences in the supply of complementary factors per worker.[6] This is particularly the case when comparison is on an international basis. It is with these reservations that I present table A3.7.

In this table, one observes significant inter-industry differences in average labour productivity, both in Tanzania and other countries. In general, Tanzania's labour productivity is lower than that of Japan, the United Kingdom and the USA. In several fields it is, however, higher than that of India. This includes fruits and vegetable canning, grain milling, sugar refining, soft drinks, tobacco manufacture, cordage, rope and twine, footwear, wearing apparel, sawmilling and plywood, paper products, printing and publishing, leather, paints, matches, cement and radio assembly. The differentials with respect to India in labour productivity may be accounted for by the differences in classification since Tanzania's figures relate to firms employing 10 or more persons, while other countries included all establishments irrespective of size. The differentials with the more developed countries must be explained largely by differences in capital utilization.

In relation to the measurement of capital productivity in the Tanzanian manufacturing industry, my task was even more difficult. Data on capital employed are fragmentary and for the largest part of industry non-existent. My survey of the thirty-six firms, arranged in appropriate industry categories below, is all I have available by way of measurement of capital productivity. I have therefore not been able to make any international comparisons on capital productivity. From table A3.8 it is seen that (a) footwear and apparel, wood products and chemicals are the most capital-productive industries, and (b) that average capital productivity as measured tends to vary inversely with the capital-labour ratio.

Before I close this long appendix on the salient aspects of the Tanzanian manufacturing sector, let me add a few words on the locational aspects. From the *Survey of Industrial Production, 1966*, I have computed the relative spatial distribution of industrial establishments and employment and the relative shares of various economic zones in the country's manufacturing activity. Table A3.9 gives the percentage distribution of all manufacturing establishments (employing

[6] Richard R. Nelson, 'A "Diffusion" Model of International Productivity Differences in Manufacturing Industry', *American Economic Review* (May 1968).

TABLE A3.8

Tanzania: productivity of capital in thirty-six firms

Industry	Firm no.	Value added per unit of capital	Capital-labour ratio (sh.)
Food	1	0.14	155,352
	2	0.18	127,092
	3	0.36	43,494
	4	0.40	33,570
	5	0.98	10,937
Beverages	1	0.62	66,115
	2	0.82	171,695
Tobacco	1	0.46	61,052
Textiles	1	0.45	14,305
	2	1.44	5,454
Footwear and apparel	1	0.58	5,575
	2	0.76	5,598
	3	0.17	24,214
	4	1.13	4,713
	5	1.15	4,630
	6	1.51	3,082
Wood	1	0.38	20,387
	2	1.33	8,067
	3	1.99	1,569
Petroleum products	1	0.23	310,605
Chemicals	1	0.48	68,690
	2	0.61	13,173
	3	1.01	42,571
	4	1.54	31,403
Non-metal products	1	0.35	102,056
	2	3.04	2,647
Metal products	1	0.30	73,133
	2	0.52	26,285
	3	0.84	18,052
Electricals	1	0.33	33,333
Miscellaneous	1	0.33	19,545
	2	0.87	10,427

Source: Survey by the author.

10 persons or more) and individual employment for the year 1966 in Dar es Salaam and three other towns, namely, Tanga, Arusha, Moshi and then the rest of mainland Tanzania. The data show that 37 per cent of the establishments and 41 per cent of the employment is concentrated in the Dar es Salaam area. It is also indicated that 69 per cent of the establishments and 65 per cent of total employment is located in the country's major urban centres of Dar es Salaam,

TABLE A3.9

Geographical distribution of manufacturing, 1966

Industry group	Establishments Ratios in per cent of total			Employment Ratios in per cent of total		
	DSM	3 main towns	Other	DSM	3 main towns	Other
All manufacturing	37.4	31.3	31.3	41.4	24.0	34.6
Food	20.8	38.3	40.9	28.0	29.2	42.9
Beverage	27.2	63.6	9.2	50.2	45.6	4.2
Tobacco	33.3	0	66.7	54.1	0	45.9
Textiles	20.0	20.0	60.0	35.8	7.1	57.1
Footwear and apparel	57.7	38.4	3.9	53.9	41.3	4.8
Wood products	22.6	43.3	34.1	14.7	60.8	24.5
Furniture and fixtures	60.7	21.4	17.9	79.0	11.0	15.0
Paper products	100.0	0	0	100.0	0	0
Printing and publishing	50.0	20.0	30.0	73.8	12.3	13.9
Leather products	30.0	20.0	50.0	45.5	17.2	37.3
Rubber products	100.0	0	0	100.0	0	0
Chemicals	30.0	30.0	40.0	34.5	32.1	33.4
Non-metal products	38.4	23.1	38.5	74.6	10.4	15.0
Metal products	84.2	5.2	10.6	9.7	1.2	9.1
Repair of non-electricals	40.0	50.0	10.0	47.9	49.5	2.6
Assembly of electricals	0	33.3	66.7	0	50.6	49.4
Assembly of transport	90.9	9.1	0	91.7	8.3	0
Miscellaneous manufacture	64.3	28.6	7.1	43.3	47.6	9.1

Source: Survey of Industrial Production, 1966.

Tanga, Moshi and Arusha. The data on small-scale and cottage industries (that is, establishments employing less than ten persons) also show that 50 per cent of the employment and 61 per cent of the establishments is concentrated in those four areas whose population is 19.3 per cent of the country's total.[7] Another aspect revealed by table A3.9 is the dispersion of individual industrial activities. For example, industries which seem to be highly congregated in Dar es Salaam in ranking order, according to the number of establishments are: the manufacture of paper products, rubber products, assembly of transport equipment, manufacture and assembly of metal products, miscellaneous manufacturing, manufacture of furniture and fixtures, and manufacture of footwear and apparel. On the other hand, food manufacturing, manufacture of wood products except furniture, manufacture of non-metallic mineral products, manufacture of leather products and printing, publishing and allied industries are not concentrated in the Dar es Salaam areas. If one compares industrial employment dispersion of the major urban centres (Dar es Salaam, Tanga, Arusha and Moshi) with the rest of the country, then the following industrial distribution pattern emerges: the manufacture of paper products, rubber products, the assembly of transport equipment, repair of non-electrical machinery, manufacture of beverage industries, footwear and apparel, metal products, miscellaneous manufactures, printing and publishing, non-metallic mineral products, furniture and fixtures and wood products are highly concentrated in the aforementioned towns, whereas food manufacturing, tobacco manufactures, manufactures of textiles and assembly and repair of electric machinery are more evenly distributed throughout the country.

[7] Karl Schadler, *Crafts, Small-scale Industries and Industrial Education in Tanzania* (Munich, Weltforum Publishing House, 1969), table 7 and appendix 1.

APPENDIX IV

THE INTER-INDUSTRY RELATIONS STUDY FOR TANZANIA, 1966

Tables were prepared from the data available from the *Survey of Industrial Production, 1966; The Annual Trade Report, 1966;* the *Background to the Budget, 1967-68;* and my own survey which is mentioned in appendix I. They were intended to reveal the internal structure of the manufacturing sector as presented in the *Survey of Industrial Production* and part II of this book. This is evident from an examination of the tables. For although the manufacturing value added constitutes less than 10 per cent of the gross domestic product, it has been accorded sixteen of the twenty-one sectors in the tables. There are other unique features of these tables which I need to spell out. These are discussed below.

(a) *An accounting model for the inter-industry relations study*

In order to unravel the methodological assumptions in constructing the input-output table for Tanzania in 1966, I will offer an accounting framework for the treatment of exports and imports with the aid of an abstract table for a two-sector economy. The two sectors are denoted by I and II and could be interpreted as manufacturing (1-16) and the rest of the economy (17-21). I and II constitute intermediate demand. Reading across the rows of this abstract table, the entries first indicate intermediate resource use (both domestic and imports) and then final demand in the form of domestic consumption or investment (both of domestic origin or imports) or exports. Using the notation adopted in the following schematic table, we have industry I's output delivered to itself in the form of inputs domestically produced

	I	II	$C+I$	E	S
I	$x_{11}+m_{11}$	$x_{12}+m_{12}$	c_1+m_{c1}	E_1	$X_1 = D_1+m_1$
II	$x_{21}+m_{21}$	$x_{22}+m_{22}$	c_2+m_{c2}	E_2	$X_2 = D_2+m_2$
M	m_1	m_2	—	—	m_1+m_2
V	V_1	V_2	—	B	
S	X_1	X_2			

228

x_{11} and imports m_{11}, output it sells to industry or sector II (x_{12} and m_{12}) and sales to final demand: domestic consumption or investment due from domestic production C_1, imports for domestic or investment purposes m_{c1} and exports, E_1. Total supply of industry I, i.e. x_1, is therefore made up of total domestic production (including inter-industry transactions), D_1, and imports m_1 of both finished products (for consumptive or investment uses) and intermediary inputs. Industry II's row can be similarly interpreted.

On the column side, it is noted that total supply for any sector x_j, represents inter-industry purchases (i.e. domestically produced inputs x_{ij} and imports m_{ij}), value added of industry i, V_j, which consists of wages and salaries, including fringe benefits, rent, interest, profits, taxes and depreciation allowances, and finally imports which may either be competing or non-competing. Let me denote the value of domestically produced output of the two sectors or industries by D_1 and D_2. It follows then that:

$$D_1 = (x_{11}+x_{21}) + (m_{11}+m_{21}) + V_1$$
$$D_2 = (x_{12}+x_{22}) + (m_{12}+m_{22}) + V_2$$

Now an imported commodity can either be purchased by a production sector as an intermediary factor of production or purchased by the final users as consumption or investment good. The former, the intermediary factor, is denoted by m_{ij}, while the latter, the imported goods which are used as either consumption or investment goods but without entering into the domestic production sector, are denoted by m_{cj}, $j=1, 2$. Thus the total imports of a commodity to be denoted by m_1, m_2 is the sum of the two types of imports, that is,

$$m_1 = m_{11}+m_{12}+m_{c1}$$
$$m_2 = m_{21}+m_{22}+m_{c2}$$

In a typical cell in column 3 of the above table, there are two entries. One entry is the imported goods used for consumption or investment, i.e. the entries m_{c1}, m_{c2}. The other entry is the domestically produced net output available for consumption or investment, i.e. the entries denoted by c_1, c_2. However, the domestically produced net output can also be exported. These outputs are shown in column 4 as E_1 and E_2.

To the extent that the total output of an industry D_1, D_2 can be used either as an intermediate factor (x_{ij}) or final demand (c_j, E_j), the allocations of these total outputs can be represented by the following equations:

$$D_1 = x_{11} + x_{12} + c_1 + E_1$$
$$D_2 = x_{21} + x_{22} + c_2 + E_2$$

The total supply of a commodity, denoted by X_1, X_2, is the sum of all entries in the corresponding row. It follows that

$$X_1 = D_1 + m_1$$
$$X_2 = D_2 + m_2$$

If we define B as the import surplus, then

$$m_1 + m_2 = E_1 + E_2 + B, \quad \text{and}$$
$$V_1 + V_2 + B = c_1 + c_2 + m_{c1} + m_{c2}$$

These equations indicate a final balance of the economy.

(b) *Application of the accounting model to Tanzanian data*

The methodological procedure indicated in the above paragraphs was, with minor modifications to be noted below, adopted in the construction of the Tanzanian input-output table, 1966, because of the preponderance of imports and exports in the productive structure of the economy as well as the nature and quality of the data provided by the survey of manufacturing industry.

In table A4.1, the entries (1-16) and (17-21) correspond to sectors I and II, except that x and m are not distinguished. This was because it was not generally easy to distinguish imported inputs. Moreover, the total supply used in determining the coefficients of table A4.2 include column 22 as well as the final demand, without separating consumption investment and exports. And looking at the columns, total supply included row 22, the value added and imports.

The entries in the tables are as follows:

1. Alcoholic beverages includes 'European beer' and *chibuku*. It excludes local *pombe* which is not recorded, and Dodoma wine was not produced in sufficient quantity to be recorded at that time.
2. Tobacco includes cigarettes and other tobacco products.
3. Food and soft drinks includes meat and meat preparations (the product of Tanganyika Packers really since local butcheries'

meat products are not recorded), dairy products, fruit and vegetable canning, grain mill products, sugar products, bakery products including chocolate and confectionery and edible oil products. It also includes soft drinks as marketed. Again, here local soft drinks that are marketed on a small scale are not included.

4. Footwear and apparel requires no comment.

5. Textiles includes spinning, weaving, finishing of yarns and fabrics; knitting mills. It *excludes* cotton ginning, cleaning and processing; kapok and coir cleaning and processing and cordage, rope and twine.

6. Paper, printing and publishing requires no comment.

7. Chemicals includes industrial chemicals, extraction of non-edible oils, paints, varnishes and lacquers, soap, pharmaceuticals, and insecticides.

8. Petroleum products include all the products of Tiper Refinery.

9. Cordage, rope and twine is self-explanatory.

10. Leather and rubber products includes tanneries, leather finishing plants, tyre retreading and tube vulcanizing.

11. Wood products include furniture and fixtures, sawmilling and manufacture of plywood.

12. Non-metal products: glass products, brick tiles, cement, concrete blocks, stone crushing and mica factories.

13. Metal products include aluminium rolling and manufacture of metal products, radio assembly and other manufacture of machinery.

14. Processing for exports includes cotton ginning, cleaning and processing, tea processing and packing, coffee curing and packing and cashew nuts processing.

15. Maintenance and repair includes repair of machinery both electrical and non-electrical, and motor vehicle maintenance.

16. Miscellaneous manufacturing as given in 39 of ISIC.

17. Agriculture includes estate as well as subsistence and peasant agriculture as given in the national accounts.

18. Mining requires no further comment.

19. Building and construction includes what is called rent, i.e. private and public rentable dwellings and construction.

20. Public utilities include electricity and water.

21. Services includes commerce, public and private services as defined in the national accounts.

TABLE A4.1

The structure of the economy of Tanzania, 1966 (in thousand sh.)

Showing the relationship of inputs and outputs of industries whose code numbers are given across the rows

Row	Column	1	2	3	4	5	6
1	Alcoholic beverages	16270.	0.	0.	0.	0.	0.
2	Tobacco	0.	0.	0.	0.	0.	0.
3	Food and soft drinks	524.	0.	10009.	0.	0.	0.
4	Footwear and apparel	0.	0.	0.	0.	0.	2.
5	Textiles	0.	106.	4173.	29267.	26982.	13692.
6	Paper, printing, publishing	0.	3093.	3886.	1461.	125.	741.
7	Chemicals	219.	67.	2642.	7.	1788.	36.
8	Petroleum products	225.	0.	2295.	64.	233.	0.
9	Cordage, rope and twine	0.	0.	0.	0.	0.	0.
10	Leather and rubber	0.	0.	0.	2684.	0.	1306.
11	Wood products	804.	457.	448.	0.	0.	0.
12	Non-metal products	573.	0.	337.	0.	14.	0.
13	Metal products	0.	0.	11709.	0.	24.	0.
14	Processing for exports	0.	0.	0.	0.	0.	2516.
15	Maintenance and repair	12300.	14037.	27247.	5942.	3170.	0.
16	Miscellaneous manufacturing	0.	0.	476.	217.	3.	0.
17	Agriculture	3876.	16164.	172456.	0.	1139.	0.
18	Mining	0.	0.	24.	0.	7.	0.
19	Building and construction	0.	0.	0.	0.	0.	345.
20	Public utilities	957.	198.	2579.	307.	630.	510.
21	Services	476.	5.	5977.	408.	336.	0.
22	Total	36224.	34127.	244258.	40357.	34451.	19148.

Row	Column	7	8	9	10	11	12
1	Alcoholic beverages	0.	0.	0.	0.	0.	0.
2	Tobacco	0.	0.	0.	0.	0.	0.
3	Food and soft drinks	0.	0.	0.	0.	0.	0.
4	Footwear and apparel	0.	0.	0.	0.	0.	0.
5	Textiles	691.	0.	92.	11.	12.	4.
6	Paper, printing, publishing	1302.	0.	883.	0.	4.	1115.
7	Chemicals	42887.	379.	904.	141.	1179.	30.
8	Petroleum products	1689.	1685.	33.	96.	479.	550.
9	Cordage, rope and twine	0.	0.	0.	0.	0.	0.
10	Leather and rubber	0.	0.	1.	0.	0.	0.
11	Wood products	19.	0.	93.	0.	4044.	28.
12	Non-metal products	99.	0.	75.	0.	0.	0.
13	Metal products	1068.	0.	0.	50.	831.	1.
14	Processing for exports	0.	0.	0.	0.	0.	0.
15	Maintenance and repair	7036.	2118.	2799.	1656.	8063.	2013.
16	Miscellaneous manufacturing	93.	0.	0.	0.	0.	16.
17	Agriculture	11761.	0.	13599.	36681.	4889.	16158.
18	Mining	0.	0.	0.	0.	0.	0.
19	Building and construction	0.	0.	331.	0.	0.	0.
20	Public utilities	1561.	0.	331.	64.	647.	668.
21	Services	137.	0.	333.	1106.	4793.	0.
22	Total	68343.	32384.	19143.	39805.	24941.	20583.

Row Column	13	14	15	16	17	18
1 Alcoholic beverages	0.	0.	0.	0.	0.	0.
2 Tobacco	0.	0.	0.	0.	0.	0.
3 Food and soft drinks	0.	0.	0.	0.	0.	0.
4 Footwear and apparel	0.	5696.	0.	0.	0.	0.
5 Textiles	31.	1084.	45.	230.	0.	0.
6 Paper, printing, publishing	449.	14.	56.	23.	0.	0.
7 Chemicals	354.	2788.	44.	17.	57000.	6700.
8 Petroleum products	492.	0.	0.	0.	0.	0.
9 Cordage, rope and twine	0.	0.	0.	0.	0.	0.
10 Leather and rubber	0.	1920.	0.	0.	0.	0.
11 Wood products	2.	0.	626.	2.	0.	0.
12 Non-metal products	0.	2428.	0.	0.	0.	0.
13 Metal products	47456.	0.	3405.	0.	0.	0.
14 Processing for exports	0.	18471.	0.	0.	0.	0.
15 Maintenance and repair	5124.	0.	0.	0.	0.	0.
16 Miscellaneous manufacturing	0.	216294.	0.	0.	0.	0.
17 Agriculture	0.	202.	1657.	1448.	115000.	7100.
18 Mining	0.	0.	0.	0.	0.	0.
19 Building and construction	0.	0.	0.	0.	0.	0.
20 Public utilities	1058.	1137.	204.	157.	14000.	1500.
21 Services	2034.	1253.	8711.	6095.	173000.	19000.
22 Total	57000.	251286.	14748.	7972.	359000.	34300.

Row Column	19	20	21	22
1 Alcoholic beverages	0.	0.	3000.	19270.
2 Tobacco	0.	0.	2000.	2000.
3 Food and soft drinks	0.	0.	2000.	12533.
4 Footwear and apparel	0.	0.	0.	0.
5 Textiles	0.	0.	0.	67067.
6 Paper, printing, publishing	0.	0.	0.	27369.
7 Chemicals	0.	0.	0.	51363.
8 Petroleum products	4500.	200.	0.	78293.
9 Cordage, rope and twine	0.	0.	0.	0.
10 Leather and rubber	0.	0.	0.	2684.
11 Wood products	25480.	4000.	0.	29137.
12 Non-metal products	0.	0.	0.	1116.
13 Metal products	4870.	3000.	0.	72860.
14 Processing for exports	56440.	8000.	3000.	57400.
15 Maintenance and repair	0.	300.	8000.	122149.
16 Miscellaneous manufacturing	0.	0.	0.	2339.
17 Agriculture	0.	0.	0.	591875.
18 Mining	0.	0.	0.	51693.
19 Building and construction	0.	5000.	32000.	32000.
20 Public utilities	300.	0.	8000.	23643.
21 Services	11610.	5000.	32000.	272784.
22 Total	103200.	25300.	90000.	1528615.

TABLE A4.2

Technical coefficients showing the relationship between inputs and outputs of industries whose code numbers are given across the rows

Row	Column	1	2	3	4	5	6
1	Alcoholic beverages	0.2942	0.0000	0.0000	0.0000	0.0000	0.0000
2	Tobacco	0.0000	0.0000	0.0000	0.0000	0.0000	0.0000
3	Food and soft drinks	0.0095	0.0000	0.0301	0.0000	0.0000	0.0000
4	Footwear and apparel	0.0000	0.0000	0.0000	0.0000	0.0000	0.0000
5	Textiles	0.0000	0.0019	0.0126	0.3938	0.1153	0.0000
6	Paper, printing, publishing	0.0000	0.0548	0.0117	0.0197	0.0005	0.2521
7	Chemicals	0.0040	0.0000	0.0078	0.0001	0.0076	0.0136
8	Petroleum products	0.0041	0.0012	0.0069	0.0009	0.0010	0.0007
9	Cordage, rope and twine	0.0000	0.0000	0.0000	0.0000	0.0000	0.0000
10	Leather and rubber	0.0000	0.0000	0.0000	0.0361	0.0000	0.0240
11	Wood products	0.0145	0.0081	0.0013	0.0000	0.0000	0.0000
12	Non-metal products	0.0104	0.0000	0.0010	0.0000	0.0001	0.0000
13	Metal products	0.0000	0.0000	0.0352	0.0000	0.0001	0.0000
14	Processing for exports	0.0000	0.0000	0.0000	0.0000	0.0000	0.0000
15	Maintenance and repair	0.2224	0.2485	0.0820	0.0799	0.0136	0.0463
16	Miscellaneous manufacture	0.0000	0.0000	0.0014	0.0029	0.0000	0.0017
17	Agriculture	0.0701	0.2861	0.5188	0.0000	0.0049	0.0000
18	Mining	0.0000	0.0000	0.0000	0.0000	0.0000	0.0000
19	Building and construction	0.0000	0.0000	0.0000	0.0000	0.0000	0.0000
20	Public utilities	0.0173	0.0035	0.0078	0.0041	0.0027	0.0064
21	Services	0.0086	0.0001	0.0180	0.0055	0.0014	0.0094
22	Total	0.6551	0.6041	0.7348	0.5430	0.1473	0.3543

Note: The last row (22) contains the sum of all industrial activities (i.e. 1-21).

Row Column		7	8	9	10	11	12
1	Alcoholic beverages	0.0000	0.0000	0.0000	0.0000	0.0000	0.0000
2	Tobacco	0.0000	0.0000	0.0000	0.0000	0.0000	0.0000
3	Food and soft drinks	0.0000	0.0000	0.0000	0.0000	0.0000	0.0000
4	Footwear and apparel	0.0000	0.0000	0.0000	0.0000	0.0000	0.0000
5	Textiles	0.0046	0.0000	0.0034	0.0002	0.0002	0.0001
6	Paper, printing, publishing	0.0087	0.0000	0.0328	0.0000	0.0001	0.0261
7	Chemicals	0.2851	0.0024	0.0336	0.0020	0.0236	0.0007
8	Petroleum products	0.0112	0.0108	0.0012	0.0014	0.0098	0.0129
9	Cordage, rope and twine	0.0000	0.0000	0.0000	0.0000	0.0000	0.0000
10	Leather and rubber	0.0000	0.0000	0.0000	0.0000	0.0000	0.0000
11	Wood products	0.0001	0.0000	0.0000	0.0000	0.0809	0.0007
12	Non-metal products	0.0007	0.0000	0.0035	0.0000	0.0000	0.0000
13	Metal products	0.0000	0.0000	0.0028	0.0007	0.0166	0.0000
14	Processing for exports	0.0468	0.0136	0.0000	0.0000	0.0000	0.0472
15	Maintenance and repair	0.0007	0.0000	0.1040	0.0237	0.1614	0.0000
16	Miscellaneous manufacture	0.0782	0.0000	0.0000	0.0000	0.0000	0.0000
17	Agriculture	0.0000	0.1812	0.5955	0.5250	0.0979	0.0004
18	Mining	0.0000	0.0000	0.0000	0.0000	0.0000	0.3788
19	Building and construction	0.0104	0.0000	0.0000	0.0000	0.0000	0.0000
20	Public utilities	0.0009	0.0000	0.0123	0.0009	0.0130	0.0157
21	Services	0.0009	0.0000	0.0124	0.0158	0.0000	0.1124
22	Total	0.4473	0.2081	0.7116	0.5697	0.4033	0.5950

Row	Column	13	14	15	17	16	18
1	Alcoholic beverages	0.0000	0.0000	0.0000	0.0000	0.0000	0.0000
2	Tobacco	0.0000	0.0000	0.0000	0.0000	0.0000	0.0000
3	Food and soft drinks	0.0000	0.0000	0.0000	0.0000	0.0000	0.0000
4	Footwear and apparel	0.0000	0.0000	0.0000	0.0000	0.0000	0.0000
5	Textiles	0.0001	0.0179	0.0002	0.0017	0.0000	0.0000
6	Paper, printing, publishing	0.0021	0.0034	0.0002	0.0002	0.0000	0.0000
7	Chemicals	0.0017	0.0000	0.0002	0.0001	0.0429	0.0265
8	Petroleum products	0.0023	0.0088	0.0000	0.0000	0.0000	0.0000
9	Cordage, rope and twine	0.0000	0.0000	0.0000	0.0000	0.0000	0.0000
10	Leather and rubber	0.0000	0.0000	0.0026	0.0000	0.0000	0.0000
11	Wood products	0.0000	0.0061	0.0000	0.0000	0.0000	0.0000
12	Non-metal products	0.0000	0.0000	0.0140	0.0000	0.0000	0.0000
13	Metal products	0.2259	0.0077	0.0000	0.0000	0.0000	0.0000
14	Processing for exports	0.0000	0.0582	0.0068	0.0000	0.0000	0.0000
15	Maintenance and repair	0.0244	0.0000	0.0000	0.0109	0.0000	0.0000
16	Miscellaneous manufacture	0.0000	0.0000	0.0000	0.0000	0.0866	0.0000
17	Agriculture	0.0000	0.6816	0.0000	0.0000	0.0000	0.0280
18	Mining	0.0000	0.0006	0.0000	0.0000	0.0000	0.0000
19	Building and construction	0.0000	0.0000	0.0000	0.0000	0.0000	0.0059
20	Public utilities	0.0050	0.0036	0.0008	0.0012	0.0105	0.0751
21	Services	0.0097	0.0039	0.0358	0.0459	0.1303	0.0000
22	Total	0.2713	0.7918	0.0606	0.0600	0.2703	0.1355

Row	Column	19	20	21	22
1	Alcoholic beverages	0.0000	0.0000	0.0023	0.2965
2	Tobacco	0.0000	0.0000	0.0015	0.0015
3	Food and soft drinks	0.0000	0.0000	0.0015	0.0411
4	Footwear and apparel	0.0000	0.0000	0.0000	0.0000
5	Textiles	0.0000	0.0000	0.0000	0.5502
6	Paper, printing, publishing	0.0000	0.0000	0.0000	0.4139
7	Chemicals	0.0000	0.0000	0.0000	0.3828
8	Petroleum products	0.0209	0.0042	0.0000	0.1677
9	Cordage, rope and twine	0.0000	0.0000	0.0000	0.0000
10	Leather and rubber	0.0000	0.0000	0.0000	0.0361
11	Wood products	0.0900	0.8333	0.0000	0.3118
12	Non-metal products	0.0225	0.0000	0.0000	0.0156
13	Metal products	0.2700	0.0625	0.0000	0.3881
14	Processing for exports	0.0000	0.1668	0.0023	0.4389
15	Maintenance and repair	0.0000	0.0000	0.0060	1.1848
16	Miscellaneous manufacture	0.0000	0.0000	0.0000	0.0177
17	Agriculture	0.0000	0.0000	0.0000	2.8549
18	Mining	0.0000	0.0000	0.0000	0.5888
19	Building and construction	0.0000	0.0000	0.0241	0.0241
20	Public utilities	0.0017	0.0000	0.0060	0.1288
21	Services	0.0675	0.1041	0.0241	0.6809
22	Total	0.4727	0.4208	0.0678	8.5242

TABLE A4.3

Table of total requirements

Row Column		1	2	3	4	5	6
1	Alcoholic beverages	1.4170	0.0002	0.0003	0.0000	0.0000	0.0001
2	Tobacco	0.0001	1.0001	0.0002	0.0000	0.0000	0.0000
3	Food and soft drinks	0.0139	0.0001	1.0312	0.0000	0.0000	0.0000
4	Footwear and apparel	0.0000	0.0000	0.0000	1.0000	0.0000	0.0002
5	Textiles	0.0004	0.0022	0.0148	0.4452	1.1305	1.3374
6	Paper, printing, publishing	0.0010	0.0733	0.0165	0.0267	0.0010	0.0268
7	Chemicals	0.0091	0.0020	0.0123	0.0056	0.0121	0.0020
8	Petroleum products	0.0123	0.0153	0.0335	0.0026	0.0016	0.0000
9	Cordage, rope and twine	0.0000	0.0000	0.0000	0.0000	0.0000	0.0000
10	Leather and rubber	0.0000	0.0000	0.0000	0.0361	0.0000	0.0361
11	Wood products	0.0260	0.0123	0.0039	0.0015	0.0004	0.0000
12	Non-metal products	0.0147	0.0000	0.0000	0.0000	0.0001	0.0028
13	Metal products	0.0094	0.0056	0.0500	0.0023	0.0007	0.0017
14	Processing for exports	0.0050	0.0018	0.0035	0.0001	0.0006	0.0698
15	Maintenance and repair	0.3249	0.2566	0.0900	0.0895	0.0162	0.0023
16	Miscellaneous manufacturing	0.0000	0.0001	0.0015	0.0030	0.0000	0.0075
17	Agriculture	0.1239	0.3162	0.5899	0.0246	0.0075	0.0004
18	Mining	0.0080	0.0029	0.0067	0.0005	0.0004	0.0004
19	Building and construction	0.0011	0.0013	0.0025	0.0004	0.0001	0.0095
20	Public utilities	0.0273	0.0081	0.0056	0.0061	0.0033	0.0177
21	Services	0.0467	0.537	0.1043	0.0146	0.0037	1.5148
22	Total	2.0407	1.7518	1.9778	1.6599	1.1782	

Note: The last row (22) contains the sum total of all the other columns.

Row	Column	7	8	9	10	11	12
1	Alcoholic beverages	0.0001	0.0000	0.0003	0.0003	0.0001	0.0005
2	Tobacco	0.0000	0.0000	0.0001	0.0001	0.0000	0.0002
3	Food and soft drinks	0.0000	0.0000	0.0002	0.0002	0.0000	0.0002
4	Footwear and apparel	0.0000	0.0000	0.0000	0.0000	0.0000	0.0000
5	Textiles	0.0073	0.0000	0.0042	0.0002	0.0005	0.0002
6	Paper, printing, publishing	0.0163	0.0000	0.0446	0.0001	0.0007	0.0350
7	Chemicals	1.3993	0.0035	0.0482	0.0030	0.0362	0.0019
8	Petroleum products	0.0215	1.0161	0.0266	0.0267	0.0166	0.0241
9	Cordage, rope and twine	0.0000	0.0000	1.0000	0.0000	0.0000	0.0000
10	Leather and rubber	0.0000	0.0000	0.0000	1.0000	0.0000	0.0000
11	Wood products	0.0024	0.0002	0.0036	0.0010	1.0902	0.0039
12	Non-metal products	0.0009	0.0000	0.0035	0.0000	0.0000	1.0000
13	Metal products	0.0028	0.0004	0.0074	0.0021	0.0280	0.0028
14	Processing for exports	0.0029	0.0003	0.0042	0.0021	0.0029	0.0045
15	Maintenance and repair	0.0679	0.0143	0.1114	0.0254	0.1802	0.0516
16	Miscellaneous manufacturing	0.0010	0.0000	0.0001	0.0000	0.0000	0.0001
17	Agriculture	0.1223	0.0006	0.5612	0.5768	0.1221	0.0046
18	Mining	0.0044	0.1884	0.0063	0.0050	0.0031	0.3943
19	Building and construction	0.0005	0.0004	0.0023	0.0023	0.0006	0.0036
20	Public utilities	0.0162	0.0013	0.0199	0.0077	0.0163	0.0193
21	Services	0.0226	0.0153	0.0954	0.0956	0.0253	0.1507
22	Total	1.6883	1.2420	1.9396	1.7486	1.5229	1.6977

Row	Column	13	14	15	16	17	18
1	Alcoholic beverages	0.0000	0.0003	0.0001	0.0002	0.0005	0.0003
2	Tobacco	0.0000	0.0002	0.0001	0.0001	0.0002	0.0001
3	Food and soft drinks	0.0000	0.0002	0.0001	0.0001	0.0002	0.0001
4	Footwear and apparel	0.0000	0.0000	0.0000	0.0000	0.0000	0.0000
5	Textiles	0.0003	0.0204	0.0003	0.0024	0.0001	0.0000
6	Paper, printing, publishing	0.0037	0.0047	0.0005	0.0003	0.0000	0.0000
7	Chemicals	0.0032	0.0008	0.0003	0.0002	0.0002	0.0001
8	Petroleum products	0.0032	0.0419	0.0000	0.0000	0.0481	0.0278
9	Cordage, rope and twine	0.0000	0.0000	0.0000	0.0000	0.0000	0.0000
10	Leather and rubber	0.0000	0.0000	0.0000	0.0000	0.0000	0.0000
11	Wood products	0.0009	0.0083	0.0030	0.0003	0.0015	0.0008
12	Non-metal products	0.0000	0.0000	0.0000	0.0000	0.0000	0.0000
13	Metal products	1.2930	0.0123	0.0184	0.0007	0.0012	0.0007
14	Processing for exports	0.0013	1.0030	0.0005	0.0007	0.0034	0.0018
15	Maintenance and repair	0.0324	0.0623	1.0082	0.0006	0.0022	0.0012
16	Miscellaneous manufacturing	0.0000	0.0000	0.0000	1.0110	0.0000	0.0000
17	Agriculture	0.0013	0.7497	0.0008	0.0006	1.0978	0.0016
18	Mining	0.0006	0.0085	0.0001	0.0000	0.0090	1.0341
19	Building and construction	0.0004	0.0026	0.0009	0.0012	0.0036	0.0019
20	Public utilities	0.0067	0.0125	0.0012	0.0015	0.0126	0.0067
21	Services	0.0150	0.1088	0.0375	0.0479	0.1489	0.0807
22	Total	1.3621	2.0366	1.0721	1.0673	1.3296	1.1580

Row	Column	19	20	21	22
1	Alcoholic beverages	0.0003	0.0004	0.0033	1.4244
2	Tobacco	0.0002	0.0002	0.0015	1.0035
3	Food and soft drinks	0.0002	0.0002	0.0016	1.0486
4	Footwear and apparel	0.0000	0.0000	0.0000	1.0000
5	Textiles	0.0056	0.0035	0.0002	1.6358
6	Paper, printing, publishing	0.0014	0.0011	0.0002	1.5665
7	Chemicals	0.0036	0.0034	0.0002	1.5722
8	Petroleum products	0.0343	0.0129	0.0011	1.3688
9	Cordage, rope and twine	0.0000	0.0000	0.0000	1.0000
10	Leather and rubber	0.0000	0.0000	0.0000	1.0361
11	Wood products	0.1008	0.0926	0.0032	1.3929
12	Non-metal products	0.0000	0.0000	0.0000	1.0204
13	Metal products	0.0352	0.0854	0.0016	1.5623
14	Processing for exports	0.2721	0.1686	0.0101	1.4922
15	Maintenance and repair	0.0347	0.0284	0.0087	2.4765
16	Miscellaneous manufacturing	0.0000	0.0000	0.0000	1.0193
17	Agriculture	0.2143	0.1362	0.0096	4.6693
18	Mining	0.0066	0.0025	0.0002	1.6829
19	Building and construction	1.0025	0.0031	0.0248	1.0565
20	Public utilities	0.0072	1.0045	0.0065	1.2100
21	Services	0.1020	0.1284	1.0288	2.3435
22	Total	1.8209	1.6714	1.1018	32.5818

APPENDIX V

CLASSIFICATION OF ISIC INDUSTRIES INTO CONSUMER, CAPI-
TAL, BUILDING MATERIALS, PRODUCERS' SUPPLIES AND
OTHER INDUSTRIES, 1966

Industrial classification	ISIC Code
(a) Consumers goods industries	
Slaughtering, canning, and preservation of meat	201
Canning and preservation of fruit and vegetables	203
Manufacture of dairy products	202
Grain mill products	205
Bakery products, chocolate and sugar confectionery	206,208
Sugar factories and refineries	207
Manufacture of edible oil, tea processing, coffee curing and packing	2091,2093–4
Cashew nuts processing, other foods n.e.s.	2095,2097
Breweries, soft drinks	213,214
Tobacco manufacture	220
Cotton ginning, cleaning and processing	2311
Spinning, weaving, printing, finishing of yarns and fabrics	2312
Knitting mills	232
Manufacture of footwear	241
Manufacture of wearing apparel	244,243
Manufacture of furniture and fixtures	260
Manufacture of paper products	272
Printing, publishing, and allied products	280
Tanneries and leather finishing	291
Manufacture of soap, pharmaceuticals, matches	3192–4
Manufacture of glass products	332
Miscellaneous manufacture	394,399
Repair and manufacture of electrical machinery	370
(b) Capital goods industries	
nil	
(c) Building materials industries	
Saw milling and manufacture of plywood	2510,2511
Manufacture of wood products	259
Manufacture of building materials	331,334,339
Aluminium rolling	342

(d) Producers' supplies industries

Cordage, rope and twine	233
Kapok and coil cleaning and processing	239
Basic industrial chemicals and petroleum refining	311,312,321
Manufacture of paints, varnishes, lacquers	313
Metal products	3500

(e) Other: intermediate and services industries

Rubber products	300
Insecticides	3190
Pyrethrum processing	3195
Repair of non-electrical machinery	360
Motor vehicle assembly	383

A few justifications of the above entries

(a) Paper products consist mostly of exercise books, which are in the nature of final consumption.

Glass products consist of glasses (tumblers) and bottles, and are closely associated with breweries.

Electrical machinery is dominated by Philips Electronics Ltd., which is a consumer durable.

(c) Aluminium rolling consists of corrugated sheets used in housing construction.

(d) Metal products consist of containers.

(e) Motor vehicle assembly consists of both private cars, and lorries and buses. Since we had no breakdown, we classified the activity under miscellaneous.

APPENDIX VI

EXPORT PROMOTION AND IMPORT SUBSTITUTION

It has been argued in the literature on the industrialization of the periphery that an encouragement of import substitution (with the tariff structure such an industrialization strategy implies) tends to discourage export promotion. It has also been argued that countries tend to export those goods which embody the more abundant factors in their resource-endowment. This subsection will not deal with these very important problems of international trade theory, if only because of the inadequacy of data, although the first issue was briefly discussed in chapter 4, the section on incentives. Here we deal with a relatively simple problem, namely, what is the nature of the goods which are exported, and how do they relate to Tanzania's resource endowment?

This problem is important for the following reason. Exports in the now developed countries were combined with a highly important factor, namely, an autonomous investment and technological innovation. This made it possible to take advantage of the opportunities offered by the external market and to diversify and integrate the domestic production capacity. In Tanzania, as well as in many of the underdeveloped countries, exports were not only the one autonomous source of income growth but were the dynamic centre of the whole economy. This type of development set up a rigidity in the production system, domestic production being differentiated from export production on the basis of the composition of output. Such a production structure differs from that of the now developed countries in that there is no dividing line between the two sorts of production capacity in the latter, one to meet domestic and the other to meet external demand. Developed countries do not therefore have an export sector as such, manufactured goods being consumed in large quantities within the country and any specialization for the external market that exists being in terms of specific products rather than of different sectors of production.

The export sector in underdeveloped countries has gradually been transformed from the basic collection of produce to some sort of simple processing. Our interest here is to find the proportion of industrial exports which have no home base, and those which could be absorbed

TABLE A6.1

Comparative structure of the exportables

Item	Consumer goods industries-I*	Consumer goods industries-II**	Construction goods industries	Producers supplies industries	Export industries
Number of establishments	16	3	8	2	7
Capital output ratio	3.7	1.6	2.5	3.7	1.5
Capital labour ratio (sh.)	41,227	84,245	43,793	151,147	21,313
Local materials as per cent of output	35.9	12.1	8.7	0.7	57.3
Value added as per cent of output	28.1	51.9	37.3	25.4	19.9
Value added per worker (sh.)	11,185	53,319	17,772	41,281	13,868

* consumer necessities
** consumer luxuries

Source: Survey made by the author.

by the internal market in case the external market went sour; the proportion of industrial output in total exportables as against import substitution, and the input structure of the exportables.

From the *Survey of Industries, 1966* we have the following export industries: slaughtering, canning and preserving of meat (95 per cent for export), manufacture of edible oil, tea processing and packing, coffee curing and packing, cashew nut processing, cotton ginning, cleaning and processing (95 per cent for export), cordage, rope and twine (90 per cent for export), manufacture of plywood (85 per cent for export), pyrethrum processing, and meerschaum smoking pipes. From the data on value added and employment, we estimate that exportables account for 33 per cent of total industrial value added and 34.1 per cent of employment; and that among these exportables, the ones with a home base make up 11.5 per cent of total industrial value added and 10.8 of employment. In other words, about two-thirds of the exportables do not have a home base. This is certainly one of the features which make the industrial structure of the Tanzanian economy inflexible.

Correspondingly, import substitution makes up 67 per cent of total industrial value added and 65.9 per cent of total industrial employment, which implies, as we suggested earlier, that the industrialization which has taken place has been of the import-substituting type. This becomes even more obvious when we consider the fact that meat exports, tea, pyrethrum, meerschaum pipes and cotton exports were established either by the forties or certainly before the mid-1950s.

The data from the *Survey of Industrial Production, 1966* do not enable us to say anything meaningful about the factor proportions problem. Table A6.1, however, which is derived from the *Survey* data I have referred to earlier, indicates that the exportables tend to conform more to the country's factor proportions than the other classifications in that table. In the table it is shown that both the capital-labour ratio and the capital-output ratio are the lowest among the various other classifications. Local material use as a percentage of output is also highest in the export sector. However, the sector tends to add relatively little (less than 20 per cent) to the economy, and its productivity, though higher than that of necessary consumer goods industries, is still relatively low. The implication for such an industrial structure of the export sector is that improvements in resource availabilities and value added should be made, if this sector is to improve its performance and become nationally integrated with the import-substituting industries.

SELECT BIBLIOGRAPHY

BOOKS

ABOYADE, O.	*Foundations of an African Economy: A Study of Investment and Growth in Nigeria*, New York, 1966.
AGARWALA, A. N. AND SINGH, S. P. (EDS.)	*The Economics of Underdevelopment*, New York, 1957.
AHARONI, Y.	*The Foreign Investment Decision Process*, Cambridge, Massachusetts, 1966.
ALEXANDERSON, G.	*Geography of Manufacturing*, New Jersey, 1967.
ALPERS, E. A.	*The East African Slave Trade*, Nairobi, 1967.
AMANN, H.	*Energy Supply and Economic Development in East Africa*, Munich, 1969.
ARCHIBALD, G. C.	*Industrialization and Capital Requirements in Greece*, Athens, 1969.
ARRIGHI, G.	*The Political Economy of Rhodesia*, The Hague, 1967.
AUSTEN, R. A.	*Northwest Tanzania under German and British Rule*, New Haven, 1968.
BAIROCH, P.	*Révolution Industrielle et Sous Développement*, Paris, 1964.
BARAN, P.	*The Political Economy of Growth*, New York, 1957.
BARRAT-BROWN, M.	*After Imperialism*, London, 1962.
BIENEN, H.	*Tanzania: Party Transformation and Economic Development*, Princeton, 1967.
BLAUNER, R.	*Alienation and Freedom*, Chicago, 1967.
BLISS, C. A.	*The Structure of Manufacturing Production: A Cross Section View*, New York, 1939.
BROWN, M.	*The Theory and Empirical Analysis of Production*, New York, 1967.
BUCHANAN, N. S.	*International Investment and Domestic Welfare*, New York, 1945.
BURKE, F. G.	*Tanganyika Preplanning*, Syracuse, 1965.
CARTER, A. P. AND LEONTIEF, W. W.	*The Position of Metalworking Industries in the Structure of an Industrializing Economy,*

	Massachussetts, Harvard Economic Research Project, 1967.
CLARK, C.	*The Conditions of Economic Progress*, London, 1957.
COLLINS, N. R. AND PRESTON, L. L.	*Concentration and Price-Cost Margins in Manufacturing Industries*, Berkeley, 1968.
CONTSOUMARIS, G.	*The Morphology of Greek Industry*, Athens, 1963.
COUPLAND, R.	*East Africa and its Invaders*, London, 1939.
DOBB, MAURICE	*An Essay on Economic Growth and Planning*, New York, 1960.
	Studies in the Development of Capitalism, New York, 1963.
DOMAR, E.	*Essays in the Theory of Economic Growth*, New York, 1957.
DUMONT, R.	*False Start in Africa*, London, 1966.
ESTALL, R. C. AND BUCHANAN, O.	*Industrial Activity and Economic Geography*, New York, 1967.
FANON, F.	*The Wretched of the Earth*, New York, 1966.
FLORENCE, P. S.	*Investment, Location and Size of Plant*, London, 1948.
FRANK, A. G.	*Capitalism and Underdevelopment in Latin America*, New York, 1969.
――	*Latin America: Underdevelopment or Revolution?* New York, 1969.
FRANKEL, H.	*The Economic Impact on Underdeveloped Societies*, Cambridge, Massachusetts, 1963.
FRIEDLAND, W. H. AND ROSBERG, C. E. (EDS.)	*African Socialism*, Stanford, 1964.
FUGGLES-COUCHMAN, N. R.	*Agricultural Change in Tanganyika: 1945–1960*, Stanford, 1964.
FURTADO, C.	*Diagnosis of the Brazilian Crisis*, Berkeley and Los Angeles, 1965.
GREEN, R. H.	*Stages in Economic Development: Changes in the Structure of Production Demand and International Trade*, Yale Growth Center, no. 125, 1969.
GREENHUT, M. L.	*Plant Location in Theory and Practice*, Chapel Hill, 1956.
GUILLEBAUD, C. W.	*An Economic Survey for the Sisal Industry of Tanganyika*, London, 1966.

GULLIVER, P. H.   *Land Tenure and Social Change among the Nyakyusa*, Kampala, 1958.

HALEY, B. F. (ED.)   *A Survey of Contemporary Economics*, vol. II, Illinois, 1952.

——   *The Allocation of Resources*, Stanford, 1959.

HAWKINS, H. C. C.   *Wholesale and Retail Trade in Tanganyika: A Study of Distribution in East Africa*, New York, 1965.

HAZLEWOOD, A.   *African Integration and Disintegration*, London, 1967.

HILDEBRAND, G. H. AND LIN, T. C.   *Manufacturing Production Function in the U.S. 1957*, Ithaca, 1965.

HIRSCH, S.   *Location of Industry and International Competitiveness*, London, 1967.

HIRSCHMAN, A. O.   *The Strategy of Economic Development*, Yale, 1957.

——   *How to Divest in Latin America and Why*, Princeton, 1969.

HOOVER, E. M.   *The Location of Economic Activity*, New York, 1948.

HUBERMAN L. AND SWEEZY, P. M.   *Socialism in Cuba*, New York, 1969.

HUGHES, A. J.   *East Africa: Search for Unity*, London, 1963.

HUNTER, G.   *The New Societies of Tropical Africa*, London, 1962.

ILLIFE, J.   *Tanzania under German Rule*, London, 1969.

ISARD, W.   *Methods of Regional Analysis*, New York, 1960.

JOHN, S. M.   *Principles of Political Economy*, London, 1929.

JONES, E. L. AND WOOLF, S. L.   *Agrarian Change and Economic Development: Historical Problem*, London, 1969.

KILBY, P.   *Industrialization in an Open Economy: Nigeria 1945–1966*, London, 1969.

KIRILO, J. AND SEATON, E.   *The Meru Land Case*, Nairobi, 1967.

KIMAMBO, I. AND TEMU, A. (EDS.)   *A History of Tanzania*, Nairobi, 1970.

KUZNETS, S.   *Modern Economic Growth: Rate, Structure and Spread*, New Haven and London, 1966.

LANDES, D. S.   *The Unbound Prometheus: Technological Change and Industrial Development in*

	Western Europe from 1750 to the Present, London, 1969.
LANGE, O.	*Political Economy,* vol. I, New York, 1963.
——	*Essays in Economics and Sociology,* New York, 1970.
LARRY, H. B.	*Imports of Manufactures from Less Developed Countries,* New York, 1968.
LEUBUSCHER, C.	*Tanganyika Territory: A Study of Economic Policy under Mandate,* London, 1940.
LOFCHIE, M.	*Zanzibar: Background to Revolution,* Princeton, 1967.
LUGARD, LORD	*The Dual Mandate in British Tropical Africa,* London, 1965.
MADISSON, A.	*Economic Growth in Japan and the USSR,* London, 1969.
MAIZELS, A.	*Industrial Growth and World Trade,* London, 1963.
MANGAT, J. J.	*A History of Asians in East Africa circa 1886–1945,* London, 1969.
MARSHALL, A.	*Principles of Economics,* 9th ed., London, New York: Macmillan, 1961.
MARX, K.	*Capital,* vol. I, Moscow, 1964.
——	*Pre-Capitalist Economic Formations,* New York, 1965.
——	*A Contribution to the Critique of Political Economy,* Moscow, 1970.
MATHUR, P. N. AND BHARADWAJ, R.	*Economic Analysis in an Input-Output Framework,* Poona Input-Output Research Association, 1967.
MERHAV, M.	*Technological Dependence, Monopoly and Growth,* London, 1969.
MOFFET, J. P. (ED.)	*Tanganyika: A Review of its Resources and their Development,* Dar es Salaam, 1958.
	Handbook of Tanganyika, Dar es Salaam, 1958.
MYINT, H.	*The Economics of the Developing Countries,* London, 1964.
NEWLYN, W. T.	*Money in an African Context,* Nairobi, 1967.
NICHOLAS, V.	*Growth Poles: An Investigation of their Potential as a Tool for Regional Economic Development,* Philadelphia, 1967.

NKRUMAH, K.   *Neo-Colonialism: The Last Stage of Imperialism*, London and New York, 1965.

——   *Handbook of Revolutionary Warfare*, New York, 1969.

NURSKE, R.   *Patterns of Trade and Development*, London, 1961.

——   *Problems of Capital Formation in Underdeveloped Countries and Patterns of Trade and Development*, New York, 1967.

NYERERE, J. K.   *Freedom and Unity*, Dar es Salaam, 1966.

——   *Freedom and Socialism*, Dar es Salaam, 1968.

——   *Education for Self-Reliance*, Dar es Salaam, 1967.

——   *Ujamaa: Essays on Socialism*, Dar es Salaam, 1968.

OJALA, E. M.   *Agriculture and Economic Progress*, London, 1952.

OLIVER, R. AND MATHEW, G. (EDS.)   *History of East Africa*, vol. I, Oxford, 1963.

PAPANEK, G. F. (ED.)   *Development Policy—Theory and Practice*, Cambridge, 1968.

PAPPENHEIM, F.   *The Alienation of Modern Man*, New York, 1959.

PEARSON, D. S.   *Industrial Development in East Africa*, Nairobi, 1969.

RASMUSSEN, P.   *Studies in Intersectoral Relations*, Amsterdam, 1956.

RAY, R. L.   *Labour Force Survey of Tanzania*, Dar es Salaam, 1966.

REUSCH, R.   *History of East Africa*, New York, 1961.

RICHMAN, B.   *A First Hand Study of Industrial Management in Communist China*, Los Angeles, 1967.

RITCHIE, E. M.   *The Unfinished War*, London, 1940.

ROBERTS, A. (ED.)   *Tanzania Before 1900*, Nairobi, 1968.

ROBERTSON, D. H.   *The Control of Industry*, London, 1923.

ROBINSON, E. A. G. (ED.)   *Economic Development for Africa South of the Sahara*, London and New York, 1964.

——   *The Structure of Competitive Industry*, New York.

RODNEY, W.   *West African Slave Trade*, Nairobi, 1967.

ROSTOW, W. W.   *The Stages of Economic Growth*, London, 1960.

RUTHENBERG, H. (ED.)   *Smallholder Farming and Smallholder Development in Tanzania*, Munich, 1968.

——   *Agricultural Development in Tanganyika*, Munich, 1964.

SCHADLER, K.   *Manufacturing and Processing Industries in Tanzania*, Munich, 1969.

——   *Crafts, Small-Scale Industries and Industrial Education in Tanzania*, Munich, 1969.

SCHUMPETER, J. A.   *The Theory of Economic Development*, Cambridge, 1934.

SEN, A. K.   *Choice of Techniques: An Aspect of the Theory of Planned Economic Development*, Oxford, 1960.

SINGER, H. W.   *International Development: Growth and Change*, New York, 1964.

SPULBER, N.   *Foundations of Soviet Strategy for Economic Growth*, Bloomington, 1964.

STOLPER, G.   *German Economy, 1870–1940: Issues and Trends*, New York, 1940.

SZENTES, T.   *The Political Economy of Underdevelopment*, Budapest, 1970.

TAYLOR, C. J.   *The Political Development of Tanganyika*, Stanford, 1963.

THOMAS, P. A.   *Private Enterprise and the East African Company*, Dar es Salaam, 1969.

TORDOFF, W.   *Government and Politics in Tanzania*, Nairobi, 1967.

TSURU, S.   *Has Capitalism Changed?* Tokyo, 1961.

TURNHAM, D. AND JAEGAR, J.   *The Employment Problem in Less Developed Countries, a Review*, OECD Development Centre, Paris, 1969, mimeo.

WEBER, A.   *Theory of Location of Industries*, Chicago, 1929.

WILSON, M. AND WILSON, A.   *Social Change*, London, 1945.

WRIGHT, F. C.   *African Consumers in Nyasaland and Tanganyika*, London, 1955.

YAFFEY, M. J.   *Balance of Payments of Tanzania*, Munich, 1970.

ZIELINSKI, J. G.   *Lectures on the Theory of Socialist Planning*, Ibadan, Oxford, 1968.

OFFICIAL PUBLICATIONS

ADMIRALTY WAR STAFF INTELLIGENCE DIVISION — *Handbook of German East Africa*, London, 1916.

ARTHUR D. LITTLE INC. — *Tanganyika Industrial Development*, Dar es Salaam, 1961.

CENTRAL STATISTICAL BUREAU — *Recorded Population Changes: 1948–1967*, Dar es Salaam, 1968.

—— *Statistical Abstract 1962*, Dar es Salaam, 1963.

E. A. CUSTOMS AND EXCISE — *Annual Trade Report.*

GOVERNMENT OF TANGANYIKA — *Development Plan for Tanganyika, 1961–1962/1963–1964*, Dar es Salaam, 1962.

IBRD — *Economic Development of Tanganyika*, Baltimore, 1961.

ILO — *Report to the Government of the United Republic of Tanzania on Wages, Incomes and Prices Policy*, Government paper no. 3, Dar es Salaam, 1967.

IMF — *Surveys of African Economics*, vol. 2, Washington, D.C.

MINISTRY OF COMMERCE AND INDUSTRIES — *A Short Guide to Investors*, mimeo, Dar es Salaam, 1967.

TANGANYIKA TERRITORY — *General Administration Memoranda*, Dar es Salaam, 1931.

—— *Report of the Arusha-Moshi Land Commission*, Dar es Salaam, 1947.

—— *Annual Medical Report*, Dar es Salaam, 1924.

UNITED NATIONS — *The Growth of World-Industry*, 1967 edition, vol. I, New York, 1969.

UNITED REPUBLIC OF TANZANIA — *The Economic Survey and Annual Plan 1970–1971*, Dar es Salaam, 1970.

—— *Second Five-Year Plan 1969–1974, Programme for Industrial Development, Part I and II*, Dar es Salaam, 1969.

—— *Tanganyika Five-Year Plan for Economic and Social Development, 1st July 1964–30th June 1969*, Dar es Salaam, 1964.

—— *Survey of Industries 1965, 1966*, Dar es Salaam, 1967, 1969.

ARTICLES

ALAVI, H.   'Imperialism; Old and New', *Socialist Register*, 1964.

AMES, E. AND YAN C.   'Economic Interrelatedness', *Review of Economic Studies*, October 1965.

AMIN, S.   'The Class Struggle in Africa', *Revolution*, vol. I, 1964.

ARRIGHI, G.   'International Corporations, Labour Aristocracies and Economic Development in Tropical Africa', University College, Dar es Salaam, 1967, mimeo.

——   'Labour Supplies in Historical Perspectives: the Proletarianization of the Rhodesian Peasantry', University College, Dar es Salaam, 1967, mimeo.

ARRIGHI, G. AND SAUL, J.   'Socialism and Economic Development in Tropical Africa', *The Journal of Modern African Studies*, vol. 6, no. 2, 1968.

——   'Nationalism and Revolution in Tropical Africa', *Socialist Register*, 1969.

AUBREY, H. G.   'Investment Decisions in Underdeveloped Countries', *Capital Formation and Economic Growth*, Princeton, 1955.

BAER, W. AND HERVE, M.   'Employment and Industrialization in Developing Countries', *The Quarterly Journal of Economics*, February 1966.

BAIN, J. S.   'Relation of Profit Rate to Industry Concentration: American Manufacturing, 1936–1940', *The Quarterly Journal of Economics*, August 1951.

BALASSA, B.   'Integration and Resource Allocation in Latin America'—paper presented at the Conference on the Next Decade of Latin American Development, Cornell University, April 1966.

BASEVI, G.   'The United States Tariff Structure: Estimate of Effective Rates of Protection of United States Industries and Industrial Labour', *The Review of Economics and Statistics*, May 1966.

BATOR, M.   'On Capital Productivity, Input Allocation and Growth', *The Quarterly Journal of Economics*, February 1957.

BECKFORD, G. 'Toward an Appropriate Theoretical Framework for Agricultural Development Planning and Policy', *Social and Economic Studies*, September 1968.

BERG, E. 'Socialism and Economic Development in Tropical Africa', *The Quarterly Journal of Economics*, November 1964.

'Backward-Sloping Labour Supply Functions in Dual Economies', *The Quarterly Journal of Economics*, August 1961.

BERRY, E. AND BERRY, L. 'Land Utilization and Land Use in Tanzania', *Bralup Research Notes*, no. 6, Dar es Salaam, 1969.

BEST, L. 'Outlines of a Model of Pure Plantation Economy', *Social and Economic Studies*, September 1968.

BINHAMMER, H. H. 'Commercial Banking in Tanzania', Economic Research Bureau Paper 69.11, University College, Dar es Salaam, 1969.

BOHR, K. A. 'Investment Criteria for Manufacturing Industries in Underdeveloped Countries', *Review of Economics and Statistics*, May 1954.

BRUTON, H. J. 'The Import Substitution Strategy of Economic Development: A Survey of Findings', Williams College, 1969, mimeo.

BYE, M. 'Self-Financed Multi-Territorial Units and Their Time Horizon', *International Economic Papers*, 1957.

CHENERY, H. B. 'Patterns of Industrial Growth', *American Economic Review*, September 1960.

CHENERY, H. B. AND TAYLOR, L. 'Development Patterns: Among Countries and Over Time', *Review of Economics and Statistics*, November 1968.

CHENERY, H. B. AND WATANABE, T. 'International Comparison of the Structure of Production', *Econometrica*, October 1958.

CHENG CHU-YUAN 'Growth and Structural Change in the Chinese Machine Building Industry, 1952–1966', *The China Quarterly*, January–March 1970.

CHODAK, S. 'Social Classes in Sub-Saharan Africa', *Africana Bulletin*, 1966.

CLIFFE, L.   'Socialist Education in Tanzania', *Mawazo*, December 1967.

CORDEN, W. M.   'The Structure of a Tariff System and the Effective Protection Rate', *The Journal of Political Economy*, June 1966.

CORRY, H. AND HARTNOLL, M.   'Notes on Land Tenure in Bukaria (Bukara)', *Tanganyika Notes and Records*, June 1947.

CUKOR, C.   'The Growth of Engineering Industries in the Developing Countries', *Acta Oeconomica*, 3, 1968.

DALTON, G.   'Tribal and Peasant Economies', *The Quarterly Journal of Economics*, LXXVI.

DEANE, P.   'The Output of British Woollen Industry in the 18th Century', *The Journal of Economic History*, XVII (1957).

DEUTSCHER, I.   'Roots of Bureaucracy', *Socialist Register*, 1969.

——   Land Tenure of the Wasambaa', *Tanganyika Notes and Records*, no. 10, 1940.

DOBRSKA, Z.   'Criteria for Public Investment in Manufacturing: Five Tanzanian Case Studies', Economic Research Bureau Paper no. 68.7, Dar es Salaam, 1968.

——   'Criteria for Evaluation of Investment Projects in Manufacturing Industry', Economic Research Bureau, Dar es Salaam, 1968, mimeo.

DOBSON, E. B.   'Comparative Land Tenure of Ten Tanganyika Tribes', *Tanganyika Notes and Records*, March 1955.

ECKAUS, R. S.   'The Factor-Proportions Problem in Underdeveloped Areas', *The American Economic Review*, September 1965.

EDWARDS, R. C. MACEWAN, A. *et al.*   'A Radical Approach to Economics: Basis for a New Curriculum', *The American Economic Review*, May 1970.

EVERSLEY, D. E. C.   'The Home Market and Economic Growth in England, 1750–80', in *Land, Labour and Population in the Industrial Revolution*, London, 1967.

FINDLAY, R.   'Optimal Allocation Between Consumer Goods and Capital Goods', *Economic Journal*, March 1966.

258

FISHER, A. G. B. 'Production: Primary, Secondary and Tertiary', *Economic Record*, March 1939.

FRANK, C. R. 'Urban Unemployment and Economic Growth in Africa', *Oxford Economic Papers*, New Series, July 1968.

GALENSON, W. AND LEIBENSTEIN, H. 'Investment Criteria, Productivity and Economic Development', *The Quarterly Journal of Economics*, August 1955.

GHAI, D. 'Territorial Distribution of the Benefits and Costs of the East African Common Market', *East African Economics Review*, June 1964.

GODELIER, M. 'System, Structure and Contradiction in Capital', *The Socialist Register*, 1967.

GRAHAMS, J. D. 'Changing Patterns of Wage Labour in Tanzania: A History of the Relations Between African Labour and European Capitalism in Njombe District, 1931–1961', —unpublished, Ph.D. dissertation, Northwestern University, 1968.

GRIFFITHS, J. E. S. 'Notes on Land Tenure and Land Rights Among the Sonjo of Tanganyika', *Tanganyika Notes and Records*, no. 9, 1940.

HAKAM, A. N. 'The Motivation to Invest and the Locational Pattern of Foreign Private Industrial Investments in Nigeria', *The Nigerian Journal of Economic and Social Studies*, March 1966.

HALPERN, J. 'Traditional Economy in West Africa', *Africana Bulletin*, no. 7, 1967.

HARTLEY, B. J. 'Land Tenure in Usukuma', *Tanganyika Notes and Records*, April 1939.

HAZLEWOOD, A. 'Economics of Colonial Monetary Arrangements', *Social and Economic Studies*, December 1954.

HAZLEWOOD, A. 'The East African Common Market: Importance and Effects', *Bulletin of the Oxford University Institute of Economics and Statistics*, February 1966.

HEINING, P. C. 'Haya Land Tenure; Land-holding and Tenancy', *Anthropological Quarterly*, 1962.

HIRSCHMAN, A.O. 'The Political Economy of Import-Substituting Industrialization in Latin America', *The Quarterly Journal of Economics*, February 1968.

HOSKYINS, C.   'Africa's Foreign Relations: The Case of Tanzania', *International Affairs*, 1968.

HOUTHAKKER, H.   'An International Comparison of Household Expenditure Patterns: Commemorating the Centenary of Engel's Law', *Econometrica*, 1957.

HYMER, S. AND RESNICK, S.   'International Trade and Uneven Development',—Yale University Economic Growth Center, Center Discussion Paper no. 83.

ILIFFE, J.   'The Age of Improvement and Differentiation: 1907-1945',—Conference on the History of Tanzania, The University College of Dar es Salaam, undated.

JOHNSON, H. G.   'Tariffs and Economic Development', *Journal of Development Studies*, October 1965.

KESSEL, D.   'Effective Protection of Industry in Tanzania', *The East African Economic Review*, June 1968.

KUZNETS, S.   'Quantitative Aspects of the Economic Growth of Nations, II: Industrial Distribution of National Product and Labour Force', *Economic Development and Cultural Change*, July 1957.

LEDDA, R.   'Social Classes and Political Struggle in Africa', *International Socialist Journal*, August 1967.

LEE III, R.   'The Hsia Fang System, Marxism and Modernization', *The China Quarterly*, October–December 1966.

MAHALANOBIS, P. C.   'The Approach of Operational Research to Planning in India', *Sankhya*, vol. 16, part I, no. II, 1955.

MALIMA, K.   Trends in the Economy of Tanzania', University College, Dar es Salaam, 1968, mimeo.

MARONEY, J. R.   'Cobb-Douglas Production Functions and Returns to Scale in U.S. Manufacturing Industry', *Western Economic Journal*, December 1967.

MARTIN, C. J.   'Some Estimates of the General Fertility and Rate of Natural Increase of the African Population of British East Africa', *Population Studies*, XII, July 1953.

MEILLASSOUK, C.   'A Class Analysis of the Bureaucratic Process in Mali', *Journal of Development Studies*, January 1970.

MODI, J. R.   'Income Tax Policy Problem in Less Developed Economies of Tropical Africa: With Special Reference to Tanganyika', unpublished Ph.D. dissertation, University of Edinburgh, May 1964.

MOHAN, J.   'Varieties of African Socialism', *Socialist Register*, 1966.

MYINT, H.   'The Classical Theory of International Trade and the Underdeveloped Countries', *Economic Journal*, June 1958.

——   'An Interpretation of Economic Backwardness', *Oxford Economic Papers*, New Series, June 1954.

NELSON, R. R.   'A "Diffusion" Model of International Productivity Differences in Manufacturing Industry', *American Economic Review*, May 1968.

NETHERLANDS ECONOMIC INSTITUTE   'Second Hand Machines and Economic Development', May 1958.

OKHAWA, K. AND ROSOVSKY, H.   'The Role of Agriculture in Modern Japanese Economic Development', *Economic Development and Cultural Change*, October 1960.

OLDAKER, A. A.   'Tribal Customary Land Tenure in Tanganyika', *Tanganyika Notes and Records*, 1957.

PACK, H. AND TODARO, M. P.   'Technological Transfer, Labour Absorption and Economic Development', *Oxford Economic Papers*, November 1969.

PERROUX, F. AND DEMONTS, R.   'Large Firms—Small Nations', *Présence Africaine*, 1961.

POLAK, J. J.   'Balance of Payments Problem of Countries Reconstructing with the Help of Foreign Loans', *The Quarterly Journal of Economics*, February 1953.

POWER, J. H.   'Import Substitution as an Industrialization Strategy', *Philippine Economic Journal*, 1966.

PREBISCH, R.   'The Role of Commercial Policies in Underdeveloped Countries', *American Economic Review, Papers and Proceedings*, May 1959.

RANIS, G.   'The Financing of Japanese Economic Development', *Economic History Review*, Second Series, 1959.

RODNEY, W.   'The Imperialist Partition in Africa', *Monthly Review*, April 1970.

ROE, A.   'Terms of Trade and Transfer Tax Effects in an East African Common Market: An Empirical Study', Economic Research Bureau, Dar es Salaam 1968, mimeo.

ROSENBERG, N.   'Technological Change in the Machine Tool Industry, 1840–1910', *The Journal of Economic History*, December 1963.

——   'Neglected Dimensions in the Analysis of Economic Change', *Bulletin of the Oxford University Institute of Economics and Statistics*, February 1964.

——   'Capital Goods, Technology and Economic Growth', *Oxford Economic Papers*, New Series, November 1963.

RWEYEMAMU, J. F.   'International Trade and the Developing Countries', *The Journal of Modern African Studies*, vol. 7, no. 2, 1969.

——   'Some Aspects of the Turner Report', Economic Research Bureau, Dar es Salaam, 1969, mimeo.

SACHS, I.   'Potential, Proportional and Perverse Growth', *Czechoslav Economic Papers*, no. 6.

SARGENT, F. P.   'Selection of Industries Suitable for Dispersal into Rural Areas', *The Journal of the Royal Statistical Society*, part II, 1944.

SCITOVSKY, T.   'Two Concepts of External Economies', *The Journal of Political Economy*, April 1954.

——   'Economic Theory and the Measurement of Concentration', *Business Concentration and Price Policy*, Princeton, 1955.

SEIDMAN, A.   'Comparative Industrial Strategies in East Africa', University College, Dar es Salaam, 1969, mimeo.

SOLIGO, R. AND STERN, J. J.   'Tariff Protection, Import Substitution and Investment Efficiency', *Pakistan Development Review*, V, Summer, 1965.

STANBOUGH, R. B. Jr. — 'The Product Life Cycle, U.S. Exports and International Investment',—unpublished Ph.D. dissertation, Harvard Business School, Boston, 1968.

STIGLER, G. — 'The Division of Labour is Limited by the Extent of the Market', *The Journal of Political Economy*, June 1951.

STRASSMAN, W. P. — 'Interrelated Industries and the Rate of Technological Change', *Review of Economic Studies*, October 1959.

SZENTES, T. — 'The System of Underdevelopment: the Roots and Qualitative Features of the System', University College, Dar es Salaam, 1970, mimeo.

—— 'Economic Policy and Implementation Problems in Tanzania (A Case Study)', Budapest, 1970.

TEMU, P. — 'Nationalization in Tanzania', *East Africa Journal*, June 1967.

THOMAS, G. — 'Agricultural Capitalism and Rural Development in Tanzania', *East Africa Journal*, November 1967.

TODARO, M. P. — 'Some Thoughts on the Transfer of Technology from Developed to Less Developed Nations', Institute for Development Studies, University College, Nairobi, 1969, mimeo.

UNITED NATIONS — 'The Growth and Decline of Import Substitution in Latin America', *Economic Bulletin for Latin America*, March 1964.

VAITSOS, C. — 'Transfer of Resource and Preservation of Monopoly Rents', Development Advisory Service, Harvard University, 1970.

VAN DER LAAR, A. — 'Growth and Income Distribution in Tanzania Since Independence', University College, Dar es Salaam, 1967, mimeo.

VERNON, R. — 'International Investment and International Trade in the Product Cycle', *Quarterly Journal of Economics*, May 1966.

WEST, E. G. — 'The Political Economy of Alienation: Karl Marx and Adam Smith', *Oxford Economic Papers*, New Series, 1969.

WINSTON, G. C. 'A Preliminary Survey of Import Substitution', *Pakistan Development Review*, Spring 1967.

YAFFEY, M. J. H. 'The Effect of Nationalization on Current External Payments', Social Science Conference, Kampala, 1968, mimeo.

—— 'External Aspects of the Tanganyika Economy Since 1949', University College Dar es Salaam, 1968, mimeo.

—— 'International Transactions Before and During the German Period', Dar es Salaam, Economic Research Bureau, 1967, mimeo.

INDEX

absenteeism 22–3
accumulation rate 184; socialist 187
Africanization 47, 57
Africanization Commission 47
agglomeration economies 166
agriculture capital goods requirements 170; conditions 2–3; economic control 65; employment in 49, 53; inputs in industrialization 81; labour productivity 86–7, 177; linkage effect 153, 156; planning 178, 188; production of farm equipment 103; and small scale industries 188; *see also* rural development
Amani Agricultural Research Institute 116
Angola 41
Arabs 1, 9–10, 13, 25, 30
Arthur D. Little Report 39
artisans 8
Arusha 29, 127, 140, 160, 162
Arusha Declaration 38, 40, 46, 57–62, 68–9, 74, 175
Asians 1, 11, 30–1, 42; businessmen 66, 115; traders 10

balance of payments 34, 44, 57, 62, 64, 115
banana culture 7–8, 71
banks borrowing system 45; and fund allocation 34–5, 39; nationalization 59, 63, 65
basic goods 181–3; *see also* wage goods, means of production
Belgium 128
beverage industries 112, 115, 133–4, 136, 145, 153, 156–7, 165
bourgeoisie African 28–9, 66, 72, 107; European 28, 30–1, 97
boycotts 32

Britain 11–13, 21, 24, 34, 36, 39, 41, 44–5, 47, 72, 79, 87, 116, 120, 122
British civil servants 30; companies 125, 128; settlers 16, 116
building materials industries 166–7
Bukoba 18, 28–9, 165
Bushiri rebellion 13

Canada 44
capital formation 82–3
capital goods 33, 82–7, 91, 93, 108–10, 166, 171, 181, 185, 191
capital goods industries 65, 84, 86, 92, 94, 96, 103, 167–70, 177, 188–9, 195
capital goods production 85, 101
capital intensity 105
capital intensive industries 106–7, 109, 113, 144–8
capital intensive techniques 64, 95–6, 103, 106, 195
capital-labour ratios 169–70
capital-output ratio 149
capitalism *see* international capitalism
car import restrictions 190
cash crop production 12, 17–18, 22, 26–9, 36, 42, 70
cashew-nut processing 128–30, 134, 165, 172
cement industry 114, 134, 136, 145
centralization-decentralization 178, 191–2
Chagga 13, 27, 29
chemical production 112–13, 115, 145, 153, 156–7, 166, 183
China 43, 45, 123–4, 186
civil servants 30, 53, 58, 102, 172
Civil Service Negotiating Machinery Bill 48

class differentiation 26, 30; formation 26-32; structure 12
classlessness 5, 70
clothing and footwear industries
112-13, 115, 131, 133-4, 136, 145,
153, 156-7, 166
clove plantations 9-10
Cobb-Douglas production function
148
coffee 15-16, 18, 22-3, 29, 33,
45, 71, 110-11, 131, 134, 165, 172
collective ownership 176-8
Colombia 141
colonialism 60, 72-3, 79, 91
colonization and the colonial period
4, 6, 8-9, 11-37, 47, 102
common market (E.A.) 45
Commonwealth 34, 39
compensation payments 62-3
competition 138-9, 184
concentration 138-9; degree of
143; industrial rates 165; ratios
142, 144; seller 141
consumer goods 33, 81-2, 101-3,
109, 133, 181; industries 73, 135,
167-9, 172, 187
consumer market 165
consumption 55, 180, 194; allocation 179; structure 188
co-operative movement 50, 178,
187
Cooperative Bank 59
cost conditions 139; curves 181-2;
levels 94; and price movements
109; structure 139
'cottage' industries 111
cotton 13, 15, 18, 20, 27, 32, 45,
110-11, 124, 134; ginning 112-13
craft industries 111
cubic dimensions 182
currency 34; common East Africa
45
customs 117
cybernetics 191

Dar Declaration *see* TANU
Guidelines of February 1971
Dar es Salaam 32, 47, 53, 124-5,

160, 162-5, 170
debt/equity ratio 140
decentralization *see* centralization-
decentralization
demand 109; pattern 150;
structure 81
Denmark 44
dependency relationships 91-2,
176-7, 181
depreciation 55, 140, 195
depression 19, 36, 116
development during colonial period
35; neo-colonial 57-8
'development corporations' 108
Development Levy 42
development of underdevelopment
36
development plans 181; *see also*
First Five Year Development
Plan; First Five Year Plan
(FFYP); Three Year Development Plan
dialectics internal 38; law of 197
distribution of production surpluses
traditional 7
distribution principles 196
Dodoma operation 67
domestic market 115, 147, 190
domestic policy post-independence
period 46-56
domestic production 106-7, 116-
17, 135, 144-9, 171
dumping 183

earnings, invisible 63
East African Currency Board 34
East African Common Services
Organization 46, 49
East African Community 46, 183,
186
East African Customs and Excise
118, 135
East African Railways and Harbours
47
education 26, 189, 191
'Education for Self-Reliance' 61,
66, 68
'educational revolution' 60-1

educational system 30

efficiency 93–4, 105, 152, 171

elasticity factor substitution 81; growth 113, 155; labour demand 20; market demand 139; price 102; supply 20, 151

electrical equipment industries 166

elitism 11, 36–7, 60

employee welfare benefits 52

employees, numbers in labour-intensive industries 146–7; textile industries 124; various establishments 142

employment conditions 192; creation of 56; growth rate 95; in consumer goods industries 172; maximization of 57; opportunities 106, 188

enclave character of economy 35

Engel's law 110

entrepreneur class 96

entrepreneurs African 50; foreign 79, 89, 91, 96–7, 102, 106, 176–7; Indian 124; local private 106–7, 149

entrepreneurship foreign 23, 42, 73

equations 114, 132, 135, 143, 146–8, 152, 158

Eastern Europe 186

Europe 9

European economics 11

Europeans 10, 25, 31

exchange rates 34, 132

exchange economy 86

exchange relations 67

excise duties 135

export duty 22; growth 115; interests 101, 168; markets 23, 94, 99, 110, 130; sector 72, 109; type 135

export enclaves 32, 35, 102–3, 107, 156, 159, 166

export-import trade 11, 33, 35, 59

export-processing industries 123–9

exports 15–16, 18, 21, 33, 55, 87–8, 91, 118–20

factor bias 94, 183; combinations 195; cost 55; endowments 101–2; inputs 151, 195; price configurations 96, 195; productivity 106–7, 147–8; proportions 185; shares 147; substitution 81

federation, East African 45

First Five Year Development Plan 39

First Five Year Plan (FFYP) 49–52

First World War 115

flow of payments 64

flow of trade 34

food manufacturing industries 112, 115, 134, 136, 145, 153, 156–7, 160, 165

foreign aid 44–6, 58

France 79

Freehold Law 27

Frelimo 43

French indicative planning method 49

fund allocation role of colonial banks 34–5

Gabon 41

geographical description 1–3

German colonization 12, 14, 17, 20–1, 29; settlers 16

German Democratic Republic 45

German East Africa Company 13

Germany 13, 15, 24, 72, 79, 116

Ghana 41

glass products 113–14, 134, 136

Gogo 13

Gotzen, Governor 20

gross domestic product (GDP) 49, 52, 55

gross national product 81

Groundnut Scheme 25

growth economic 56, 83, 138, 181; elasticities 113, 155; of national income 178–80; of output 184

Hadimu 9–10

Hallstein doctrine 44

Haya 29

health care 190–1

Hitler 116
Holmes Commission 31
home markets 88, 92, 110
Hong Kong 45
housing 191
Hypothesis 1 105–6, 138–44
Hypothesis 2 106, 144–7
Hypothesis 3 107, 147–9
Hypothesis 4 107, 150–9
Hypothesis 5 107–8, 159–66
Hypothesis 6 108–10, 166–72

ISIC classifications 141–2, 166–7, 172
import data 183; duties 22, 135; price index 110; prices 44
import-replacing industries 98–9
import-substituting industrialization 101, 103, 122–3, 129, 154, 156
import substitution 86, 102, 113, 133
imports 21, 33, 55, 57, 74, 85, 116–20, 171; capital requirements 188; dependence on 150; in industrialization process 98
incentive schemes inventions 187; incentive structure 192–3, 196–7
incentives economic 187
income allocation 179; distribution 55, 73, 109; drains 65; government 55; investment 21, 57, 63, 93; levels 81; property 55; real growth 52; rural household 54–5; from sale of labour 21; subsistence 55
independence, attainment of 31, 38, 42, 46–7, 50
India 129
Indians 10-11, 128-9
indirect rule 27, 29
industrial capitalism 90; development 3, 58, 69, 73–4, 104–5; economics 82; growth 111–20; investments 97, 130; location 165; output 114, 132–3; patterns 88, 101; production 133, 166; stagnation 116; upsurge 123
industrialization 74, 82, 88–90, 97,

117, 122, 159, 178; pattern 175; policy 105; process 23, 80, 86, 102–3, 107–8, 154; role in development process 80–2; strategy 78
industries competitive 109; nationalization of 59; small-scale 187–8
industry, pattern of 78, 80
input requirements 153
inputs 150–2, 163, 166
insurance 59, 65
insurance companies 35, 63
input/output data 133; ratio 182
inter-industry linkage 107; relations 105
interest charges 140
intermediate goods industries 167
international corporations and subsidiaries 57; investments 99–100; trade 87
international capitalism post-independence period 38–46, 51; Tanzania's involvement 72
investment allocation 179, 187–8; bias 168; decisions 99–101, 107, 169, 177–8; distribution 73; income 21, 57, 63, 93; motivation 98; patterns 35, 64, 72, 102, 122–30; planning 49–50, 120, 183; policy 105; projects 195; structure 62; of surplus 95
investment autonomous 87; commercial 50; foreign 24; government 50; industrial 50, 57; private 55; public 55
Iringa 165
iron and steel production 155, 183
irrigation 3, 8, 191
Italian industry 129–30
Italy 153–4, 156
Ivory Coast 41

Japan 45, 78, 86, 125–7, 130–1, 153–4, 156, 169–70, 186

Kampala Agreement 45–6, 118–19, 125
Kenya 20, 22, 32, 41, 43, 45, 104, 116–20, 123, 133, 167

Kibosho 13
Kilimanjaro area 7, 16, 18
Kilosa 20
Kilwa 13
Korean War 120
kulak class 48, 56

labour 'aristocracy' 106; division of 72, 90, 187, 191; force 17, 56; forced 20–1; hired (colonial) 28; international division 79–80; market 6, 26; migrant 12, 22–3, 28, 188; productivity 81, 84, 148, 177, 185; sale of 21; scarcity 109; shortage 17; skilled 132; stabilization 23, 52; supply 19–22, 110; surplus 28; training 47; unions 23, 109
labour-capital substitution 96
labour-intensive industries 84
labour-intensive methods 94, 195
labour-saving techniques 96–7
Lake Victoria 29
land alienation of 16; holdings 71; nationalization 48; tenure 4–5, 7–8, 27–9, 48
Latin America 116
leather industry 84, 112, 115, 153, 156, 165
Leontief matrix 151, 157
leverages (debt/equity ratio) 143–4
life expectancy 49
linkage effects 101, 103–4, 107, 150–4, 156–7, 159, 189
living, standard of 55
localization 160–3, 165
location of industries 105, 108
location quotient 159–60
locational patterns 163, 166
London 34–5, 116
luxury goods 102–3, 108–10, 133, 135, 166, 171–2, 181

machine-building industries 166
machinery 131, 140, 144, 155; foreign made 149; manufacture 129, 186; over-invoicing 124; production 84, 92, 96, 171; repairs 112–13, 115, 166, 188
Maji Maji rebellion 13, 21
Malawi 42
management 23, 187
management-worker relationships 192–4
managerial decisions 192
manufactures 88, 120
manufacturing 81, 97, 100, 111–12, 170
manufacturers, overseas 33
market areas 99; characteristics 166; demand 97, 139; dependency 176–7; domestic 98, 101; exchanges 6; expansion 56, 123; forces 72; imperfections 195; internal 67, 106, 109; mechanisms 17; price 184; size 122, 163; strategy 131; structure 100, 105, 138, 142
market threat hypothesis 125
markets 91, 105; national 91–2; world 74
Marx, Karl 80, 180, 184
Marxism Leninism 52
Mbulu 56
meat products 32, 133–4, 136
merchandising groups 33
merchant class 28–30
Meru area 16
metal products industries 112–13, 115, 131, 134, 136, 153–7, 165–6; *see also* iron and steel production
metropolitan centres 13–14, 25, 72, 79, 88, 91, 109–10, 117, 190
Middle East 9
migrants *see* labour, migrant
mineral products (non-metallic) 112–15, 145, 153, 156–7
minimum wage 47, 53
Ministry of Commerce and Industry 131
missionaries 12, 26, 29
Mkwawa rebellion 13
Mombasa 125

money (as source of development) 58

monopolistic market 130; structure 93

monopoly 32–3, 59, 79, 109, 125, 138–9, 141; profits 142, 144

Morogoro 20–1

Moshi 29, 71, 156, 160, 162

Mozambique 41, 129

Mpwapwa 116

Mtwara 165

Muscat 9

Mwanza 18

Mwongozo *see* TANU Guidelines of February 1971

NUTA 48, 53, 193–4

Nairobi 32

National Bank of Commerce (NBC) 59

national credit allocation 65

National Development Corporation (NDC) 59-60, 108, 123-4, 128, 170

'national ethic' 51

National Housing Corporation 191

National Insurance Corporation 64

National Milling Corporation (NMC) 59

National Union of Tanganyika Workers Bill 48

nationalization 62, 64–5, 178, 192; compensation 60; of industry (drawbacks of) 64–5; policy 59–60

native reserves 16

natural resources 2–3, 155, 183

Netherlands 125–8

Ngoni 13

Nigeria 41, 98–100

Northern and Central Railways 26

Norway 44

Nyakyusa 27–8

Nyamwezi 8, 20

Nyarubanja 8

Nyerere, Julius 36, 48, 65, 68, 73, 189

oligopolistic structures 101, 103, 105, 109, 130, 138–9

one-party state 48

output gross industrial 140–2; levels 23, 138–44, 150–1, 181–3; pattern 81; real growth 52; sectoral distribution 105

outputs 152, 163, 166

over-invoicing 105–6, 138–44

'overseas economy' 13

overseas merchandising 33

ownership means of production 192; state 65, 196; structure 178–9; in tribal societies 4–6

Pangani 13, 22

paper, printing and publishing industries 84, 112–13, 115, 134, 153–4, 156–7, 166

peasantry 4–8, 12, 16–22, 26–7, 29, 32–3, 48, 54, 56, 58–9, 61, 66, 68, 176, 193

per capita consumption 52

per capita income 49, 52, 91, 114, 155, 165

per capita value 155

periphery 80, 85–6, 89–91, 95–7, 101

periphery-centre 117

periphery-satellite 104, 117

petroleum industry 114, 125, 145–6, 153–7, 166

phamaceutical industry 134, 191

planning economic 176, 178; *see also* industrial planning

plantation system 12, 14–25, 32, 35

political democracy 58; leaders 58; orientation 46; parties 30–1; power 72, 91, 122

politicians 102

population 1, 91; density 1–3, 66; growth 52, 81; pressure 8; racial distribution 1–2

Portugal 43

'power of dispersion' 158

pre-colonial economy 3–9

pre-independence period 1–37

Presidential Commission on the Establishment of a Democratic

One Party State 50
Presidential Special Committee of Enquiry into Co-operative Movement and Marketing Boards 50
price-cost ratios 138–9
price shifts 81
private enterprise system 50, 108
production capacity 81, 118; costs 132, 140, 149, 184; domestic 102; industries 121, 183; levels 182; methods 185; modes 70–2; output 195; pre-capitalist 4; relations 3, 6, 17, 70–1, 176–8, 192; scales 92–3; stimulus 57; structure 40, 88, 120, 188; surpluses 67; techniques 27, 84, 95–6, 101, 180; theory 151; unit 79; value 152; workers' control 65
productive forces 3; investment 74
productivity 92, 148; increases in 110; low 56
profit hidden 140; maximization 20; motive 89; over-invoicing 105–6; rate 138–9, 144; transfer to home base 141
proletarianization 20, 22
proletariat 27, 147
protective shelter 23
protectionist policies 101
public transportation 190
purchasing power 35; growth 123
pyrethrum 32, 165

radio assembly 114, 131, 134, 136, 145–6
radio assembly industry 119, 125–7
rates of return 137
raw materials 11, 13–15, 79, 89, 131–3, 137, 144, 151, 155, 163–5, 181, 191, 193; local 154, 166; over-invoicing 141
real product, growth of 49
regional integration 182–3
regression equation 114
regression model 148
rent-earning buildings, socialization of 61
reserves, lowering of 44

resource allocation 46, 48–51, 55–7, 132, 178, 188, 191
Rhodesia 22, 41, 44, 116
Ruanda-Urundi 43
rubber 15, 112–13, 115, 166
rural areas 188–90; development 66–8, 73–4, 191; electrification 191; sector 56–7, 61, 66, 73, 109; transformation 61, 67–8, 74

SITC classifications 118–19
satellites 116–17; *see also* periphery-satellite
scale, economics of 148, 181–3
school leavers 54, 60
Schumpetarian view 97–8
Second World War 24, 31, 36, 79, 116, 120
segregation 30
self-reliance policy 58–9, 62, 73–4
settlement schemes 54, 56, 67
Seyyid Said 9–10
shadow prices 147–8
Shambala 20
shipping agents 63
sisal 15, 20, 23, 32, 39, 45; declining market 52–3, 110; estates 36, 47–8; industry 23–6, 52–3, 111–12, 128–9, 145; nationalization of industry 59; price 44, 52–3, 57; products 121, 134, 136, 145, 153, 156; pulp project 124
slavery and slave trade 9–12, 25, 91
social class 48; differentiation 46–8, 52–7, 70–1; facilities 67; strata 30; welfare 165
socialism 48, 58, 62, 65–71, 74, 175–8; *see also* ujamaa socialism
Socialism and Rural Development policy directive 61
socialist goods 175–8
South Africa 41, 116
South West Africa 41
sphere of influence 14
spread effects 117
State Trading Corporation (STC) 59, 66
sterling 34; devaluation 34, 120;

exchange 39; reserves 34
Stillmann 13
strikes 32
subsistence farming 27; income 54; production 70–1; wages 17–19
sugar 16, 134, 136
Sukuma 20
surplus 8, 140, 195; rate 139–43; variables 144; variation 142
Survey of Industrial Production, 1966 160–1, 167
Sweden 44

TANU 31, 47–8, 51, 59, 62
TANU Guidelines of February 1971 62, 66, 69
Tabora 13
Tanga 47, 53, 128, 160, 162, 165
Tanga area 20
Tanganyika Federation of Labour 48
tariff protection 94, 98, 100, 102, 105, 109, 125, 129–37, 144
tariff structure 116, 169
tax, hut 21
tax incentive structure 123
tax protection 134
taxation colonial 21; progression 50
taxes 55, 88, 140–1
tea 23–4, 33, 111, 165, 172
technical assistance 50; improvements 195; progress 184–6
technological advancement 35; change 25, 87; dependency 91–5, 101, 176; diffusion 83–4; threshold 98–100, 122, 155
technology 85, 87; transfer 101
Territorial Industrial Licensing Ordinance 119
textiles and textile industry 22, 33, 84, 112–15, 121–4, 131, 134, 136, 145, 153–7
Three Year Development Plan 39, 48
tobacco 111–13, 115, 131, 133–4, 136–7, 145, 153, 156–7
trade deficits 123; elimination of

barriers 116; gains 110; patterns 34, 119; socialization of 61; terms 110, 120; unions 47–8
trade and industry interterritorial imbalance 118
trade and trading precolonial and early colonial 8, 10, 28, 32–5
Trade Disputes Bill 48
Trade Unions Ordinance Bill 48
traditional economy 3–9, 12, 17; medicine 191; society 3–9, 19–20, 23, 25, 28, 70–1, 111
transition period (to socialism) 179–80, 196–8
transport equipment 112, 115, 166; facilities 26, 103; industry 170–1, 190; networks 190
transportation 35, 86, 163, 166

U.N. Conference on Trade and Development 87
USSR 45, 186
Ubena 16
Uganda 41, 43, 45, 117, 119, 123
Uganda Coup 62
Uganda Railway 26, 29
ujamaa socialism 67–73, 188, 191; villages 61, 68, 191
United Arab Republic 104
United Kingdom 37, 117, 126–8
United States 9–10, 15, 31, 79, 83, 87, 123, 125, 129, 153–4, 156, 163
United Tanganyika Party (UTP) 31
Unyamwezi 13
Unyanyembe 13
Upper Kitete 56
Urambo 13
Usambara 7, 20, 71
Usambiro 13

value added 102, 167–8, 172
value law 195
village community 4–7, 19
villagization 66–7

wages average 172; differentials 53–4; earners 49; employment

21–2; fund 149; goods 181, 189, 191; labour 5, 11–12; rates 20, 95, 129

wages 47, 52, 86, 94, 106, 109; *see also* subsistence wages

weltanschauung 51–2

West Germany 44, 126–8

West Lake 7–8, 71

wood products industries 112–13, 115, 134, 145, 153, 155–7, 165

work organization 6–7; process 192–4

working participation in production 192–5

workers 58–9, 192

working class 176, 187

World Bank 49, 54, 61

World Bank Report 39

Yao 8, 13

Zaïre 41–3

Zambia 41–2, 63, 125

Zanzibar 1, 9, 11, 30–1, 43

Printed by Kenya Litho Ltd., P.O. Box 40775, Changamwe Road, Nairobi, Kenya. Prepared for press, designed and published by Oxford University Press, Eastern Africa Branch, P.O. Box 72532, Electricity House, Harambee Avenue, Nairobi, Kenya.